The Great
White Elephant of
Maplin Sands

The Great White Elephant of Maplin Sands

The neglect of comprehensive transport planning
in Government decision-making

Peter Bromhead

Professor of Politics, University of Bristol

Paul Elek London

To my wife

First published by Elek Books Ltd. 1973
54–58 Caledonian Road
London N1 9RN

ISBN 0 236 15491 5

Printed in Great Britain by
Clarke, Doble & Brendon Ltd.
Plymouth

Contents

Contents

List of Tables

7

List of Tables

Maps and Figures

Preface

This book makes some claim to be a case-study in decision-making. What are the decision-makers' values? What determines those values? Given that knowledge relevant to decisions must be inadequate, how far do the values determine the scope of the efforts to obtain relevant knowledge?

The immediate object examined is the British Government's decision in 1971 to set machinery in motion so that work could begin as soon as possible on the construction of a new airport for London; not so much the decision to put it off Foulness Island, Essex, rather than somewhere else (which is a straightforward matter), but the decision to build it as soon as possible, and the depth and direction of the assessments on which that decision was based.

In so far as it looks at the quality and orientation of decision-making, this book is also conceived as a severely practical and limited contribution to the great surge of debate about man and the environment, which found some expression at the United Nations conference at Stockholm in June 1972. It does not explicitly take one side or the other in the controversy which found rather extreme expression in 'Blueprint for Survival', the January 1972 number of *The Ecologist*, and in the reply offered by the journal *Nature*. It does assume, though, that the evidence now available suggests that the steadily increasing rate of change in the biosphere carries such dangers that it is prudent and desirable to look now for practical ways of minimizing these dangers. It reflects the latest trend in the argument between optimists and pessimists over the prospects for future oil supplies; here, even during 1972, new developments suggested that these supplies will indeed soon be under serious pressure, and so any practicable way of reducing future consumption deserves urgent attention.

We have to recognize that it is unrealistic to advocate policy

11

options which involve a real sacrifice of immediate public satisfactions for the sake of long-term conservation. But it is realistic to look very hard for options which are environmentally preferable without demanding unacceptable sacrifices of current consumption. Just how far can such considerations affect a government's approach to problems? How far did they in this case? What conflicts were involved?

The airport question has been argued over for more than ten years, and in 1970 the Roskill Commission, which had been set up to examine it, reported with the advice that a new airport should be put at Cublington. Until that time I had been a supporter of the Foulness alternative; the Roskill Report made it clear that every possible site was so bad that a further appraisal of the need for any new airport was needed. However, early in 1971 the Government finally decided that preparations for the building of a third major London airport must begin at once, and that the airport should be on Maplin Sands, just off Foulness Island, fifty miles from London down the Thames estuary. Preparations went ahead. During the next two years much work was done, but only at the planning and administrative level. Meanwhile, the scheme was widely criticized. However, by February 1973 the Government was still insisting that the new airport would be needed and that the whole scheme should go ahead.

This book sets out to examine the airport decision as an example of governmental activity. It asks how much care was taken in examining the consequences that would follow from the building of the airport, how the Government reacted to the pressures affecting the issue, how far it compared alternatives, and what criteria were set up. In other words, it discusses the decision in terms of the dichotomy between synoptic and incremental approaches to problems, a dichotomy well shown by Professor Charles Lindblom's defence of incrementalism where it is appropriate, and by governmental claims to act synoptically.[1]

The decision to build a new London airport was based on detailed and expensive inquiries, made with the most sophisticated techniques for calculating runway capacity and the demand for it. Yet the terms of reference given to the expert inquirers did not invite them to ask what changes in the pattern of transport might occur, subject to choices among a whole range of feasible investment options in different modes. The findings of the inquiries were therefore quite

inadequate as guides to action. The Government itself had, up to the
Second Reading of the Maplin Development Bill in February 1973,
taken no measures to fill the gap. The studies of the Channel tunnel
and of Midlands airports, initiated in 1971, were not said to involve
a questioning of the third airport decision; thus they were con-
demned in advance, by compartmentalism, to failure as contributions to transport planning. Yet Mr Heath's action in setting up a
Central Policy Review Staff in 1970 seemed devised precisely for
the purpose of filling gaps of this kind.

Thus the airport decision was essentially incremental, though the
partial use of synoptic methods may seem to give the decision an
appearance of a more serious rationality.

This book will seek to show how the broader options could have
been identified, even without the use of sophisticated techniques. It
will also suggest why the gap remained unfilled, because of the
combined force of a narrow value-system, at several levels, within
the executive branch of government, and of the failure to break down
the boundaries between administrative compartments.

The book is in three main parts.

Part One takes note that the airport and its access routes would
use more resources, and cause more environmental damage, than
any single project ever undertaken in this country, and that it could
soon be made obsolete by new technologies now being developed.
It suggests reasons why it would have been rational, before taking
any decision, to examine thoroughly and simultaneously two devices
for holding in check the future London airports' load: a more
rational distribution of air traffic, and full exploitation, with the
indispensable help of a Channel tunnel, of the railways' new
potential.

Part Two concentrates on detailed analysis of figures, noting that
the Roskill Commission had available to it only data which were
inadequate for a full understanding of the possible spontaneous or
induced changes in the pattern of traffic. It examines various consequences which might flow from a commitment to railways within
the EEC, including the Channel tunnel.

Part Three examines the airport decision in terms of values and
procedures, administrative and parliamentary, and of the conflict
between the search for 'a new style of government', profoundly
assessing alternative programmes, and the old habits of muddling

through by finding the most workable compromise between the most potent and clamant interests.

Not enough attention is paid, in Parliament or elsewhere, to numbers. Once prepared by statisticians, they tend to be accepted, even though their basis may be questionable. The Government's decision was based on traffic-projections which assumed fixed annual percentage increases in traffic by air, rail, etc., slightly modified to take account of possible changes in the pattern. This procedure is deficient when it fails to take into account much bigger changes in the pattern which might occur in certain circumstances; and in this case the likelihood of change depends on the use made by Governments of the choices open to them. The crudely based figures suggested in this book are offered with no claim to be authoritative, but as a set of speculations designed to throw a light on the possible effect of a new approach to transport planning.

The need for haste in preparing this book has left no time for the discussions which would have been desirable, and I have gratefully to acknowledge only the help of some public officials who have kindly discussed a number of issues with me. I should also like to thank Nevil Johnson and Allen & Unwin for permission to quote two passages from *Parliament and Administration*; Denys Munby and the proprietors of the *Political Quarterly* for permission to quote from that journal; the proprietors of *New Society* for permission to republish (on p. 93) a map, slightly amended, which accompanied my article of 5 August 1971; and the Controller of Her Majesty's Stationery Office for permission to quote from the Report of the DTI's Working Party on Traffic and Capacity at Heathrow, 1971. I should also like to give my warmest thanks to Jan Nicholas and Mary Woods for all their unstinting help, and to my wife and daughters for their forbearance.

PETER BROMHEAD, Bristol, May 1973

PART ONE

'The Third London Airport will be needed by 1980'

1

The background: from Stansted to Maplin

The Government's decision to start building a new airport at Foulness can adequately be interpreted only in the light of the Stansted saga. That story, up to 1968, has been told elsewhere,[1] so it will be repeated here as briefly as possible.

After 1945 the Government came into possession of many airfields. It took over Stansted from the US Air Force in 1951, along with some others during this period. It looked forward to a huge growth of civil air transport, and in the meantime accepted a large financial burden from its small-scale operation of all these aerodromes. No public corporation was set up, because there was then no hope that an airports corporation could pay its way. From 1950 some municipalities began to operate airports. In 1955–6 the House of Commons Select Committee on Estimates recommended that municipalities should be encouraged to own and operate airports; it wanted to reduce the burden on the national exchequer. Five years later the Estimates Committee examined the London airports and its criticisms of the waste of money at Stansted made a considerable impression. The administration's defence was that Stansted was being kept available for development at a later stage as a major London airport in addition to Heathrow and Gatwick. It has been argued that the criticism stimulated a determination to see that Stansted would indeed be so developed.

The administrative machine's identification with the need for a third airport was confirmed, and set in its unshakeable mould, by the Report of the Interdepartmental Committee on the Third London Airport, presented in June 1963 and published in March 1964.[2] The Committee's chairman was the Under-Secretary, Ministry of Civil Aviation, Aerodromes (General) Division, and it included seven civil servants of that Ministry, one from the Ministry of Transport and one from the Ministry of Housing and Local Govern-

17

ment. The remaining members were representatives of the airlines and of the Air Traffic Control services. (The British Airports Authority had not yet been set up.) The Report contains a review of the expectations regarding growth of traffic at existing airports. Paragraph 14 of the Report ends as follows : 'On the basis of these

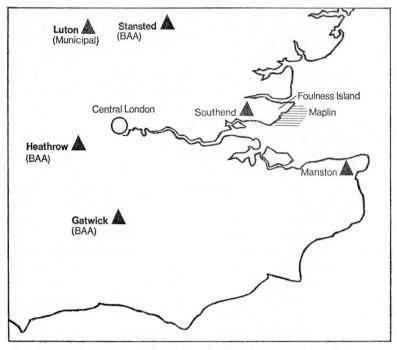

Existing airports in south-eastern England. 'London-area' airports are shown in bold type

figures, therefore, we believe that a third airport will be required for London by the early 1970s.'

The rest of this 1963 Report was mainly concerned with comparison of possible sites, and the conclusion was that Stansted was the best of the sites that had been considered and 'the only one with clear prospects of making a good airport for London.' Paragraph 68 concluded : 'We are accordingly unanimous in recommending Stansted as the site for London's third airport.'

Public concern at the possible choice of Stansted had already been growing; now a substantial opposition movement formed, with the North West Essex and East Herts Preservation Society 'dedicated to resisting the Third London Airport at Stansted'. Eventually, £23,500 was collected for this resistance.

Two years later the Ministry of Housing and Local Government held an inquiry into the local objections to the proposed development of land at Stansted as the third airport for London. The inquiry lasted from 6 December 1965 to 11 February 1966.[3] The terms of reference governing the inquiry were quite clear that neither the need for a third airport nor the date when it would be required were 'proper subjects for discussion.'[4] The Assessor referred to this point in the Report,[5] but he did suggest that with larger aircraft the need for runway capacity might grow much less fast than the number of passengers. In general he considered that there should be 'a more general examination in depth before any firm discussion was taken' (para. 77).

The Report itself (para. 49) concluded that the evidence for Stansted was inadequate: 'In my opinion, a review of the whole problem should be undertaken by a committee equally interested in traffic in the air, traffic on the ground, regional planning and national planning.' The Inspector found that there were strong arguments against Stansted on five counts: planning, access, noise, environmental damage, and loss of agricultural land.

The Inspector presented his Report in May 1966, but the Report was not made public until a year later, together with a White Paper, *The Third London Airport* (Cmnd. 3259), in which the Government answered the Inspector's objections and concluded (para. 72) 'that a major new airport to serve London should be developed at Stansted.'

A great outcry followed and there was criticism of the delay over publishing the Report. On 29 June the House of Commons debated an Opposition motion calling on the Government 'to set up an independent committee of inquiry into national airport policy in the context of which a decision on a third London airport could be taken, and to delay a final decision on the siting of such an airport until the committee had published a report on the issue.' The question was decided on party lines, but with a Government majority of only 74 (ten less than normal at that time); some Government supporters abstained, including Mrs Renée Short, who spoke strongly against her own front bench. She complained that the civil servants involved had been 'judge and jury in their own case'.[6] and she argued for transfer of future traffic to regional airports, particularly Birmingham (in her own area). The next Labour speaker, Mr Newens, also spoke against the Government, partly on the same lines, and only two speeches supported Stansted. None raised the possibility of transferring passengers to rail, but this was not surprising, as the new railway potential had not yet been developed. The main Opposition front bench argument, put by Mr Carr, in opposing Stansted, was that the capacity of the existing airports could be increased enough to deal with increasing traffic pending a further inquiry.[7] This has indeed been done. The swamping of the existing airports that was then predicted for 1974 was soon put off to 1980 and further deferred until 1985.

A full day's debate in the House of Lords on 11 December 1967 was almost entirely hostile to Stansted.

The Government now faced a continuing and determined battle, in which its decision for Stansted won very little public support. Most of the constructive public argument favoured a site in the Thames estuary, and at that time, and on the basis of the information then available, so did the writer of this book. Public preference for Foulness was becoming evident.

In autumn 1967 a new Minister, Mr Anthony Crosland, took over at the Board of Trade, formerly presided over by Mr Douglas Jay. Mr Crosland was not personally involved with the Stansted decision. After some processes whose nature has not been divulged, the Cabinet soon decided that the substance of the Opposition's motion of the previous summer was correct. On 27 February 1968 Mr Crosland announced the Government's intention to set up a new commission, and on 20 May the appointment of the Commission, under Mr Justice Roskill, and its terms of reference were announced.

Mr Crosland observed, in announcing that there was to be a new inquiry, that 'nearly all the critics of the Stansted decision have conceded that a third London airport in the South-East will certainly be necessary. Therefore I think that it is essential that the inquiry should concentrate on that.'[8] Although eight months earlier the Opposition had demanded a much wider inquiry, in the questions on Mr Crosland's statement no Opposition speaker rebutted his claim, which was the foundation of the narrow terms of reference. Only Mr Lubbock, for the Liberal Party, now argued specifically for a widening of the inquiry to cover airport policy as a whole.[9]

20

The terms of reference, announced on 20 May, asked the Commission 'to inquire into the timing of the need for a four-runway airport to cater for the growth of traffic at existing airports serving the London area, to consider the various alternative sites, and to recommend which site should be selected.'

The Commission's attention was directed specifically to issues of general planning, including population and employment growth, noise, amenity, and effect on agriculture and existing property; of aviation, surface access, defence and cost, including the need for cost-benefit analysis.[10]

We need not diverge here to discuss the constitutional points about the Commission (interesting though these are).[11]

The full terms of reference were circulated with the official Report, but, as Mr Crosland said, they were drawn up in consultation with the official Opposition and there had been broad agreement.[12] Lord Dilhorne, as a Cross-bench peer, had been brought into the discussion.

The absence of any scope for discussing a national airports plan had by now been accepted by the Opposition; its spokesman, Mr Corfield, said nothing about this in his welcome of Mr Crosland's statement.[13]

During the short discussion which followed, thirteen Members raised various points. Only one, Mr Robert Howarth (Labour, Bolton East) referred to the need for a national airports plan, and Mr Hooley (Labour, Sheffield Heeley) asked if the new airport might be outside the South-East.[14]

As Mr Howarth said, the Commission would not be able to make a really adequate judgement on the timing of the need without taking wider issues into account, but it was likely to be deterred from any really broad survey by the very fact that its terms of reference omitted any such task. Mr Crosland gave a clear signal when he replied that there was no doubt that a third airport in the South-East was necessary. His implication was that there was no point in cluttering the terms of reference with unnecessary directions.

Thus the Commission was asked to estimate when the new airport would be needed, or, in other words, when it was reasonable to expect that, as a result of growth in traffic, aircraft movements would exceed the capacity of the existing London airports. But it was not asked whether the growth in London air traffic might be affected by new developments in alternative means of transport. It was not asked whether such new developments were desirable, or how they might be fostered or prevented. Still less was it asked to consider the effects that different levels of investment in railways, in France and Benelux as well as in Britain, would have on the future demand for travel by air to and from London airports. Nor was it asked to study the future role of regional airports in Britain.

The Commission thus considered the question whether, or when, a third London airport would be needed, only within the narrow framework imposed by trends in demand over the previous few years, making some allowances for slight modifications to the picture which could already be seen. Nearly all the Commission's efforts, which cost about £1·5 millions, went into the comparison between the locations at which the airport might be put.

By this time it seemed unlikely that Stansted would be recommended. The opposition to it had been so determined and so long-sustained that it seemed that any new review must find another site. As the Roskill Commission pursued its inquiries, new opposition groups were formed at all the inland sites. By early 1970 every available wall and bridge in the area of Thurleigh, for example, was yelling out the message of the inhabitants of the threatened area : THURLEIGH, NO AIRPORT HERE.

It was against this background that the Roskill Commission eventually recommended Cublington, another inland site, where the local opposition was just as great as at Stansted and the national sympathy potentially just as vigorous. They decided for the inland site because, for all its obvious and popular advantages, Foulness was shown to be a very bad place for an airport.

It is not necessary here to describe the pressure-group activities in opposition to the inland sites; they were all concerned with location, not with the question whether an airport was needed. But it was clear that the opposition was formidable; substantial organization developed and a big public-relations exercise was mounted. Parallel activities in relation to the Foulness site were on a much smaller scale and opinion in the nearby town of Southend was by no means all hostile. There was positive enthusiasm over the prospect of development and new employment in the area.

Opposition to inland sites, beginning at Stansted, had a real effect on politicians' thinking. The Conservatives in opposition had moved into a position of hostility to Stansted for obvious political reasons, although they had supported it in office before 1964. But hostility to Stansted, in sympathy with the local (mainly Tory-voting) pressure, necessarily implied hostility to other inland sites where similar problems would arise. Clearly the Conservative Government wanted the Roskill Commission to find in favour of the Foulness site. The fact that it did not, in spite of heavy pressure, showed the strength of the arguments against Foulness.

The objections to Foulness had been familiar for a long time, but they had after all been expounded by aviation interests and by official spokesmen, supposedly on a narrow basis. Those objections were given a completely new dimension by the Roskill Report. On the question of site-comparison the terms of reference had been irreproachable, and the Commission had reached its conclusion on the siting issue by an impartial balancing of arguments, using every conceivable measuring device. Its finding in favour of Cublington created a new situation. If Foulness was so bad (for so many reasons, among which bird-strike and the Shoeburyness firing range were relatively unimportant) and Cublington intolerable, the new message was that a search for any possible means of doing without the airport had gained an importance such as it had not had before.

The Roskill Commission's Report was debated in the House of Lords on 22 and 23 February 1971, and in the Commons on 4 March. The Government had not yet decided what to do about the Roskill proposals and ministers were ready to be influenced by these debates. Out of some forty contributions in each House only one favoured Cublington for a new airport. A few thoughtful speakers suggested grounds for deferring the decision yet again, but the ministers who spoke all indicated that they did not intend seriously to look at the possibility of deferment. Their only task now, as they saw it, was to decide, as politicians, between Cublington (or Thurleigh) and Foulness.

Two months later Mr John Davies, then Secretary for Trade and Industry, announced that the Government had chosen Foulness and that the first administrative preparations for building a new airport there, and means of access to it, would begin immediately. A team of civil servants was assigned to the task. In August plans for a second runway at Gatwick were dropped. In June 1972 the location of the runways on Maplin Sands was published and in August a public body was established to carry out the work. As far as the Government was concerned, discussion of the timing of the need for the new airport had been closed long before – indeed, since before 1965 the answer has always been the same: the new airport will be needed as soon as we can have it ready. No new calculations reflecting the new railway technology, or possible variations in the pattern of travel, have been allowed to affect this settled doctrine.

It seems clear that no thorough inquiry into broader transport options had been undertaken before the debates on Roskill; if there had been such inquiries, or if ministers had been aware of the results, they could not have spoken as they did in the two debates. (After all, Roskill had been, theoretically, examining the question of timing, so it was hardly appropriate for the Departments to run a rival inquiry at the same time; but then Roskill's terms of reference precluded a full inquiry.) Nor can the Government have done any serious work on the options for deferment during the two months between the debates and the announcement of the decision for the Foulness site. There was no time; if there had been any such new inquiry it would have been Mr Davies' duty to disclose it, and he made no such disclosure; and the wording of his announcement suggests that his mind was already closed.

In 1971 the Government set up an inquiry, jointly with the French, into the technical and economic questions concerning the possible building of a Channel tunnel, and in the summer of 1972 the inquiry moved on to a second stage, which was to cost £4 million and was expected to be completed by the summer of 1973. In November 1972 the Civil Aviation Authority started an inquiry into the role of airports in the British Midlands and Lancashire.

One of the principal proper functions of both these inquiries would have been to assess the contribution that the tunnel (with energetic investment in railways) and the regional airports might make to transport needs; to weigh the two together against a third London airport as options worthy of consideration, and to compare the costs of the options. As both inquiries were set up on the assumption that the decision on the third airport was a *fait accompli*, both were prevented in advance from performing their respective functions in relation to rational planning.

Meanwhile, during 1971 and 1972, the Government went ahead with the creation of the administrative machinery for planning Maplin Airport, and some progress was made. By early 1973 some old difficulties were still unsolved: no satisfactory new site had been found for the Ministry of Defence firing range that the airport would displace; in late January there were rumours that the sand had been found to be 80 feet deep, but the Department of the Environment preferred not to release a report on this matter until it had thoroughly studied the implications.

At just the same time the Maplin Development Bill was due to come up for Second Reading in the House of Commons. It was first scheduled for Tuesday 31 January. In the previous week strong opposition was shown in the Conservative Members' aviation group. The Second Reading was put off for nine days, but went through on 8 February, after some controversy.

By this time nothing had been divulged about the planned line of the road and rail access routes to Maplin. If the fixing of the route was delayed until after serious work on Maplin Sands had begun, it would be more difficult for objectors to the access routes to prove that the routes were unnecessary because the airport itself was unnecessary.

Ministers continued to insist that the airport was needed, though in doing so they made no attempt to answer the claims that alternative transport solutions should be studied.

Meanwhile the newly established Civil Aviation Authority had been pursuing its inquiries, evidently at greater depth and breadth than its predecessors. On 21 April 1973 the *Guardian* published an article by David Fairhall, reporting that a draft report from the CAA, not yet published, would show that the existing London airports would still have a little spare capacity in 1985; a Channel tunnel would increase that spare capacity, but the amount of the increase would depend on the quality of the railway service. A Mark II tunnel, with a $2\frac{1}{2}$-hour rail-journey to Paris, would leave substantial spare airport capacity.

A month earlier, on 23 March, the Department of the Environment had published a Green Paper on the Channel Tunnel (Cmnd 5256), claiming that a Tunnel would have no significant effect on the total volume of air travel. It appeared to assume only a poor-quality railway (the CAA's Mark I). It did not even raise the question of the differential effects of different qualities of rail service. As the CAA took cognizance of this question, the Department of the Environment's failure to do so was seriously disturbing. Both this Green Paper and other Government statements omitted or distorted important items in the argument.

2

The snags of Maplin

Superficially, the scheme to build a new airport on Maplin Sands, at the edge of Foulness Island, is exciting and attractive. It is quite pleasing to contemplate the main body of London's future air traffic taking off and landing at this rather useless bit of the Thames estuary, fifty miles from London, disturbing relatively few people. There is a positive attraction in the scheme for reclaiming land from the sea and in the associated developments which are planned. The scheme for a new city of over half a million people fits in with the South-East planners' hope to develop South Essex and reduce London's population.

Roskill's rejection of Foulness in favour of Cublington, in the South Midlands, was courageous, in that it was bound to provoke a great outcry. The long battle against Stansted had been based on justified fear of damage to the environment of a populated inland area, and the proposal for Cublington was bound to produce a new and repetitious battle. It did. Sir Colin Buchanan became a folk-hero for his one-man dissent in which he argued that any inland site would be an environmental disaster.

The Commission as a whole would no doubt have preferred to recommend Foulness, but the weight of evidence against it was so great that they felt obliged, in all honesty and no doubt with reluctance and trepidation, to recommend Cublington instead. Even so, the Government deserved the acclaim that it won for deciding against it. Its decision for Maplin was almost universally welcomed, because of public relief that all the inland sites were at last abandoned. The Government's earlier insistence on Stansted had built up a great wave of emotional opposition, not only to Stansted but to other inland sites as well.

Amid all the cheering for the rejection of Roskill's recommendation that an airport should be put at Cublington the enormous disadvantages of Maplin were overlooked. These disadvantages were well set out in the Roskill Report, and one argument for looking for ways of dispensing with a third London airport rests on the fact that every imaginable site for it is very bad.

A good summary of the objections to the Foulness site was given by the Chairman of the British Airports Authority, Sir Peter Masefield, when, in his evidence to the House of Commons Select Committee on Nationalized Industries on 19 January 1971, he summarized the reasons why the British Airports Authority considered it the most disadvantageous of the four sites which had been short-listed by Roskill:

. . . first, it was relatively inaccessible, it was very difficult to get to and had no roads or rail service in existence; they would have to be created. Secondly, it would conflict in a serious degree with European air traffic control. It would certainly affect the capacity of airports like Schiphol and Brussels, and this would be disadvantageous in the European context as a whole.

Thirdly, he mentioned the danger of bird-strike, and then continued:

And there are serious doubts about the meteorology, the weather features of Foulness. There is a great deal of evidence that sudden fogs come up and go down which would make it a good deal worse than other sites. When we add to this the financial problems and the fact that Roskill has pointed out in his summary that it would inevitably be less attractive to air traffic – very much less attractive to air-lines than any other site – it would or could court commercial disaster not only for us but for everyone else concerned in its propagation and operation.[1]

More specifically, there was the point that by 1991, according to the BAA's calculations, Maplin would have 26 million fewer passengers than would use Cublington in that year if it were built.[2] However, this calculation should be treated with a good deal of scepticism.

Distance from London and general inaccessibility are the first and most obvious of the objections. Roskill did attempt a thorough evaluation of the cost of access to each of the sites considered, and found that passenger-user costs, discounted to 1982, would be £167 million or £207 million more for Foulness than for Cublington.[3] (In addition, Roskill put the excess of freight-user costs at

£14 million, or road capital at £4 million, and of rail capital at £13 million.)

Without going into any detailed discussion of Roskill's findings, or of Professor J. Parry Lewis's critique of the methods used,[4] we may observe that the location of Maplin involves large capital expenditure in building a rapid-transit system and roads to reach it, and the expenditure of large resources in conveying people over this long distance. All passengers travelling by train will have to go into a central London rail terminal and the great majority will have to cross London. The road and railway (or other mass-transit system) will cause immense environmental damage, including the demolition of many thousands of houses to make room for them. A railway could be put in a tunnel for the first few miles within London, at a cost, but it would still have to go through Essex.

An Advanced Passenger Train system with one track each way could apparently carry up to 15,000 passengers an hour in each direction, given clearway running and no stops. If some of the trains were to serve other transport demands in the area, or even to stop to pick up airport passengers, a four-track route would be needed. The non-stop trains could do the journey in under 30 minutes. If some other system, such as tracked hovercraft, were used, the time might be reduced to 20 minutes, but no new alternative would be of any use unless it could equal the conventional railway's hourly load-capacity.

The difference between 30 minutes and 20 minutes for the journey is in any case unlikely to be very important. If there were a single mass-transit terminal station at the Maplin end, and the number of users were great enough to make the airport worth while, most of the passengers would have a long way to travel at Maplin between the rail terminal and their airport building. A better solution would be to have numerous rail terminals within the Maplin area. In this case it might be most convenient for trains to fan out, one to one Maplin terminal, one to another; but then the frequency of trains to each terminal would be reduced and the cost of construction, with the need for multi-level junctions, would be high. Alternatively, there could be a series of Maplin stations on a circuit, with all trains passing all of them, but if each train stopped at each station it would take up to half an hour to go round the circuit.

For the road access, the British Airports Authority's Report for 1971–2, published in September 1972, envisages only an eight-lane motorway from London as a first-stage need. But both this Report and Roskill put the airport's maximum passenger load, at some date in the future, at 125 million passengers. On this basis, if more than one-tenth of the passengers from London tried to go to the airport by car or taxi in a busy hour, or more than one-fifth at a normal time, they would be delayed by congestion. The main body would need to use the mass-transit system. If the mass-transit system were used by 80 million passengers a year to and from London, the daily average would be about 220,000, which is the number handled by Victoria Station in 1972. Even if the peak loads were much reduced in relation to the total load, it would be difficult for a single town terminal to deal with such a number of people, nearly all of them with baggage. Severe congestion on the roads and in underground stations would seem likely.

Some of the passengers would terminate their journeys outside the South-East and travel by surface means. A fairly large proportion of these would presumably travel by road. Their demands for road space would add to the load on the road system round the north of London and inevitably produce a vicious circle of more congestion-delays (to themselves and others) and more road-building to alleviate the congestion. The large new community in Essex would in its turn require communications to London and elsewhere, and would add much to the burden on the Essex transport system.

Travel to the airport by the persons working there will present ever-increasing difficulties. The BAA Report for 1971–2 mentions preparations for a secondary road system to the airport for the staff and for travellers from points north of London. Heathrow now needs 50,000 staff for 20 million annual passengers. The BAA estimated 37,000 staff in the year 2000 for 75 million passengers. This was by projecting into the future the 4·3 per cent annual increase in staff productivity achieved at Heathrow before 1970.[5] The projection looks highly suspect. The Ministry of Transport's *Report of a Study of a Rail Link to Heathrow* (1970) estimates that in 1981, on a typical day, 40,000 personnel will travel into the Heathrow airport enclosure, and that 28,000 to 31,000 of them will go by car. (The exact number using cars is assumed to depend on the number owning cars, and that is likely to increase.) We seem then to need to think of 20,000 staff entering the Maplin zone by car on a typical day. Presumably at least one-third would enter it during the busiest hour; even at two per car they would need three lanes of road one way for the last few miles. Their demands for road space and parking space might be reduced if a bigger proportion travelled by bus, or by a rail service additional to that for passengers from London. But we still have to provide for lorries, and for the private cars of passengers from East Anglia and the Midlands; and perhaps more than one-tenth of the passengers from London would try to come by car. It looks as if twelve lanes of road for the few miles at the Foulness end, with numerous and complex flyovers, would be scarcely enough to prevent intolerable congestion.

The Ministry of Transport's evidence to the Roskill Commission assumes between 2,250 and 3,000 passenger-car units travelling from the airport to London in the evening peak hour (depending on a modal split). This is apparently for a total load of about 30 million passengers assumed for 1990. (If Maplin's load were as small as that in 1990, Heathrow and Gatwick would be very fully loaded.)

By the time when Maplin is dealing with 100 million passengers a year, this estimate would involve around 6,000 to 9,000 passenger-car units one way, demanding a total of about 16 lanes of road all the way to London.

The whole scheme seems likely to require, in the long run, between 400 and 1,200 lane-miles of road and 250 to 400 track-miles of new railway, partly within London in each case. If there is only one railway terminal in London, the problem of access to that terminal, and its effects on London's road system for a long distance from it, might in itself be as serious initially as the whole question of the London Maplin access routes. It is just not practicable to provide eight additional lanes of road for passengers' taxis to and from the London terminal. Two or three quite widely separated terminals would bring some alleviation on the town-side, but would demand the construction of ten or twenty additional track-miles of new railway within London. The only hope for a solution which might be practicable would be through a boat or hovercraft service down the Thames to Maplin, with at least eight landing-stages in London.

There is also one serious objection, which applies not just to Foulness in particular, but to any major airport for London in addition to Heathrow. For obvious reasons, airlines do not like to split their operations between airports serving the same area; splitting increases their cost and thus damages not so much the airlines themselves but either their passengers, who must ultimately pay the price of the reduced efficiency through higher fares, or taxpayers who subsidize publicly owned airlines. So long as Heathrow has been the London area's principal airport most airlines have been reluctant to use Gatwick. BEA eschewed Gatwick 'for many years' until very recently,[6] but with a third major London airport in the offing they developed a 'new-found love' for it,[7] and began to argue that Gatwick should have a second runway to increase its capacity.[8] Rather similarly, the group of foreign airlines supported a second runway at Gatwick, though they 'had shown a marked reluctance hitherto ever to use the airport and some had even pressed their governments to take action against British airlines when they had been pressed to use it.'[9]

Both BEA and the group of foreign airlines were much concerned about the links between airports, and in particular between any third airport and Heathrow and Gatwick. BEA disliked Foulness even more than Cublington, because it envisaged the journey-time between Foulness and Heathrow as four hours; and the foreign group of airlines considered that 'adequate inter-airport communications would be a crucial issue for ten or fifteen years at least.'[10] But any reduction of the journey-time would involve new environmental damage along the lines of the new roads which would be needed in order to reduce the congestion.

Nobody can yet estimate the probable size of the demand for inter-airport transfer. If Maplin airport is built there will be some such demand, but the number of persons wishing to transfer between airports in a year will be small in relation to the ordinary London people desiring better local transport. In the competition for the improvement of transport facilities as a whole in the London area, inter-airport transfer ought probably to come a rather long way down in the priority order.

In all this any third airport is undesirable, but Foulness is even more undesirable, as a device for getting people between aeroplanes, than the inland sites that were considered.

The airlines, British and foreign, were realistically arguing against Foulness for their own interests, and ultimately for the interest of travellers. They were emphasizing two undeniable and inescapable facts; first, for air operations and for air travellers, an airport close to the centre which it serves is better than one farther away; secondly, one airport is better than two, and two airports better than three; the fewer airports for any given centre the better. For the public, in so far as it is not travelling by air, nearer airports are worse than more remote ones, but their interest on the whole agrees with that of airlines and travellers in preferring fewer airports. A corollary of all this is that there are strong arguments against attracting more traffic than necessary to a major population-centre. But Roskill and the Government saw things differently; they seemed to think that it would be a terrible thing if there were 'a shift of traffic to competing continental airports such as Paris, Amsterdam and elsewhere and hence to competing foreign airlines.'[11] This is a curious doctrine. If somebody wants to go to London, why should he go to Amsterdam? If he wants to go from Teheran to Pittsburg and has to change planes in Europe, it may not really be worth taking the trouble to get him to change planes at a London airport rather than at Amsterdam, if Amsterdam has spare accommodation.

Although the environmental damage to people and villages on the site would be less than at any of the inland sites, it would still be colossal. An airport on Maplin Sands, even with a minimum of associated development, would totally change one of the few parts of south-eastern England which have managed to survive until 1973 without drastic man-made encroachments.

At Maplin, aircraft would have to face an uncertain and incalculable danger. Sooner or later a plane might come to grief through hitting a large bird in one of the aircraft's vital spots. A few disasters have already been caused by 'bird-strike' at airports outside Britain. The Roskill Report concluded, after a thorough study, that 'there must be a greater risk of a major disaster due to of bird-strike at Foulness than at an island site' (8.41). In comparison with inland sites there were some compensating safety factors (e.g. a crashing plane would fall into the sea), so the bird-strike danger was 'not a major influence on the choice of site' (8.42). But there was no comparison of this danger with much smaller dangers of rail movement.

Maplin airport must be disastrous to the birds themselves which now frequent the place, and not only ornithologists would deplore this special damage. Appendix 4 to the Roskill Report was contributed by Mr A. S. Hunt, a member of the Commission and a Principal Planning Inspector in the Department of the Environment, summarizing local hearings. We may well quote his words in para. 13 of that Appendix:

Foulness was a site of national and international importance as a habitat of large numbers of birds. One-fifth of the world population of the dark-bellied Brent Goose wintered at Foulness. Large numbers of waders and other birds used the marshes and mud flats during winter migration. There was no satisfactory alternative habitat for the Brent Goose displaced by an airport.

Note also Appendix 4, para. 12:

The local cockle industry would be completely lost. There is no source of cockles comparable with the Maplin Sands within accessible distance. The Leigh-on-Sea cocklers collect about 27 per cent of all cockles landed in the United Kingdom. Aside from the national implications, those engaged locally in the industry have considerable investment in boats and other equipment and would suffer irreparable hardship.

It is easy to shrug off arguments such as this. The cocklers can be given money to compensate them. It is possible that there will be no bird-strike accidents. The certain damage to the birds can only be adequately discussed in language which would be dubbed emotive or sentimental, but there is a growing and proper concern at the changes in the balance of nature caused by man's more brutal or heedless assaults on whole animal species. 'The consequences of dredging up millions of tons of estuarine mud and dumping it on the Maplin Sands will be to pour nutrient-rich water into shallow seas. This could lead to algal blooms, perhaps of a species which release toxic by-products (the so-called red tides for example) . . . an impact on the North Sea spawning grounds is not unlikely.'[12] We may observe that, 200 miles to the west of Maplin, there are great schemes afoot for the Severn estuary which might include a national airport. Here the possible effects on the estuarine ecology are engaging a group of experts on long-term research which is considered necessary before any new interference is undertaken.

The agricultural land in the Foulness area is of exceptionally high quality and much of its production would be sacrificed to the airport and its associated works. This point has been copiously referred to in Parliament and the press, and in para. 11 of Mr Hunt's Appendix 4 to the Roskill Report.

The question of amenity was mentioned in para. 14:

Fears were expressed that large-scale urbanization would greatly increase pressure upon the limited open areas which would remain. The unusual qualities of the estuary lands adjoining the Crouch and the Roach would be harmed by the surface access routes. Facilities afforded to yachtsmen and fishermen by the River Crouch could be impaired. The existing open character of the Dengie peninsula merited stringent protection.

There are also dark stories about vast numbers of unexploded shells embedded in the sand, some of which can never be neutralized, and there can be no absolute certainty that one of these might not suddenly go off.

These add up to quite an impressive collection of objections to the Maplin site as such.

One of the advantages attributed to Foulness is that it produces conditions favourable for associated industrial developments, of which the most important is an oil port. However, there are two serious grounds for doubt about the oil port. First, by the early 1980s Europe's energy supplies, in the form of oil and natural gas, can be expected to come more and more from European sources, so that the need for more tanker berths is likely not to grow significantly.[13] Secondly, in the longer run, as the 1980s progress and pressure on world oil supplies develops, energy will need to be derived more from coal and nuclear sources, rather than from oil, as far as is practicable. The decision, in December 1972, to maintain the coal industry's capacity in Britain reflects a need to keep options open. The contribution of tidal water-power may become important. (All this creates an argument for preferring railways, which can be driven by electricity, to aircraft which are wholly dependent on petroleum products, in cases where the two media are interchangeable.) Thirdly, even if more oil berths are needed, expert opinion tends to favour development on Britain's West coast rather than on the East.[14]

Quite apart from the doubts about the need for a new oil port at the Foulness site, there has been no demonstration of any real advantage to be expected from new urban developments bringing a million residents to this part of the South-East within about 25 years from now. The area as a whole has consistently had a lower unemployment rate than any other region in the UK. Southend may have some seasonal problems, like other seaside towns, but

34

the airport is an over-heavy solution to these. The new activities would be additional to the existing industrial and commercial activities of the South-East; there would be a net addition to the normal diversion of population to the South-East.

It will be argued in Chapter 3 that the present dominance of the south-eastern airports in Britain's international air traffic is not healthy, and that some change in the pattern would be in agreement with the regional policies that all Governments proclaim. Further encouragement to the concentration in the London area of air-borne freight operations can only damage importers and exporters in the regions. As with passenger operations, a major airport at Foulness is bound to be worse in this respect than one at a place such as Cublington, though Cublington too would have been rather bad, and much less good than a diffusion of traffic among regional airports. There has been no means of expression of regional views on the matter.[15] As we shall see later, the occasional regional voice raised in parliamentary debate was brushed aside.

Finally, there is one environmental objection which tends to be overlooked, because it works indirectly. Maplin airport will displace the Shoeburyness firing range. It is impossible to find another coastal site to accommodate a new firing range to replace Shoeburyness except at the cost of damaging some other section of the already overburdened coastline. There is a certain irony here. In the pre-Roskill years, which we may now call the Stansted period, the Ministry of Defence earned opprobrium for defending the Foulness site against those who advocated an airport there rather than at an inland site. Mr Crosland rightly congratulated the Roskill Commission for treating the Defence Ministry's evidence 'with a great deal of scepticism'.[16] Roskill's rejection of the Foulness site was not influenced by the Defence Ministry's protection of its interests. But the Foulness birds can live with the firing range, and it is sad to contemplate the harm that would follow from the establishment of the range at another site.

Some support the present Maplin airport scheme because they hope that, if Maplin is built, all the London air traffic will eventually be concentrated there, so that Heathrow, Gatwick, Stansted and Luton will be closed down. By this means, in some distant future, London's umbrella of noise and danger would be taken away to the lower Thames estuary and not-too-populous land areas beside it.

At first sight this plan might seem to deserve support as a piece of admirable land-use planning. But there are valid objections. The existing airports already represent a huge investment and, in order to enable them to cope with developing traffic on the existing pattern, vast further investments must be put into them in the next few years, including new access transport systems. They must be prepared to handle over 50 million passengers in the last year before Maplin is ready – nearly three times the present load. Once this apparatus is in place it would be a pity to throw it all away.

Technology is about to give us much quieter aircraft. That particular source of noise pollution will soon be reduced anyway, so that it will be insignificant in relation to road traffic. To scrap Heathrow and Gatwick would be so extravagant in terms of resources that it would be difficult to justify on the grounds of noise alone.

A variant of the plan to abolish Heathrow, once Maplin becomes fully operative, might be to expect Heathrow to be converted into a VTOL/STOL airport for the air traffic up to about 1,000 miles. By this means the equipment and access routes for Heathrow would not be wholly wasted. Total air traffic would presumably grow at the rate envisaged by Roskill, but there would be a rationalization as between London airports for the 1990s.

An obvious objection is that Heathrow is so far out of London that the advantage of VTOL aircraft would be wasted if they operated there rather than at an airport nearer to the central area. The objection is not wholly conclusive, but in any case if we used rail and a national airports policy to take care of the demands of the 1980s we would still have open the option of starting a new third national conventional airport at a later stage, after a more complete and modern reassessment than Roskill was able to provide. We could then keep the Thorne (Humberside) and Severnside options open in the meantime, for comparison with Maplin. The aspiration to take the long-runway aircraft movement away from the existing London airports would have as good a chance of being realized then as it does now that it has been decided to build Maplin.

We should also remember that Maplin's construction will use up enormous resources. It is certain to affect railway development directly or indirectly. On that side three main possibilities can be envisaged :

Either (1) we should not build a Channel tunnel, but leave air to continue as the main provider of public transport between Britain and Europe. Rail would then run down and the impact would affect all Europe, which would drift towards the American pattern of middle-distance public transport based on road and air.

Or (2) we should built a Channel tunnel as well as Maplin and also commit full resources to the railways. In this case we should use up even more resources and the result would be over-provision. If the air services were fully used the railway would provide relatively infrequent services at relatively high unit cost.

Or (3) we should build a Channel tunnel and not invest much in the railways. In that case they could not compete with air for the public transport traffic. The tunnel's main function would be to carry cross-Channel cars, to the detriment of the Channel ports and Kent.

The hope that all London's air traffic might ultimately be removed from the London area is an admirable hope, but probably forlorn. Ironically, the building of the new airport in the 1970s must surely damage the chances of that hope's realization.

Once Maplin airport is in use there will be no incentive to stem the growth of London air traffic. On the contrary, there will be an immediate incentive to encourage an increase in it so as to make the new airport economically viable. Railways and regional airports will be likely to be stunted, and the relief which they could give to air traffic at London frustrated.

The accepted projections foretell a total London air traffic of 150 million passenger movements a year by some date in the 1990s, and 200 million by the year 2000. Could one airport deal with such a load? Probably not. The maximum capacity of 125 millions estimated in the BAA Report for 1971 could almost certainly not be exceeded, if only because of the access problems. The difficulties of access to Maplin, dismissed above (p. 30), would be brought forward in time, and the saturation of Maplin would occur soon.

It just looks as if it would be quite inconceivable to move all the London air traffic down to Maplin unless the total growth of that traffic were slowed down. The best way to slow it down would be by developing alternative routes and modes of transport as fast as possible. The deferment of the airport would have been the best device for achieving these other developments.

3

A preliminary discussion of the alternatives

The Roskill Report showed that Maplin is a bad site for a new London airport, unattractive to passengers, damaging to the environment and sure to disturb a vast population along its access route. The Government chose it because all the other possible sites were even more damaging, and it is to be congratulated on this choice.

The message of Roskill's investigations was clear: any new major London airport would be very undesirable. Mr Noble, Minister for Trade and Industry, acknowledged this when he introduced the Report in the House of Commons. The Report led him to 'question seriously the possibility of doing without a third London airport'.[1]

Such a 'serious questioning', if it had really been serious, might have started with a recognition that all the assumptions of Roskill, and of official thinking up to then, had neglected one obvious principle: that there is in reality no such absolute thing as demand for transport in aeroplanes to or from London-area airports. In fact there are demands for transport between A and B, C and D; this street in Hampstead to that office in Stuttgart, Yeovil to Accra, Bedford to Corfu, Milan to Kensington; for each person demanding transport there may be a choice of routes or modes; and where there is a choice, the preference is determined by a combination of price, time consumed, reliability, safety, comfort and convenience. In 1971 a serious questioning of the need for Maplin would have involved a new and synoptic assessment of future transport needs.

The inquiries conducted by the Government, the Roskill Commission and its advisers were incremental rather than synoptic with reference to this fundamental question, because they started with the existing traffic at London-area airports and made projections into the future from these narrow data, instead of starting with much fuller information about possible or desirable changes in the pattern

38

of transport of which London air movements are only a part. Nor did they take full note of the changes in the pattern of transport which new technologies were already producing, or of the challenge which these technologies presented to any Government concerned with rational planning.

Even an incremental approach, starting with the current London airport traffic, was bound to take into account three factors, each of which is certain to reduce the future rate of increase in aircraft movements at London airports. First, regional transfer : as total air traffic increases, so the direct international services to and from British provincial airports will improve, and a smaller proportion of provincial travellers will need to use London. Secondly, transfer to rail : improving rail services will undoubtedly take over many of the travellers over short distances, as rail extends the ring of journeys on which it gives quicker door-to-door journey-times. Thirdly, load factors : the average size of aircraft will increase, so the demand for aircraft runway-space will not rise as fast as the number of passengers.

All these three factors were taken into account by Roskill's inquiries, and the first projections of the London airports' future load were corrected so as to allow for them. Or so it seemed. The validity of the corrections was questioned in Parliament, but no questioner succeeded in denting the official confidence in their scope or comprehensiveness.

One single figure, 3·5 million passengers in 1981, was assumed as a likely reduction in the London airports' load through the availability of the improved direct flights at the major airports in Scotland, the North-West and Midlands;[2] improved railway services within Britain were assumed to produce a reduction of 2·5 million London-airport users.[3] Both figures were for 1981 only; no allowance was made for a possible increase in the number of travellers who would or might desert the London airports after 1981. No allowance at all was made for transfer to rail of traffic with the European continent through a Channel tunnel, because it was not known whether there would be a tunnel, or, if there were a tunnel how much would be invested in the railways feeding it. In any case, it was argued, the rail tunnel could hardly take more than 5·5 million passengers away from the London airports by 1981.

On the basis of Roskill's somewhat casual assessment, these possible reductions in the London traffic, through diversion, by a little over 10 per cent, looked relatively insignificant. The number involved was less than the difference between the higher and lower estimates of absolute passenger demand, derived from mere uncertainty about the annual rate of increase in total propensity to travel on journeys of the type currently performed by air. They were also less than the difference in demand for runway-space which would arise from a difference between 120 and 140 as an average passenger load per aircraft.

The most nearly fixed element in the situation was that the maximum capacity of Heathrow's runways looked likely to be around 300,000 air-transport aircraft movements, and Gatwick's around 100,000. These capacities could be increased through the acceptance of some 'overload', but there were many good reasons for avoiding this.

The range of uncertainty about absolute passenger demand by 1981 seemed about 20 per cent – or the equivalent of two or even three years' future growth; the range of possible loads per aircraft was at least as great as this and probably more. The third source of uncertainty, through transfers of traffic to regional airports or domestic rail services, looked to be no more than half as great as either of the first two. The Roskill Commissioners' relative neglect of this last relatively minor variable thus seems to have been perfectly reasonable.

Why then should a whole book now be devoted mainly to this third issue? The first answer, in principle, is that even in 1971, when work on this book began, it was clear that, with up to half of the London airports' traffic potentially railable, and with the future role of regional airports not yet thoroughly examined, the range of conceivable transfers was very much greater than Roskill had assumed it to be. The second answer is that the extent of that range was not just a matter for speculation. It could be immensely influenced, and to some extent determined, by governmental decisions which, in their turn, would affect the whole shape of European transport, and notably the ability of railways to play their full potential role in producing a given quantity of transport with relatively low environmental damage and consumption of irreplaceable scarce resources.

Developments in 1971–3, discussed elsewhere in this book, have brought further reinforcement to these arguments of principle. But, to return to the uncertainties mentioned above, the trend in the

40

increase of absolute demand for air transport has been downwards since 1969, and the trend in average aircraft size has been upwards. Revised projections in 1973, made on the same basis as the four-year-old projections used by Roskill, seemed likely to defer by two to five years beyond 1980 the date at which saturation would be reached on the existing runways, even without transfer on a scale bigger than Roskill's. There seemed therefore at the time of writing (February 1973) to be ample time for at least a deferment of the start of actual construction work on Maplin Sands, so that the British Government, together with others, could be enabled to work out an integrated transport policy.

A synoptic approach in 1971 would have started with a recognition that future traffic at London airports will be only a part of the whole movement of people and freight by public transport to and from and within Britain. The development of this package of traffic will depend on what is done about other airports and railways, and the distribution of the traffic will depend heavily on the distribution of transport investment, which in its turn would need to be determined against a background of a full appreciation of the options.

It is certain that much the greatest part of air movement at British airports will be in traffic with places overseas. A synoptic view would begin with a total projection for Britain to overseas, then project the proportions likely to terminate in the South-East and outside it; then, having established a non-South-East sub-total, ask how it might be distributed among British airports. Supposing that X would be likely to terminate in the Midlands, what variety of direct services could Midlands airports provide (including charter), and how many travellers would use their regional airports as a result? There is a chicken-egg effect which demands close analysis. We might then go further and ask whether some of the travellers terminating in London might make their flights to or from regional airports, comparing the detriments to their convenience with the gain to the regions.

The potential contribution of railways could also be examined synoptically. The nationalized railways of France, Belgium, Holland, Germany and Italy all have schemes to provide for linking major cities at start-to-stop speeds of over 100 mph. They do not know whether or not the necessary investments are justified without estimates of the traffic, and adequate estimates can only be made

on an all-Europe basis, on a whole series of assumptions, includ-
ing various possible distributions between air and rail. The potential
British element in the traffic is an important factor, particularly in
France and Benelux.

The relative costs of the various possible distributions would have
to be considered; and the prices charged to travellers would influence their choices between routes and modes. The environmental
consequences of the options are a major factor to be taken into
account.

The range of variables is wide, but essentially not very resistant
to measurement, which would have a reasonable chance of producing sound predictions. The measurements could proceed by stages,
beginning with fairly rough common-sense estimates, which might
give some indication of the worthwhileness of proceeding to a more
sophisticated stage.

It could be objected that we just do not have the time or the resources for synoptic inquiries into every set of options. Such an
objection would be weakened by the nature of the Roskill inquiries.
Having proceeded incrementally and within the confines of a single
compartment on the primary issue (the timing of the need for a
third London airport), the Roskill Commission then went on to
bring into operation the whole armoury of synoptic inquiry for the
secondary issue, that concerning the location. The Government's
rejection of Roskill's recommendation suggests that the question
was not a particularly favourable one for the full synoptic treatment. The fault, if there is one, lies with the terms of reference
given to the Roskill Commission, rather than with the Commissioners – though they did have scope for being more imaginative
than they were. Roskill's narrow terms of reference were given by
the Labour Government, but they did not carry out the principles
admirably stated by Mr Ernest Davies in an article published shortly
before the Commission was set up : 'Transport must be considered
as a system, not as a number of modes unrelated to each other.' Mr
Davies also claimed that, at that very time, 'a planned transport
policy was being developed based on socio-economic considerations,
more vaguely defined as the national interest.'[4]

Mr Davies' words expressed aspirations which are still far short
of fulfilment, though they are not wholly novel; only in their environmental implications did they go beyond the objects set forth
by the French law of 5 July 1949, which provided (in article 7) 'for

the use of the means of transport which minimize the national pro-
duction-cost'.

In an important French production of 1972 the heads of the
national transport undertakings argue for a rational transport plan;
the chiefs of the Société Nationale des Chemins de Fer and Air
France both plead for avoidance of duplication of infrastructures
and of pointless competion.[5] The German *Programm zur Gesün-
dung des deutschen Verkehrswesens* ('Leber Plan'), approved by the
Bundestag in 1968, is perhaps the nearest approach to a concrete
rational policy that has yet been seen, but until now its application has been rudimentary and confined within West Germany's
borders.

No fully rational transport plan for any part of Europe can be
developed for any single nation; but piecemeal bits of national
planning such as that for the third London airport present elements
of frustration in the way of any general plan, by introducing dis-
tortions of a total policy. As the London airport involves a large
part of a European transport, the distortion which it produces is
particularly serious.

The market for which the airport is planned is only in part European, but the domestic and long-haul sections are highly susceptible to Britain's own planning decisions. In the light of a combination of this element with the European element (including, obviously,
a Channel tunnel), an approach to the London airport question
might usefully have proceeded as follows:

First, regarding transport as a whole, identify the factors which
might reduce the growth of London airport traffic, and quantify the
reductions.

Secondly, construct a model showing the effect of these reductions, separately and together, on the traffic and demand for runway space at London airports.

Thirdly, regard each of the reductions as an option within the
transport model and assess the likely consequences, social and
economic; in other words, assess their desirability, the costs and
benefits involved.

Fourthly, examine the feasibility of the reductions, one by one;
just who must do what in order to achieve each one of them.

Fifthly, put the reductions in an order of priority based on merit.

Sixthly, work out a time-scale for the reductions.

In spite of Mr Noble's words, there is no evidence that anything of this kind was done. On the contrary, there is ample evidence that the government machinery was determined to have no truck with any such stuff as this; that it had identified itself with the need for a third airport and regarded any evidence against it as an irritation to be brushed aside.

Both transfer to regional airports and transfer to rail are proper objects of planning policy. Public authorities own and control the major infrastructures and most of the vehicles and their operations. Roskill's spontaneous incremental reliefs to London's airports (already showing signs of outrunning earlier expectations) could be increased by a positive approach to the planning of the transport system.

Details concerning possible transfers, spontaneous and stimulated, planned and unplanned, and their possible consequences, will be discussed in the succeeding chapters, but it may be useful here to offer a preliminary summary of these sections of the London airports' future market from which some passengers might transfer to regional airports or to rail. By putting together the findings of the Board of Trade's survey conducted in 1968 (published in 1970 as *Passengers at London Airports*), the various statistics of airport movements (mainly in the BAA annual reports) and the projections for the future used by Roskill (particularly those published in the DTI Working Party's *Report on Traffic and Capacity at Heathrow* (1971), we can identify nine markets from which some of the future travellers might be expected to transfer to other airports or to rail. The size of each of these nine markets can be roughly measured as a proportion of the London airports' projected future total. Then, by adding together the proportions of all these markets which might be deflected from the London airports, we can arrive at a preliminary estimate of the proportion of their total passenger load which they might 'lose' by about 1985.

Among these groups of transfers the least attractive would seem to be those involving the use of non-south-eastern airports for travellers to Europe (groups 3, 4 and 5). It is most unlikely that these would be needed.

The overriding assumption is that no travellers would need to add more than an hour to their door-to-door journey-time, assuming the availability of overnight rail where appropriate. The need to avoid double-counting is borne in mind. We shall begin with a paragraph on each market, leading to a tabulation, in which the percentage deductions made by Roskill will be entered for comparison.

1. Passengers terminating outside the South-East but using London airports now amount to almost a fifth of the London airports' load. Most of these are British holiday-makers, for whom a much greater variety of destinations will be available from their local airports by 1985. The great majority can be expected to use direct flights from regional airports. Most scheduled journeys from British regions will still require two bites, but in some cases an interchange at (e.g.) Amsterdam (likely to be served directly by 1985) may be as good as an interchange at London and much better than an interchange at London demanding an inter-airport transfer. We can also assume that very little region-to-North America traffic will need to use London airports. The feasible 'loss' to London airports might be put at 10 to 15 per cent of the uncorrected total by 1985, compared with Roskill's 7 per cent for 1981.

2. A sixth of the DTI's unrevised estimate for 1985 is for North America. (The upwards revision for 1980, made after a year's further study, would imply a raising of this proportion.) Another tenth is other long-haul. We should now leave out the element terminating in the British regions, as we have allowed for this already.

If a third of the London–North America travellers went by train to a British regional airport, probably Liverpool, the loss to London airports in 1985 would be 5 per cent of the total load; if half, plus some other long-hauls, it could be as high as 10 per cent.

3. Some of the travellers between London and parts of Europe which will still be inaccessible by rail might use regional airports in appropriate geographical locations. Much of this market consists of British holiday-makers, mainly to the Mediterranean. The possibilities are complex and will be discussed in Chapter 4. The whole market amounts to almost a quarter of London's total load. The scope for relief might range between 5 and 10 per cent of the whole.

4. Much or most of the London–Channel Islands traffic could be switched to a southern airport. Loss to London airports: 1 to 2 per cent.

45

5. Some of London's traffic with Ireland, including Belfast, could be switched to Birmingham or Liverpool or a southern airport. Let us assume one-half. Loss to London airports: 2 per cent.

SECOND GROUP: CONSEQUENCES OF TRANSFER OF
PASSENGERS TO RAIL

6. Transfer to rail of 90 per cent of the projected air traffic between London and places in northern England, which will be able to be served by frequent trains in under $2\frac{1}{2}$ hours by the early 1980s, subject to adequate investment in railways, which would bring other valuable advantages, besides the relief for air routes. The overall journey-time will be less by rail than by air for the vast majority of travellers; rail will be more convenient and much cheaper. Loss to London airports: 2 per cent.

7. Transfer to rail of 60 per cent of the traffic with Glasgow and Edinburgh, which will be reached by train in about 3 to 4 hours by the early 1980s, at much lower cost than by air. This modest rate of transfer still leaves much of the business traffic moving by air. Conceivably the transfer might be greater. Loss to London airports: 2 per cent (perhaps 3 per cent).

8. Transfer to rail of 90 per cent of the traffic with Paris and Brussels, which will be accessible more quickly door-to-door by rail than by air, more cheaply and more conveniently. Loss to London airports: 10 per cent.

9. Transfer to rail of 60 per cent of the traffic with Holland and Cologne–Ruhr: rail journey-time varies between equality with air and one hour longer, but price much lower. Loss to London airports: 3 per cent (maximum 5 per cent).

10. Transfer to rail of 60 per cent of the traffic with places in Europe between 400 and 1,000 miles away (mostly overnight, though some passengers to Switzerland and mid-Germany would opt for day-service in under 8 hours). Loss to London airports: 10 to 15 per cent.

Groups 6 to 10 include some regional terminators travelling by train, mainly through London but not changing stations there, assuming adequate rail links between the Channel tunnel and places north of London.

All these transfers together, at the lower rates envisaged, would

46

reduce the London airports' passengers load by 50 per cent; in the following list we shall call these reductions at the 'moderate' rate, but include the higher figures too.

Transferable groups (Nos 3, 4 and 5 as last-resort reserves)	Percentage of total passengers lost to London airports		
	1985 Moderate	1985 Maximum	1981 (Roskill)
(1) Spontaneous transfer to regional airports	10	15	7
(2) Regional airports' national role for long-haul charter	5	10	
(3) Diversion of long charter-trips to Europe	5	10	
(4) Diversion of Channel Islands air traffic	1	2	
(5) Diversion of half of Irish air traffic (including Belfast)	2	2	
(6) Switch to rail of 90 per cent of traffic with northern England	2	2	
(7) Switch to rail of 90 per cent of traffic with Glasgow/Edinburgh	2	3	5
(8) Switch to rail of 90 per cent of traffic with Paris and Brussels	10	11	
(9) Switch to rail of 60 per cent of traffic to Europe, 300–400 miles	3	5	
(10) Switch to rail of 60 per cent of European traffic, 400–1,000 miles	10	15	
Loss to London Airports, total percentage	50	75	12

It was assumed in 1971 that, in the absence of any of these reductions, except those allowed for by Roskill, demand for runway space would overtake supply by about 1981–3. That situation now seems likely to be deferred until 1985–6. If all the reductions were brought into effect at the lower of the rates indicated here, the existing airports could cope with the projected traffic until well beyond 1995. The maximum rate attainable is far beyond anything that is necessary. There is ample room for flexibility. Even without some of the changes listed we could manage with no new airport. By early 1973 the changes in trend since 1970 could be seen to give time for a full study of the whole problem as a part of European transport needs, and time for Britain to take a lead in developing an integrated and intelligent plan, preferably within the framework of the EEC.

We could thus quite safely afford to wait for at least ten years before *beginning* to build the third airport. It would not be necessary to bring all the transfers into effect at once, and some or all of them could be brought in gradually in the 1980s. British and continental railways will not be ready to take all this new load at adequate overall speeds by 1980, though they should be amply ready by 1985 or 1988, subject to investments whose worthwhileness needs to be examined in a broad context. French, German and Italian railways already have the necessary development plans.

Each of the transfers, in both main groups, involves the provision of an alternative service for a group of potential air travellers. Each of the alternative services would be more attractive the greater the commitment to it, so the aim should probably be to achieve at least the lower suggested level of transfer fairly quickly once the alternative had been chosen.

Suppose these transfers should enable us to do without a third airport only until about 1990. It could be argued that even so we might as well go ahead with the new airport now, though it would be a strange investment policy indeed that created a costly (and harmful) infrastructure six to ten years before it was required. It would be strange even if we were sure that the new airport would be needed by about 1990.

But once the 1980s were taken care of, we have no means of knowing at the present time whether or not the airport would be needed even in the 1990s. Even now, we can identify four factors which seem quite likely to take care of the 1990s too.

1. Today's projections for a period so far ahead are almost useless. The rate of increase in demand for public transport travel experienced in the 1960s is unlikely to continue. As far as we can reasonably foretell, it is more likely to decline than to rise, as saturation begins to take effect. The official projection allows for a decline in the 1990s, but its rate and timing must be highly speculative. People's choice of travel times is likely to flatten the summer weekend peaks.

2. Vertical- or short-take-off aircraft may be operating on a large scale, almost certainly up to 1,000 miles, perhaps beyond this. They will want airport facilities close to the centre of London; to send them to Foulness would be absurd. They may be expected to win passengers from growing railway traffic, but also to reduce the demand for long runway space.

3. If air travel increases we are likely to have yet bigger con-

ventional aircraft. The number of movements is likely to continue to grow less quickly than the number of passengers.
4. New factors, as yet unforeseen, could invalidate many assumptions which seem valid now. For example, we could have surface public transport at 200 mph or more. In this case Thorne Waste on Humberside could look to be a better place than the Thames estuary for a new national long-haul airport, if one were needed, particularly if our regional policies were bearing fruit. Severnside is another possibility

All this about 1990 and beyond is highly speculative. But it does show that the uncertainties about Maplin in this remote future strengthen the case for deferring its construction if we can possibly take care of the 1980s without it.

The biggest item in this package is the transfer to rail of most of the potentially railable passengers within Britain and Europe. The direct and obvious environmental advantages of this option, and its benefits for non-travellers, as compared with the accepted plan to build Maplin airport, could well lead on to indirect advantages by inducing some travellers to use rail instead of road because of the enhanced attractiveness of rail services.

The balance of advantage for the travellers needs some study, but *prima facie* evidence suggests that the rail option would be more convenient (less changing, less waiting round in limbo), more reliable and much cheaper. All the rail travel would be on major routes; with heavy use these tend to show infrastructure, vehicle and current operating costs less than half of those by air. The Japanese have estimated the total unit costs of their Tokaido rail operations at one-fifth of the cost of the equivalent air cost, after allowing for the cost of building a complete new railway system. The British and European package is comparable in many ways, with some pluses and some minuses.

The full exploitation of rail would slightly reduce the expected growth in demand for the sacred products of the aircraft industry, but an expanded rail-equipment industry would compensate for this and use some interchangeable resources, and it could well produce a better overall net effect on the balance of payments.

One argument against transferring passengers to rail has already been put by Mr Noble: the alternative railway services would not be frequent enough.[6] But the published projections for 1985 imply at least five million passengers a year between London and Paris, and another five million between London and Benelux.

Every 200,000 passengers on a route in a year correspond roughly with one 500-seat train each way per day, with average seat occupation of 55 per cent, or 275 passengers. So five million passengers a year require 25 such trains each way per day, or a half-hour daytime service, given sufficient investment to make this feasible. Is a half-hour service too infrequent for a two- or three-hour journey? The use of this argument by a Government spokesman significantly illustrates the quality and prejudice of the Government's thinking.

More broadly, ministers' speeches in 1971 made use of arguments which had been repeated with little change since 1965, though they paid more verbal attention to the bane of aircraft noise, in response to public and parliamentary complaint. But by 1973 the prospects for the 1980s had changed. There was already a prospect of substantial alleviation of noise through quieter engines; railway technology had made new advances; traffic at regional airports was growing spontaneously faster than at London. The ministerial objections to a reassessment came to look even thinner in 1973 than in early 1971.

In April 1973 the Civil Aviation Authority, appointed in the previous year, produced a new assessment of runway capacities and needs, indicating that even without relief from Liverpool, etc., or from railways through a Channel tunnel, the existing London airports should be able to cope with the expected load until 1985.

This new finding gives much more time for a full examination of the practicability and extent of the obvious diversions suggested in this book. It takes away the urgency but gives no excuse for dilatoriness. It now seems that the diversions could take care of the growth of air traffic until 1995 or later, even without the help of a new VTOL airport. In the long run it is probably desirable to restrain the growth of London's air traffic; there is now time to look at the means of doing so.

PART TWO

Comprehensive Transport Planning: Neglected Options

4

The original projections reconsidered

The official acceptance of the need for a new London airport by about 1980–2 is based on projections of total numbers of passengers, and of the aircraft movements required to accommodate them. However, even without any transfer of passengers to other airports or to rail, the date at which the new airport would be needed might conceivably be deferred as a result of new developments for which allowance has not been made. (*a*) Most obviously, the increase in demand might slow down; there are several possible, and indeed quite likely, sources of such a decline. (*b*) Peak-period demand might rise less rapidly than total demand. (*c*) Average aircraft size might increase more rapidly than in Roskill's projections, so the number of aircraft movements associated with any given number of passengers would decline, particularly after 1980.

The arguments of this book do not depend on these developments, which are hypothetical and cannot be measured; there is no means

TABLE 1

Millions of air journeys 1969–2006
(Roskill Research Group forecasts)

| | British residents | | Non-British | | Working Party forecasts | | |
	Non-business	Business	Residents	Total	Lower	Likely	Upper
1969	5·2	3·4	8·5	17·1			
1975	11·1	6·1	15·0	32·2	29·2		36·9
1980					46·1	55·9	65·1
1981	24·8	10·6	22·7	58·1	48·6		70·3
1985				82·7	67·4	88·4	106·7
1999	74·8	26·7	36·8	137·9			
2006	138·0	37·0	58·0	233·0			

by which their probability can now be tested. However, there is enough likelihood of change in these directions for them to be mentioned as reinforcements of the main arguments.

Roskill had available estimates by several authorities, but the Commission paid most attention to those of its own Research Group.[1] These may be set beside the forecast of the Department's own Working Party on Traffic and Capacity at Heathrow.

However, the Roskill Report itself gave figures which took account of certain revisions, according to which British residents would make fewer journeys by air to and from London airports and non-British residents more. The revised estimates were published in the Report (p. 191, Appendix 6, Table 5).

TABLE 2

Terminal passenger demand at all London airports
(Roskill estimates 1969–2006)

| Year | British residents | | Non British residents | Total |
	Non-business	Business		
1969	5·2	3·4	8·5	17·1
1975	9·3	6·1	17·8	33·2
1981	15·8	10·6	29·4	55·8
1991	43·9	26·7	51·9	122·5
2006	132·4	37·0	90·5	259·9

It will be useful also to reproduce a fuller range of forecasts presented to the Roskill Commission and set out in Appendix 6 to the Report (para. 18):

TABLE 3

Summary of projections submitted to Roskill:
Forecasts of air-traffic demand currently being served
at Heathrow, Gatwick, Luton and Stansted airports
(Total passengers–millions)

	1975	1981	1985
Roskill Research Team	36·1	60·7	82·7
WPTC	32·5–40	56·4–78·6	78·5–118·8
BEA	32·3	53·4	73·4
BAA	33·9–38·2	53·9–68·2	75·7–100·2
BAA's consultant	34·1	57·7	79·0

We are particularly interested in the figure for 1985, as the mid-point of the period for which postponement seems to be feasible on the basis of the predictions made from trends up to 1970. At the time of writing (1973) it looks as if the situation expected for 1985 will not be reached until 1988. We might have concentrated on the projections for 1990, but these are too remote.

The arguments which follow will be based on the rather high estimate of 88 million, given as a middle figure in the Report of the DTI's Working Party on *Traffic and Capacity at Heathrow*. There are two reasons for this choice : first, the DTI's paper (though admittedly mere extrapolation after 1980) breaks down the total into major origin and destination groups; and secondly, it agrees with the Roskill figure, after taking into account Roskill's allowance for the deduction of 3·5 million transferring to regional airports and 2·5 million to domestic rail services. If we project to 1985 the upward revision of the DTI's Working Party on the North Atlantic route and its own deduction for domestic routes, we get a 1985 total of 90 million rather than 88 million, but a new revision of the North American projections would bring the total back again to 88 million.

There are big differences between the lower and the higher estimates, and the difference reminds us of the room for error in this operation. One factor to notice is that the projections are made from a period in which air travel has increased very rapidly, partly as a result of the introduction of new cheap rates for package trips in jet aircraft. These have been made possible by the curious overall fare-structure; the package trips are cheap because they are well filled and the regular operations have some spare capacity. The proportion of cheap-rate charter trips cannot go on rising indefinitely.

The London projections are influenced by recent experience and there are some grounds for doubting their validity.

1. Is it really likely that business journeys will almost treble in the next ten years, while new methods of communication, not requiring long personal journeys, are developed and become established? A possible slow-down in the increase would affect the total of non-British residents, who are not here broken down into 'business' and 'non-business'.

2. Non-business travellers from overseas to Britain have been increasing of late to an exceptional extent by reason of a swing of fashion to London, and this trend is not likely to continue indefi-

nitely. Indeed, there was already a sharp decline in the rate of increase in foreigners' holiday visits to London in 1971. A good thing too. With five times the present number of summer visitors London would lose its attractiveness to them. This part of the projected increase looks unlikely to be realized.

3. British residents' holiday travel abroad by air has recently exploded, encouraged by newly developed charter flights. The Spanish market doubled in 1967–70. The price reductions will not continue: by 1971–2 they were already bringing heavy losses to successful operators whose tours were fully booked. The summer peak demand, which imposes the heaviest burden, is likely to spread itself more evenly. As we move towards two fortnights of holiday a year, more people who go abroad once will be inclined to eschew the torrid South in July and August, and go there earlier or later.

4. A slow-down in the rate of increase in summer-peak holiday trips to the Mediterranean is likely to be made necessary by the sheer inability of the holiday resorts to absorb indefinitely increasing numbers of peak-period visitors. The Roskill projections tend to assume that air travel in this market will increase by more than five times in 1970–85. Such an assumption cannot be sensibly made without a thorough examination of the ability of the resorts to accommodate such an increase. It is not only that over-crowding would tend to make the conditions miserable; there are also problems of water-supply, pollution, etc., which would most probably produce an absolutely insuperable barrier to increases beyond a given maximum, first in one resort-zone, then in another. The question has not been thoroughly studied yet. We do not know whether Majorca's maximum capacity to receive July–August visitors would be two, or three, or five, or ten times the present number. But there is enough evidence about the probable existence of a limit to make it plain silly to base plans on an assumption that the number *will* be quintupled by 1985, decupled by 1992, etc. We should remember too that on Roskill's purchasing-power criteria the increase in demand for Mediterranean holidays from Britain would be likely to be exceeded by the increase from those other parts of northern Europe which have a higher GNP growth-rate.

5. The biggest rate of increase projected is on the transatlantic route. Few British residents now go across the Atlantic for summer holidays. They may increase tenfold by 1985, but if they do it can be assumed that at least three-quarters of these British travellers

would be worse served by a London airport than by one nearer to their homes, and Maplin would be almost the worst possible starting point. (Only Dungeness would be worse.) At least three-quarters would prefer an airport outside the South-East. Even the South-Eastern residents could be very reasonably served by a non-London airport.

American and Canadian visitors to Britain are likely to be far more numerous. The island of Great Britain would not sink if their numbers were multiplied ten- or even twenty-fold. But London's capacity to absorb tourists does have a limit, and even a trebling of the 1973 July–August numbers would be getting very near to that limit. The tourists in their turn are much more likely to enjoy Britain if London absorbs only a small proportion of their time in the country.

It is already amply recognized that Britain's policy of attracting foreign tourists needs to aim at attracting them to places other than London. The first tool of such a policy, particularly for North American visitors, is a vigorous promotion of one or more airports *outside* the South-East for arrival in the UK. The Maplin airport scheme directly and totally contravenes all avowed policies for encouraging foreign tourists to spread out from London to other parts of the country.

People do not now, and will not in the future, make air journeys to or from London airports just for their own sake, but because they have some purpose in travelling. Whenever we look into the projections of future London air travel, broken up into its various directions, we tend to find at least one major ground for doubt: either the market, at least at peak periods, is unlikely to grow at the rate predicted; or, if it does, some of the predicted growth ought to be diverted away from London airports, could be diverted and probably will divert itself.

Thus scepticism about the whole market merges into arguments for diversion, and this chapter is not dealing with the desirability of, or scope for, particular diversions. But it is right here to mention some special reasons for preferring to minimize the growth of air traffic, apart from the obvious arguments about noise, pollution and access to airports.

First, we should remind ourselves that aeroplanes necessarily depend on oil, and Europe is likely to have difficulties with oil supplies around 1980–2000; therefore, if a given objective (in this case some type of transport) can ultimately be achieved either with or without an absolute dependence on oil, the means not requiring oil is to be preferred.

Secondly, there is the question of the crowding of air space. The projection of 120 million passengers at all London airports around the year 1990 might involve serious difficulties of air traffic control. West German estimates suggest that a total of 80 million passengers, curently projected for the airports of the whole of West Germany by 1980, would produce 'a degree of saturation which will make further expansion nearly impossible'.[2] This argument suggests that before the total London airport load reaches a figure great enough to enable Maplin to break even financially, the crowding of air space over Britain and Europe will be causing serious difficulties. According to this thesis, air traffic considerations alone make it desirable to reduce the rate of growth of air travel in the 1980s. A positive plan to develop surface transport to relieve the load looks like a positive response to this problem; but the development of air transport presupposed by the development of Maplin is incompatible with that response.

On 29 November 1972 a further escape clause was suggested in a paper read by Mr Richard Graham (a member of BEA's planning department who had formerly been involved, as a civil servant, in airport policy) to the Institute of Air Transport's fifth international symposium at Paris. Mr Graham argues that Roskill made insufficient allowance for the increasing size of aircraft. Mainly because of this factor alone, Mr Graham argued that Heathrow and Gatwick could deal with the London airport's traffic up to 1990.[3] The Civil Aviation Authority's draft report, mentioned in the *Guardian* and other newspapers on 21–23 April 1973, gave new support to the claim that Heathrow and Gatwick could handle the aircraft movements up to 1985, even without diversions.

However, for the argument which follows, the 1971 projections will not be disputed. It will be suggested that even if the projections are valid, a redistribution of the traffic on rational lines could make the new London airport unnecessary, and that, irrespective of the validity of the 1971 projections, some redistribution is desirable for the sake of London, the regions, the environment and a healthy transport system.

5

Relief from other British airports

There is nothing new about the idea that there should be a national policy for the distribution of traffic among airports in the London area and the regions. At the very beginning of the postwar period the Parliamentary Secretary to the Ministry of Civil Aviation said in the House of Commons: 'If we are to secure the orderly development of transport aerodromes in the right places and up to the right standards it is necessary to have a central plan.'[1] A White Paper of 1945 put forward the view that the airfields required for scheduled air services should be acquired and managed by the then Ministry of Civil Aviation.[2] The Civil Aviation Act of 1946 gave the Minister power to obtain land required for airport development, and during the reign of the Attlee Government plans were developed for taking over a large number of aerodromes for civil aviation purposes. At first it was supposed that over eighty such airports would be needed, but by 1947 the number had fallen to 44.[3]

The Attlee Government did not carry through its plans, largely because of the economic difficulties of the time. Mr Doganis has told the story of the 1950s in his article in *The Political Quarterly* for 1966 (pp. 416–28); it became convenient for the central government to reduce its commitments in this area, and most development was left to those municipalities or other agencies which were prepared to undertake it. As Mr Doganis puts it, 'With the exception of the London area airports, which became the subject of a number of White Papers, reports and inquiries, there was no clear Government or Ministry policy on the location and development of the country's airports.'[4]

By 1961 the Government decided that the time had come 'to decentralize the ownership and management of state aerodromes'.[5] The British Airports Authority was set up by the Airports Authority Act 1965, to take over Heathrow and Gatwick, together with Stansted and Prestwick (30 miles from Glasgow); these were then regarded as 'the principal gateways to the country for normal scheduled services',[6] and the absence of any wider policy almost certainly contributed to the Government's indifference, in the next few years, to any approach to a general plant for airports.

The main cities developed their airports under local authority or private ownership. Those above 150 miles from London developed quite substantial scheduled services to London, used partly as feeder-services for international journeys. Except on the Irish routes, direct scheduled regional-international and inter-regional services were still rather few in 1970, though by that time the regional airports' international holiday charter-flights were developing fast.

In 1966 Mr Doganis argued that a national airports programme was urgently required. He was not alone in this. In June 1967 the Conservative Opposition in Parliament advocated a national policy in their motion of censure against the Stansted decision. Meanwhile Sir Peter Masefield, Chairman of the British Airports Authority, made some detailed suggestions about the form that a national policy could usefully take.[7]

The 1967 White Paper on the need for a third London airport at Stansted dealt with the prospects of passengers transferring to regional airports, and concluded that there was no scope for such transfer to give relief to London. (Cmnd. 3259, paras. 18–23). The main conclusion was in paras. 22 and 23 :

22.   If, then, say 20 per cent of London's international passenger traffic is generated by regions outside south-east England this might amount to a demand for direct services between the regions and abroad of a little over one million one-way seats a year at present traffic levels, or about 3 million one-way seats a year by 1975. In fact, of course, some of the international travellers generated by the regions will always wish to pass through London for personal or business reasons. It is, therefore, only the residue that represent the true frustrated demand for direct air services between regional airports and abroad. But these passengers do not represent demand at any one regional airport; they are spread throughout all parts of the United Kingdom. Moreover, the potential demand at any one regional airport is further greatly fragmented because of the very many different destinations to which passengers wish to travel. Thus, the potential demand for new direct services between regional airports and overseas is split up into fragments most of which are so small as not in the foreseeable future

economically to justify a direct air service. It is likely that, at most, a fifth of the total potential demand – say 250,000 one-way passengers now, rising to 600,000 in 1975 – represents demand that it may be practicable, by one means or another, to divert from London to regional airports. Passenger traffic of this order, however, corresponds to no more than half of one year's growth of traffic through London, so that its diversion to regional airports could only defer the requirement for a third London airport for, at the most, one year.

23. There is no doubt that the number of services operating directly between regional airports and overseas will continue to increase, as in the past. The Government welcomes this trend, and has taken full account of it in the traffic forecasts given earlier in this section; but it is nevertheless forced to the conclusion that this factor will not significantly affect the need for a third London airport or the date by which it will be required.

These arguments looked sound enough for the period to which they related, up to 1975, but scarcely convincing for the next ten years. It is now clear that, on the basis of developments in 1967–72, the 'transfer' of 1·2 million passengers by 1975 was an underestimate.

The question was quite fully discussed at the hearings of the House of Commons Select Committee on Nationalized Industries[8] on 26 January 1971, just after Roskill had reported and before the Government had made its decision. Mr J. E. Barnes, Under-Secretary, Civil Aviation, in the Department of Trade and Industry, explained the difficulties. His evidence gives a useful illustration of the departmental approach and is reproduced in part, together with the relevant section of the Report itself, in Appendix 1. In explaining the difficulties Mr Barnes made the interesting statement that 'everyone had hoped that the Roskill Commission would in effect plan a very great part of our aviation infrastructure in the south-east and the areas adjoining the south-east.'

Professor Robson, in his review of this Report, comments: 'The decision on the Third London Airport had to be taken in the absence of a plan, and the plan, when it is eventually prepared, will have to be constructed around the existing fact of the Third London Airport – a complete reversal of the proper order of events.'[9]

The Roskill inquiries did pay a little attention to the prospect that some of the future travellers terminating in Britain outside the South-East might use nearby regional airports instead of London, because increasing total traffic would make possible a greater range and variety of regional operations. Appendix 6 of the Report (para. 20, p. 193) quoted the 1968 origin and destination survey. About 18 per cent of total passengers using London-area airports in 1968 originated in regions outside the South-East. 'Assuming that distribution remains constant, the total number of passengers who might be diverted from London area airports in 1981 would be about 10 million.' This was only slightly followed up :

A more realistic assessment of the amount of London area traffic susceptible to diversion to provincial airports might be one half the amount of that traffic at present originating in regions with major airports – Scotland, north-west, west midlands – and one-quarter of that traffic at present originating in other regions. In 1981 this could represent a maximum loss of some 3·5 million passengers to the London area airports and a gain of some 3 million to the provincial airports.

No convincing argument supports the claim that these small transfers would be 'realistic'. All projections in this area must include a big element of conjecture, but an assumption that the distribution will remain constant seems, on common-sense grounds, rather unlikely to be fullfilled. It is surely more realistic to begin by noting that the South-East in 1970 generated five times as many international air journeys per inhabitant than the rest of Great Britain; it is to be expected that the imbalance between the regions will be soon modified. The causes of the imbalance have not been thoroughly studied.

It is indeed not surprising that London's role as the national capital should generate business and foreign-visitor traffic well above the national average, but a Government concerned with 'regional policy' might be expected to find the present imbalance so great as to be unhealthy. It might well observe that one probable cause of it is the very fact that a large proportion of international flights terminate at London airports; that the mere availability of international air transport at London's airports has tended to generate travel to and from London, while its non-availability in the regions has reduced the propensity to travel to or from the regions.

Even in the narrow context of aviation policy it was not possible, in 1970 or 1971, to plan London's airport needs except on a nation-wide scale. However, the Roskill Report itself (5.44, p. 32) explains the Commissioners' reasons for paying such scant attention to the scope for regional transfer. One reason is environmental. The regional airports tend to be close to heavily populated areas, so that any increase in traffic causes more people to suffer from noise. Birmingham's Elmdon Airport is mentioned in this connection. However, the Report does not add that some of the airports are not really very bad in this respect; and we are on the way towards a partial cure of noise as quieter engines become the norm.

Another reason is London-oriented:

Further to limit the growth of capacity at London's airports deliberately in the hope that a minority of current users – those travelling to or from places outside London and the south-east – may as a result find air-services developing at nearer airports would be detrimental to the interests of the majority of users who do live in London and the south-east.

In the light of often-repeated Government claims to be concerned with regional development, this sentence could be considered controversial.

Roskill's assumption that $3\frac{1}{2}$ million regional-terminators should be deducted from the first projected London load for 1980, because they would use regional airports instead, was not carried forward to 1985. If it had been carried forward, the 1985 figure should have been entered as about 6 million, or nearly 8 per cent of the most likely total of about 90 million in the DTI Working Party figures.

Roskill's estimate for 1980 was not fully worked out. An important factor likely to influence the rate of regional transfer is the diversity of services available from regional airports. As an alternative to Roskill's method, it will here be suggested that it would have been useful to project a total figure for all travellers ending their journeys outside the South-East. From this total, rough estimates could have been made of the distribution of the total among areas served by existing regional airports. From the maximum potential load of each it would then have been possible to find the number of aircraft movements implied and thus (less definitely) the number of destinations likely to be served.

Such a procedure could have provided a basis for calculations of the likely numbers of travellers able to find direct air transport from their local airports. Figures reached in this way would be only a first guide. In 1970, as we shall see, few regional residents made international air journeys, as compared with residents of the South-East, and very few foreigners made journeys by air to Britain for the purpose of ending their journeys outside the South-East – though some who stayed for only two days in London, but then went to a British region, were classified as terminating in London.

The relatively low level of international journeys terminating in regions in 1970 can reasonably be assumed to reflect the low availability of international air services at regional airports. Any increase in regional–international air services can be expected to encourage further travel which would not otherwise have taken place. Thus the regional-terminating total could be expected, by 1985, to rise by an amount greater than that implied by the reduction of regional journeys via London. But the consequent increase in services at the regional airports would increase the variety of services available. This in its turn would further reduce the number needing to go to London.

By 1971 over $3\frac{1}{2}$ million people actually travelled in international services to and from regional airports, an increase of over 50 per cent in two years. The excess of their traffic growth over London's in the years 1969 to 1971 was greater than the excess which would have been expected from a beginning of the process of spontaneous transfer assumed by Roskill – and the rate of transfer could be expected to increase during the 1970s, feeding on itself. Direct flights from Bristol, Castle Donington, etc., to Palma and less obvious places were already flourishing. The 1967 Report failed to take into account the attractiveness of this new product. By 1975, assuming no political or economic catastrophe (which would affect London airports too), between 5 and 8 million people can be expected to travel between regional airports and places abroad. At the lowest figure, this will represent a 'transfer' during 1967–75 of 3 million passengers, or $2\frac{1}{2}$ times the volume which the 1967 White Paper confidently predicted. Its predictions have not been fulfilled.

The whole argument about regional transfer can easily be misunderstood. On 10 February 1973 *The Times* air correspondent, Arthur Reed, wrote that 'nobody could be found in the [aviation] industry with any enthusiasm for the plan to put off Maplin and cater for the overflow of traffic by spreading it over provincial airports'. What is proposed here is not just to 'spread the traffic'. It is to analyse the spread that has been taking place spontaneously over the past three years, and to frame a new estimate of its future development, based on dynamic research which seeks to understand the reasons for it. This chapter uses the data which are available in order to suggest a preliminary assessment of the likely development after 1981 of the process which Roskill allowed for up to that year.

High and low figures for spontaneous transfer will be suggested, on a basis slightly less arbitrary than that used by Roskill. The result for 1981 will not differ much from Roskill's, but it will suggest reasons why the basis which Roskill used for 1981 is not likely to be adequate for calculations relating to 1985 and beyond. A much more thorough analysis, based on surveys of passengers, would produce more reliable results. Our figures may not be solidly founded enough to serve as a basis for policy (nor were Roskill's), but they do suggest that a more thorough survey is needed before we have adequate predictions to include in the totals to be used for any rational assessment of the need for a third London airport.

The next chapter will suggest a special role for Liverpool, and conceivably for one or two other airports, based on specific reasoned argument, but it would be a gross distortion to describe this as merely 'spreading the traffic over provincial airports'.

The aviation industry in general would have given its first preference to the extension of Heathrow and Gatwick, its second preference to a third airport at an inland site. These solutions are excluded on environmental grounds. We do know the Government recognizes that the industry's preferences are not the only element in the situation; the choice of Foulness as a site for the third airport was made against the wishes of almost every interest in the aviation industry, including its customers, who had no voice. On 10 February 1973 Arthur Reed reported, in the article just quoted, that 'hardly a company could be discovered ready to approve Maplin'. As the Maplin solution is so widely disliked, on highly rational grounds, it is absurd to discard other solutions without looking at them; if they have wide implications for regional policy, for the development of road traffic and the use of resources, these implications should also be taken into account. There may indeed be grounds for giving positive encouragement to the provincial airports, and the views of the aviation industry are only part of that picture, not the whole of it.

Even so, there are still difficulties, attributable in part to the haphazardness of development over the past twenty years. The regional airports already established are not ideal. They come in pairs, each pair thirty or forty miles apart: Glasgow and Edinburgh, Tyneside and Teesside, Manchester and Liverpool, Birmingham and East Midlands (the latter dating effectively only from 1965), Bristol and Glamorgan. It can reasonably be argued that each pair could advantageously be replaced by a single one, either in a new intermediate location or at only one of the two established locations.

In the Midlands there is also an airport at Coventry, in West Yorkshire one at Yeadon (Leeds), which is ill-placed for access from most of its region. Further south we find Hampshire served (in 1972) by Southampton and Bournemouth, with a further airport at Portsmouth; of these three the old Southampton airport is well located for access, but it is scarcely capable of extension and is now expected to be abandoned.

In Scotland, where large investment on Glasgow and Edinburgh airports was authorized in 1972–3, there is a strong demand for the establishment of a wholly new airport at a new site between the two cities. Elsewhere, as at Bristol and Leeds, there is uncertainty whether to invest in an existing airport which has poor access, or to go to a new site. Planning in Yorkshire is complicated by the availability of an excellent new site, with good access, at Thorne Waste (near Goole); in the South-West there is the possibility that a new airport of Foulness dimensions might be put on reclaimed land in the Severn Estuary in a rather remote future, as part of a scheme which probably ought to involve several other projects, including a tidal-power dam, if it is to be carried out at all.

It can reasonably be argued that, for twenty years to come, Britain would do well to concentrate international traffic on the London system and only one airport outside the South-East. Even fast-growing projections would not justify a wide range of scheduled services from each of several regional airports. On this basis one, probably Manchester, should be developed as the main regional centre, with feeder service or surface transport from other points.

This line of argument has many deficiencies. Manchester is probably too far north of the other midland and northern conurbations for economical air operations in conditions of the future. Liverpool (which is less bad for noise) is somewhat better for westwards international journeys, and a more southerly place would be better for southward journeys. In many ways a Severn Estuary site would be preferable on grounds of geography and the long-term attractions of that solution (which could serve London as well as the Midlands) provide an argument against the presently planned Maplin development.

The merits of Thorne or Severnside as a site for a major new national airport for the 1990s or later would be increased if a tracked hovercraft system were developed for surface transport, enabling people to be brought to one of these places by a purpose-built route in 30 to 45 minutes. (No other obvious role for a 300-mph surface transport system, requiring new track separate from the railways, is in sight.) As a long-term prospect Severnside could well be a better site than Maplin for an international airport to serve national needs in the twenty-first century.

For the nearer future there may well be an argument for heavy development of scheduled regional–international traffic at, say, Manchester, but such concentration should not preclude an international role for eight to ten other regional airports. They seem to have two roles for international air transport in the future. The first is for holiday-makers' journeys, mainly by outgoing British residents, but partly too by foreign visitors. Their work in this market has increased rapidly in 1968–73. The advantages are twofold: great convenience for the travellers, through finding their air transport near their British terminal points, and small demand for road space by vehicles going to airports. Air operators may dislike this diffusion among several airports, because they prefer to concentrate their operations. It may also be a little wasteful to run a plane on a Manchester-based scheduled service during the week, and then use it for holiday charter-trips from another airport at weekends. But it would not be unthinkable for such a plane to take on some holiday-charter passengers at Manchester for its first weekend journey, stopping to pick up others at another British airport on the way.

Another international role for a regional airport such as East Midlands might be to provide a scheduled service to one appropriate continental airport, such as Amsterdam, from which services radiate in many directions. Bus-stop international services have scope for development well beyond their present rather modest level.

All this needs detailed study and analysis. The whole range of consequences needs to be compared with those of the conventional assumption that the regional traffic must mainly pass through London, possibly relieved a little by Manchester.

As late as the summer of 1972 none of this seems to have been in the mind of the Department of Trade and Industry. At that time the

DTI produced a White Paper (Cmnd. 5082) in reply to the observations of the Select Committee on Nationalized Industries. Its comments on Recommendation 3 deserve reproduction in full:

The Committee recommended that preparation of a national airports plan should be started in earnest, without waiting for the establishment of the Civil Aviation Authority [para. 37 of HC 275 of 1970–71].

The Department has undertaken preliminary economic studies and further studies on the origins and destinations of airport passengers which are essential to the formulation of any national airports plan. Moreover, since the Committee reported, the Government has decided to build the Third London Airport at Maplin to be open for traffic in 1980. This decision, together with the Government's consequential decision that the construction of new runways at Heathrow, Gatwick, Stansted and Luton would be unnecessary for the foreseeable future and that the latter would be unnecessary to cater for air transport movements when Maplin is available, has in effect provided a strategic plan for major airport development to 1985 or 1990 in the South East. This is the area in which about 80 per cent of the national aviation effort is concentrated. It will fall to the Civil Aviation Authority to complete the studies begun by the Department and to decide the nature of the advice to be given to the Government and airport owners on airport development within the framework of a broad national airport strategy.[10]

This paragraph does not explain the delay; if the delay has caused irreparable damage there may seem to be no remedy. The Select Committee's basic complaint had been:

The decision on the siting of the Third Airport will be taken before there is a national plan. This, when it is prepared, will have to be built round the existing fact of the Third Airport. Your Committee regret the present dilatoriness in starting to prepare a national plan.

The reply contains no apology for the failure which the Select Committee eloquently exposed. On the contrary it says, in effect: 'Well, the Government has taken its decision on the third London airport, and that is that. The decision may have been taken blindly, but because the decision has been taken there is no point in reopening any discussion about it now. Even though nothing much in the way of resources has been committed to the Maplin development yet, even though we could still cut our losses and draw out of it, our whole authority is committed to it, and an admission of error now, after the huge concession we have already made by choosing the Foulness site, would really be too great a retreat to expect of us for the sake of rationality or the public interest.'

In this reply one concrete defence is offered: that 80 per cent of the national aviation effort is concentrating in the South-East. The use of the present tense implies the future too; it seems to intend to describe a permanent and unchangeable state of affairs. Yet those responsible for this statement must have been aware of the recent rapid rise in international passenger traffic at those airports. The trend showed signs of confirming the arguments which they themselves had rejected; it was to be expected on the basis of any common-sense assessment, and to be desired for the sake of regional development, as well as for the promise of relief to London's excessively growing load.

The regional spiral seems to be only at its earlier stages. However much it may deserve encouragement, this spontaneous movement can be frustrated by the use of negative powers towards the expansion of regional airports. Present Government policy could conceivably be vindicated as a result of its own action to frustrate spontaneous regional growth.

The first requirement for a national plan is a series of projections of the whole of British international traffic, from which we could derive proportions of the total who in future might be expected to terminate their journeys outside the South-East. A picture of the total future load could then provide a basis for assessing the likely demand for each major airport's catchment area, and hence the variety of direct services that each might be able to support.

If the 1968 origin and destination survey, used for *Passengers at London Airports* (BOT, 1970), had been repeated two and four years later, we should now have more information on which to project international traffic according to areas of origin and destination within Great Britain. It may well be that the regional terminators have been increasing faster than those terminating in the South-East, and that the imbalance between the South-East and the rest of the country has been tending to be reduced. If so, there is even more scope for the regional airports to increase their load and to relieve London.

It may be useful to study a list of regional airports, showing the traffic in 1970 and 1971. Making use of the partial projections for the London airports, we may then produce estimates of the possible regional traffic in 1980 and 1985. From the total we may derive some idea of the number of flights per year and per week that most of these airports might supply – and hence a nation of the range and choice of routes, itself a factor likely to influence the potential travellers' choice between local airports and London.

Those who lived in or wished to visit London and the South-East were indeed a majority of all international travellers at all British airports in 1970. In that year international passengers at British airports were divided as follows:

TABLE 4

International terminal passengers at all British airports

	1970 Thousands	Per cent change on 1969	1971 Thousands	Per cent change on 1970
South-East Airports				
1. Heathrow (BAA)	12,599	+11·3	13,455	+6·8
2. Gatwick (BAA)	3,684	+24·4	4,146	+27·6
3. Luton	1,971	+31·9	2,668	+38·7
4. Stansted (BAA)	474	+138·2	(474)	
5. Southend	406	+5·7	441	
6. Lydd	46	−35·2		
Total – Nos. 1–4	18,728		21,000	(approx.)
Total – Nos. 1–6	19,180		21,500	(approx.)
Total – all GB airports	21,580		25,000	(approx.)
Non-South-East Airports				
Southampton	14	−22·2	11	−26
Bristol	108	+30·1	150	+38·9
Glamorgan	117	+67·1	141	+20·5
Birmingham	394	+23·1	553	+40·4
E. Midlands	60	+25·0	172	+186·7
Manchester	1039	+17	1,419	+36·6
Liverpool	121	+7·1	158	+30·6
Glasgow	348	+24·7	415	+19·3
Prestwick (BAA)	311	+5·4	309	−0·6
Leeds	43	−34·8	48	+11·6
Newcastle	128	+19·6	155	+21·1
Edinburgh	61	+19·6	61	—
Total Non-South-East	2,759	+25 (approx.)	3,598	+28 (approx.)

Source: British Airport Authority: Annual Report, 1970–1 and 1971–2

70

Thus in 1970 about 6 million international air journeys teminated outside the South-East; the table shows that $2\frac{1}{2}$ million of these were direct and $3\frac{1}{2}$ million via a London airport. As Roskill showed, if the distribution of terminal points and of routes used both remained unchanged, about 11 million passengers would use London airports in 1980 for journeys between British regions and abroad. Next, Roskill suggested that some change of the distribution of routes would be likely, so that $3\frac{1}{2}$ million of these would use regional airports instead of London. He did not carry the calculation forward beyond 1980. If he had done so he would have reached a figure of about 6 million for 1985, assuming no further change in distribution. But he would also have projected the trend.

The guesswork figures used by Roskill for 1980 would seem to give us the following pattern of British airports' international traffic in 1985 :

(*a*) South-East terminators using London airports : 65 million.

(*b*) Regional terminators using London airports : 10 million.

(*c*) Switching to regional airports : 6 million.

(*d*) Regional terminators served by regional airports : $12\frac{1}{2}$ million.

In other words, the regions outside the South-East would still generate under a third of Britain's international air traffic (28 million out of 93 million).

These figures would be unsatisfactory for two reasons. First, the *proportion* of regional terminators using direct flights can be expected to increase in response to the growth in the variety of destinations which will be available as a consequence of increased total traffic. Secondly, the growth of direct regional–international traffic will feed on itself, and that process is likely to be further accentuated as more attractive services generate completely new direct traffic. Such a trend should be welcome to anyone concerned with the socio-economic health of the British regions, or with relieving the London airports of their excessive load – and ministers of both parties have claimed to be concerned with these objectives.

People terminating in the South-East already have a wide variety of destinations available from London airports, so in their case there will be little lengthening of the menu and very little generation of new traffic from this cause.

If (as Roskill assumes) 60 to 65 million international passengers terminate their journeys in the South-East in 1985, the number of regional terminators is likely to be more, perhaps much more, than

28 million, simply because improved services are likely to generate new traffic at a faster rate than for the South-East. We might moderately begin by putting the figure at 35 million, of whom perhaps 5 million might transfer to rail. In this case, if the number using London airports were 5 million, 25 million might use direct services from regional airports, and a regional airport with 4 per cent of the direct regional load would deal with a million international passengers a year.

Propensity to use regional airports depends on the availability of services. Therefore, the greater the variety of international services at a regional airport, the greater the proportions of the people in its catchment area who will use it. But the greater the total load at a regional airport, the greater the variety of services. Therefore, we cannot begin to make a 'realistic' calculation of the scope for 'loss' to London airports without first looking at the prospective total international loads of the regional airports. What proportion of the catchment area traffic would, then, be provided for by an airport with a million, or two or three million, passengers a year?

In 1971 each of nine non-South-Eastern airports accounted for at least 4 per cent of all the direct regional–international passengers. These nine airports between them could provide a more accessible service than Heathrow, a much more accessible service than Gatwick, and a very much more accessible service than Maplin, for about 90 per cent of the non-South-East population. The variety of destinations to be served from each airport would depend on the total load at that airport, taking into account the average number of passengers per aircraft.

If the total number of regional terminators amounted to 30 million in 1985, and five-sixths used regional airports, and if all these nine airports shared proportionately in the increase, we would expect the smallest of these airports to deal with a million international passengers in that year.

We may reasonably assume that by 1985 the regional airports' international services would be provided by a mixture of small and large aircraft. If we assume 140 persons per aircraft (say an average aircraft capacity of 220 persons), a million passengers a year would require roughly 70 flights each way per week.

The regional airports' international traffic is at present heavily concentrated in the summer, though out-of-season charter business is now making progress too. The summer peaks will almost certainly be flattened out somewhat. With the aircraft loads assumed above, an airport with a million passengers a year might then provide 100 to 200 flights a week each way during peak periods.

The numbers of flights per week, average, maximum and minimum, would be increased if the number of small aircraft used were greater than we have supposed, and if some flights served two British regional airports (at present many flights serve, for example, both Glamorgan and Bristol).

We do not know how far people contemplating air journeys are influenced by the proximity of services available. It seems likely that almost all Derbyshire residents, offered a choice between say 50 foreign airport destinations within a summer week from Castle Donington (and thus, say, 300 resorts, scattered all round the desirable holiday areas), would be satisfied by the menu offered by their own airport; very few would think it worth trailing to London in search of more esoteric holiday-locations, particularly at peak periods.

Even the thousands unable to find services from the local airport directly to the final destination (Adelaide or Caracas or Santander) need not all be tied to London; London's airports' dual role as both South-Eastern terminal and interchange centre becomes absurd as soon as it implies a distribution of services between several London airports.

The exact future pattern of development of the regional airports has not yet been determined, and only in December 1972 was it announced that a survey of the needs of the Midlands, Lancashire and Yorkshire would begin. This survey is too late; to be meaningful it should have been part of a wider survey including the rest of the country, and no decision on the new London airport should have been taken in advance of its findings. It would be absurd to argue that the whole of the regions' international traffic could be expected to distribute itself comfortably among the nine existing airports which took at least 4 per cent each of the regions' direct international traffic. But the general argument looks convincing.

There are some uncertain situations. The Leeds–Hull area, with around 8 per cent of the non-South-East population, has no immediate prospect of being well served; Leeds (Yeadon) Airport is well placed for the residential areas of Leeds and Bradford but not easily accessible from most of the West Riding; in 1972 the Government refused to authorize a planned extension. An immediate start with a new airport on Thorne Waste might be a solution, with the idea that it might be expanded as a national airport, if necessary, twenty or thirty years hence; but the Maplin decision is now an obstacle to any long-term plan for Thorne.

The South-West is also a problem; a journey from parts of the area to Heathrow by train and bus via Reading is probably more eligible than a road journey to Bristol Airport. Also, Bristol needs to be expanded, and there are good grounds for a decision against expansion. This problem will be discussed later, in a different context.

Meanwhile, Scotland will soon be fully equipped. The airports' facilities at Glasgow and Edinburgh are both being hugely expanded. Their air services to and from London are likely to grow until about 1977 or 1980, and then to decline with the cutting of the rail journey-time to under four hours. Their expansions will be justified only if their inter-regional and direct international services grow rapidly. As Edinburgh's catchment-area population is small, its airport will need to attract heavy direct foreign-visitor traffic, diverted from London, if the new facilities are to have enough work. The thinking behind the expansion of Glasgow and Edinburgh may envisage a big growth of feeder air traffic with London, but if London terminals are spread to Maplin in addition to the existing London airports, then feeder services will not be able to be conveniently organized. These Scottish expansions could have made sense as part of a British national plan; taken in isolation they do not look so rational.

From every respectable point of view – the convenience of travellers, the demands on transport facilities in and near London, the congestion of air space in the South-East, the development of the regions, the pattern of foreign tourism to Britain – it is desirable that the highest practicable proportion of regional terminators should use direct flights rather than routes via London. And it seems to be highly practicable that the proportion not needing to go to London, by the 1980s, should be increased far beyond that envisaged by Roskill on the basis of an arbitrary figure which was put down without any consideration of wider possibilities or consequences.

There is also the question of freight traffic. By 1969 Heathrow was already, by value, Britain's third largest cargo port, and the value of imports, exports and re-exports amounted to over 10 per cent of the UK overseas trade.[11] In January 1971 the BAA did not know what proportion of these airborne exports via Heathrow originated outside the South-East. Its Chief Executive, Mr Hole, said however that London was 'a very attractive centre for freight because there are such large numbers of movements from London'.[12] Obviously, shippers in the regions would prefer to send their goods through nearer airports if services were available. Everybody else would prefer it too, because Heathrow-bound lorries add to the load on the most congested part of the road system. But in January 1971 the question had not been examined.

Freight and passenger traffic cannot easily be separated, because much freight is carried in passenger planes. We should note here, though, that the main part of the load susceptible to increasing spontaneous regional transfer would be holiday traffic, mainly British residents, with the Mediteranean, giving some relief to London's overstrained radial roads.

The traffic with the nearer parts of Europe would be less well adapted to such transfer, but for that the railways could have a major role, giving some relief also to the regional airports in their turn.

6

Regional airports in a national role

In Chapter 3 a second device was suggested by which regional airports could relieve the London airports. Some passengers terminating at London could travel by train (or road) to a regional airport to find their flights. The language used by official spokesmen suggests that they would regard as heretical any such 'detriment' to the convenience of London passengers.[1] However, the detriment involved in an increase of surface journey-time by up to an hour would not be very serious, particularly if it were compensated by a reduction of flight-time. The main possibilities to consider would seem to be (a) long-haul routes and (b) some short routes southwards and westwards across the English Channel and Irish Sea.

The use of Liverpool as a major national secondary base for transatlantic travel is the most obvious case for examination, particularly for the cut-rate flights which are taking an ever-growing share of the transatlantic market.

Liverpool airport is close to rail and road, and quite well placed in other respects. There is ample scope for development as a transatlantic terminal. The cost of the rail journey, even for passengers from London, would be balanced by savings in the costs of the airoperators as compared with London. The addition of half an hour to an hour to the overall journey-time (at least 10 hours) of travellers terminating in London would scarcely be significant to them.

As at least one airline may be operating Concordes we must see how they would fit into the pattern. It might seem strange to suggest that Liverpool might be a useful English terminal for some Concorde flights, but a little examination suggests that the small addition to their journey-time would not be absurd, particularly in relation to New York's stacking times. For the operators of the Concorde on some routes a departure from Liverpool would have the advantage of reducing the distance to be covered subsonically over land, and thus bringing substantial advantage for economical operation.

There are several special arguments in favour of substantial development of Liverpool airport for traffic originating outside the area. They fit in so well together that it is surprising that, even without a national airports policy, the central Government has neglected them.

Even in 1971 it had, in Sir Peter Masefield's words, 'a magnificent runway recently built', 'very fine terminal buildings', 'first-class services and no traffic'.[2] In the 1980s when advanced passenger trains could cut the London–Liverpool rail journey to $1\frac{1}{2}$ hours, the air service on that route is likely to wane. Other domestic traffic may grow; the growth of international charter-traffic will be complicated by the proximity of Manchester, which is an obvious major growth-point for this. Normal growth of this type will not fully exploit Liverpool airport's potential advantages.

The location is exceptionally favourable from the point of view of noise disturbance to local residents. If the runway were extended to 10,500 feet, the 31 existing dwellings lying within the 50 NNI contour would in any case have to be removed.[3] It would be relatively easy from a physical viewpoint to develop the airport substantially, with a second runway and ultimately a capacity equal to that of Heathrow, if that should be desirable at some future time.

The construction of a railway branch-line into the airport would be cheap and simple. If 5 million passengers a year between London and America and other continents were routed via Liverpool, and nearly all travelled by train (as they probably would), there would be a need for 25 or 30 trains a day in each direction serving the airport alone, and their times of movement would be somewhat concentrated in late morning in both directions, assuming subsonic aircraft were used. The annual rail-load would amount to 800 million passenger-miles. The figure of 5 million could be achieved by 1985 if about one-third of London–America passengers travelled via Liverpool at that time. But if the railway between London and Crewe is to be developed so as to realize its full potential for uninterrupted running for domestic journeys, it is at least worth looking seriously at the investment that would be needed to enable the route and the London terminal (or terminals) to accommodate up to 15 non-stopping trains an hour northwards from London, in addition to stopping traffic using the additional tracks. Present indications are that the cost would not be great.

If Liverpool took part of the London–America traffic, it would also serve traffic between America and the English Midlands and North – far better than any London airport could do so. American visitors to Britain wishing to tour the country would be better served. They would also be more likely to spread around the country and to concentrate themselves less in London; such a development would be in full agreement with the well-founded current policy towards tourism.

It is well known that Merseyside is an area of high unemployment, and a large potential labour force is already on the spot. With the decline of the need for people to work in the docks, there will be many workers with experience analogous to that needed at an airport. An incidental social benefit to Merseyside would thus be one consequence, not artificially induced merely in order to create employment, but creating employment with a sound economic basis.

However, for an indication of the Government's thinking about Liverpool we may quote Mr Barnes' evidence to the Select Committee on Nationalized Industries :

Those in Liverpool see the Government in some way, whether by bribery or direction, boosting the traffic very greatly at Liverpool. . . . Although our powers are . . . limited to planning permission and loan sanction, we have in that negative way restrained some development at various places. . . . I think we have dissuaded Liverpool, for example, from spending even more than the sums they have committed at present.[4]

So we see the implication that in January 1971 the Department thought that financial incentives in support of a piece of transport planning with a social purpose would be inadmissible interference with liberty. However, when financial incentives, through discriminatory charges, looked likely to be needed in order to coax traffic to Maplin, the Government's view was quite different. On 26 April 1971 Mr Davies, in announcing the Government's decision for the Foulness site, said that he recognized that these inducements to use the new airport would be needed, and they would be used.[5] What was bribery for Liverpool became accepted policy for Maplin.

Liverpool's potential role for transatlantic and some other long-haul traffic is the most obvious case for study. Somewhat similar considerations apply to the airports at Birmingham and Castle Donington (East Midlands). Both are beside motorways, and Birmingham is beside the main railway line, accessible by train from London in 70–80 minutes by 1985. The main London–Sheffield railway line passes four miles from Castle Donington, but the value of a direct rail link there would depend on the total volume and origin and destination of the traffic.

These Midlands and Lancashire airports could logically take part of London's traffic with Ireland or Scandinavia and beyond, in addition to their own regional loads. But they would be less viable, except for their own regional purposes, for the much larger volume involving the main part of Europe, to the south. As Mr Barnes pointed out, it would be absurd for a person to go from Reading to Paris via Liverpool.[5] It would indeed, and the choice of this extreme example was not helpful to constructive discussion. It would be less absurd, but still unsatisfactory, for a package holiday-maker from London to go via Birmingham or Liverpool to southern Spain. But a south-western airport would not be absurd.

Unfortunately there is no existing airport in the South-West or South Wales which could easily be provided with adequate runways as well as good rail and road access from outside its own area. However, the region itself suffers from the lack of a substantial and accessible airport. One possible device might be to develop Exeter towards a capacity of 5 to 10 million passengers a year by 1985. The catchment-area population is rather small, but part of London's holiday traffic with the Channel Islands, Spain, and northwest Africa might well be routed this way. The railway to Exeter via Salisbury would have to be revitalized, but this new traffic could justify its continuance, which is now in doubt. (Alternatively, an airport link could be built from the main line via Taunton.) Meanwhile, a strong south-western airport could be expected to attract foreign tourists to an area where they would be particularly welcome. The South-West's potential domestic traffic with other British regions might seem too small to justify substantial air services by the mid-1980s, but bus-stop inter-regional flights via Exeter, with good feeder connections increasing the load and continuing to western France and Spain, could produce a very different picture. The existing airports at Bristol–Lulsgate and Glamorgan–Rhoose are too inaccessible; Bristol–Filton, not a public airport, would be very good if developed.

For the 1990s and beyond, if air transport continues to grow at the rate now predicted, there is always the possibility of developing a new major airport on Severnside, though this would depend on other plans for the area, including a possible Severn barrage, and decisions on this cannot be taken in a hurry.

For the 1980s it would be reasonable to envisage the diversion of perhaps 5 million passengers to a southern airport by around 1985, with the option of some increase in 1985–90. Exeter is rather too far from London to be ideal for the purpose; some other location might well be better.

This particular group of diversions might well be unnecessary, because the London load might be held within the capacity of the existing airports by the other means suggested in this book, without the need for this reinforcement. However, if diversion of a relatively small group of London passengers were necessary, and no south-western solution could be found, one feasible but unpleasant compromise might be found through a new approach to Maplin. An airport might be built there up to the dimensions of a typical regional airport to take over and develop the work now done at Southend, assuming the existing Southend airport itself to be unsuitable for such development. The location has at least the merit of being fairly convenient for people ending their journeys in Essex and part of East Anglia.

Whether the Maplin scheme was wise or not, we are now faced with the fact that much work has already been done in preparing it. The chances of abandonment must be small. This being so, it might be as well to develop it in a small way, as a reserve airport for use by people terminating in London and the South-East, particularly those on charter flights. A single runway might be built for use during the 1980s, with the expectation that traffic would rise at once to 5 million passengers a year. The option of further development much later would then be open if this should become necessary. A railway line might be provided into the airport zone, together with some improvement to the existing system in Essex, but the airport traffic would not absorb the whole of the new capacity, which could then also serve the local community.

There would be environmental damage, but much less than that which would arise from the wholesale development now envisaged. The scheme would not be a particularly good one, but in the circumstances of the mid-1970s it might be considered as a practical one, combined with a strong policy of diversion of London's traffic to rail and to regional airports, to which the reduced Maplin might itself be analogous.

The concentration of British air travel, with only one provincial centre chosen for substantial growth, must work to the detriment of the regions. It may be inevitable now, but the more total air travel grows, the less inevitable the concentration will become. The greater the choice of services available at several regional centres, the more attractive it will become to travel to and from these centres.

A comparison of the situation in Britain with that in West Germany casts doubt on the assumption that, even with the present volume of traffic, concentration is inevitable. Spatially West Germany resembles Britain very closely. It has a few more people, in a slightly greater area, and there are major centres of population distributed through the country in a rather similar way. The population has slightly greater real purchasing power, more cars, and a slightly greater propensity to travel. None of the differences is large, except that road passenger miles are 30 per cent greater than in Britain.

Like Britain, West Germany has one urban concentration, North-Rhine-Westphalia, surpassing all others in populations and including the national capital city. In many respects this area resembles Lancashire and Yorkshire, with no single municipality containing more than a million people; it includes one 'metropolitan area'[6] with about six million people, four others with one to two million each, and two somewhat smaller ones, Bonn and Krefeld, just off the main fringe. Also, this big agglomeration has no national dominating role in culture, tourism, commerce or sentiment. But in total population and area the whole complex resembles the British South-East.

Other major German conurbations have close parallels with those in Britain, with respect to population and distance from each other and from the single biggest group. West Berlin has 40 per cent more people than Northern Ireland, and is separated by an obstacle which, like the sea, gives air transport a special advantage as compared with other modes – but we had better not pursue other differences or similarities.

Yet the distribution of air traffic among the centres of population is quite different from that in Britain. The principal airport is located in the second largest population centre, Frankfurt, which in spatial terms could be regarded as having its British equivalent at Birmingham, though in the Frankfurt region the population is slightly smaller, counterbalancing its commercial importance.

In West Germany in 1969 the total air passenger traffic amounted to 26·6 million, compared with the British total of 29 million. In Britain, Heathrow and Gatwick alone accounted for 60 per cent of the total; in West Germany the two airports serving the biggest population, Düsseldorf and Cologne, accounted for under 20 per cent of the total. The busiest German airport was Frankfurt, with 8 million passengers. This does not imply that Birmingham *ought* to be the main British airport (an important difference is that Frankfurt's airport is right on the main national road and rail trunk route, while Birmingham's is a little off the equivalent British artery; and Birmingham has special objections on account of noise). But it does suggest that, whether the German solution is good or bad, the air traffic of a country like Britain and Germany does not need to be very heavily concentrated on the airports close to the one biggest population-centre. Indeed, Düsseldorf and Cologne airports are both more favourably situated for a national role than any of the existing London-area airports, let alone Maplin.

In Britain only two 'provincial' airports exceeded a million passengers (Manchester with 1·9 million and Glasgow with 1·7 million); in Germany, in addition to Frankfurt, Munich and Hamburg dealt with over 2·5 million each, and Hanover almost 2 million. All these three exceeded Manchester and Glasgow, and Stuttgart with 1·4 million ran them fairly close. West German air traffic was thus mainly based on six major centres, one of them with two major airports. In addition, Bremen and Nürnberg dealt with half a million passengers each, West Berlin with 4 million. There is heavy inter-regional air traffic, apart from that with Berlin.

The difference between Britain and Germany can perhaps best be illustrated by a list of airports, or pairs or groups of nearby airports, showing first the approximate percentage of the national population living within about 40 miles of each airport and then the percentage of the national air traffic using the airport. Berlin and Belfast are omitted, as both places, though classed as 'domestic', are separated by obstacles from the main parts of the countries.

The major long-distance international traffic was concentrated on Frankfurt, which is better placed than Liverpool in relation to the rest of the country's population, but not so very much better. The population within 50 miles is actually greater at Liverpool than at

Frankfurt. Frankfurt's links with the major 'provincial' centres, by air, road and rail, are much better than Liverpool's, which cover routes (like Newcastle–Liverpool) that would not be likely to be covered at very high overall speeds by rail. Such inter-regional air services would be part of a substantial improvement in the whole domestic inter-regional communications system, supplementing the

Britain Airport	Distance from first population centre in miles	Local population as percentage of national population	1970 terminal passenger air traffic as percentage of national air traffic
All London incl. Luton	0	30	70
Manchester and Liverpool	200	10	7
Birmingham	120	8	3
Glasgow	400	5	6
C. Donington	120	4	0·8
Leeds	200	4	1

Germany Airport	Distance from first population centre (Düsseldorf) in miles	Local population as as percentage of national population	1970 terminal passenger air traffic as percentage of national air traffic
Cologne and Düsseldorf	0	20	15
Hamburg	250	5	10
Frankfurt	150	8	30
Munich	400	4	10
Stuttgart	250	4	5
Hanover	200	3	7

rail services which, though they could be improved, would never approach the overall speed and frequency of the major rail routes radiating from London. Any Newcastle–Liverpool train is bound to stop at least six times, taking three hours or more. Some 'feeder' air traffic could justify an air service, though probably with moderately small planes; access to local airports is much easier than for London.

There is ground for believing that the British regional airports' weakness in international services may have been influenced by the lack of any positive policy towards them. That weakness is currently being reduced, by charter runs rather than by scheduled routes; but the building of Maplin, and the need to give it business when it is in service, is likely to damage any trend towards that increase in contact with the world outside which better international air links could foster in the British regions.

7

The new capabilities of railways

In the past thirty years the railways have had a dreary image. On the one hand deficits, closures, strikes, demoralization; on the other hand, as the traveller sees them, dirt, horrible stations, unreliable services. Compare the platform litter-bins and old benches (or lack of them) with the furniture in airport lounges; and the staff whom the traveller sees lack both youth and femininity. A train journey can well be a frustrating and even humiliating experience. All this is sad, because railways are, or can be, the most effective device for moving large numbers of people on major routes: cheaper and safer than other modes, and less annoying to people who are not travelling. The new inter-city services are already good.

Now we are on the brink of a major transformation of their role. For travel between Britain and Europe the Channel tunnel is the first condition; the second is the exploitation of the new capabilities which railways have just discovered for themselves. Inter-city travel, as developed in the past few years, has already begun to show the way. But a tremendous new potential is now being developed.

The railways have already within their grasp an advance in capability which could transform their role in carrying passengers for most journeys above 100 miles in Europe. British Rail have developed their Advanced Passenger Train, of new design, capable of running at 150 mph on the existing tracks, on most of the length of the routes now covered by domestic air services to or from London airports. Trains of conventional design can run at 120 mph – and are already doing so in France and Germany – though on the Continent some new rail-routes are planned, allowing speeds of 150 to 180 mph and clearway running to make them sustainable.

Start-to-stop averages of well over 100 mph can become the norm over major British and continental routes by the early 1980s, subject to sufficient investment, which could set in motion a spiral of improvement like that which has characterized air transport in the past twenty years.

During the last few years, at the cost of a few million pounds, railway technology has quietly and cheaply produced the means for a transport revolution which will cut a 400-mile rail journey-time by the same amount as Concorde will cut the London–New York flight. The railways can soon supplant the long-runway aeroplane as the best medium for trunk-route public transport journeys up to 400 miles. Overnight they will provide travel up to 1,200 miles without loss of usable time. Before 1990 at least a third of the travellers now expected to go by air to and from London's airports might conceivably go by rail instead. For this to be feasible, government transport policy would need first to plan its investments and their direction. London's airport problems could not have been solved simply by asserting that transfer to railways will take place on this scale; but we should not regard the problem as solved without thoroughly calculating the contribution that the new railways might make, subject to what conditions, what investment, and with what effects on the economy and the environment.

It is of course wrong to assume that trains capable of 150 mph maximum speeds will automatically be able to maintain overall average speeds of 120 or even 100 mph without some new investment in the tracks. On the existing railway system the average speed of a train, even between stops, is reduced by the needs of other trains using the same track, by curves and other obstacles on which speed limits are necessary, and from time to time by repairs and maintenance. The British 'Advanced Passenger Train,' now in an advanced experimental stage, is likely to cause less deterioration of the tracks at any given speed than trains of types now in use. With its tilting system it can maintain 50 per cent higher speeds through curves than existing trains, but this particular device alone can produce only a relatively small and variable reduction of journey-times. On a route with virtually no curves the APT system would not reduce journey-time, though its British version would reduce track wear. On a route with numerous small-radius curves, increases of permitted speeds from 30 to 45 mph at some places, and from 50 to 75 mph at others, would reduce the overall journey-time, but not enough to make the railway fully competitive with road and air. Quadrupling of track on heavily used routes, and elimination of the need for trains to cross tracks on the same level, or to reduce speed to pass through junctions, would be needed in order to accommodate frequent high-speed trains.

On the whole the major British trunk routes are already fairly free of sharp curves and equipped with quadruple tracks on the most important sections. The main routes north of London have spare capacity. It is only between London and the Channel tunnel that very substantial investment in new permanent way would be needed in order to allow unimpeded movement by fast trains. But the same is not true of the routes in France and Benelux, which would be crucial for effective operation through the Channel tunnel.

European Railways already have their plans for building or developing lines suitable for running at 155 mph, even without the tilting system. They await government authorization. *Railway Gazette International* (March 1972, p. 105) lists the routes which could be open for 155 mph by 1985, subject to positive decisions by Governments:

Calais–Belgium and Paris, joined by Belgium–Paris link.
Brussels–Amsterdam.
Cologne–Frankfurt (gap)–Munich.
Paris–Lyon.
Milan–Rome.

Other routes in Germany are planned, but they do not connect with the Channel tunnel route.

The key Brussels–Cologne section is currently planned only to be improved to 125 mph standards. Apart from these new schemes, most other major existing routes extending outwards from the primary section, to Bordeaux, southern France and Copenhagen, will accommodate running speeds of 125 mph.

The new European trainways would complement the existing system much as motorways complement the road system – and they would cost no more per mile than six-lane motorways. Unlike the Japanese Tokaido system, they would be extensions of the existing network, not separate from it, but rejoining it for city terminals. Within towns they can use existing railway space, which tends to have surplus capacity because of the reduction of services on minor routes. The existing routes will continue to provide for the trains with intermediate stops, and even with their curves many parallel existing routes are now taking trains at over 80 mph average speeds between stops. These plans are the continental answer to the intractable problem of track occupation. Quadruple-track main lines may be a better answer still, and that is on the whole the British answer. The most heavily used sections north of London are quadruple already.

Apart from the special schemes, most of the major main lines in Britain and Europe can be equipped for services averaging 120 mph by the mid 1980s.

Taking the European system as a whole, the new speed capability of trains is not the whole answer. For this capability to be fully exploited, much new track construction and other capital work will be necessary. For the whole of West Germany a capital expenditure of £1,300 million is estimated to be needed to bring 1,200 miles of major trunk route up to the full capacity needed for the new fast services (500 miles of new route construction, 700 miles of improvement, including quadrupling of track, on existing alignments). Similar schemes are planned in Italy and work began on the first of them (Rome–Florence) in 1971.

Decisions in northern France and Benelux depend heavily on the Channel tunnel and the associated British contribution. If the tunnel is not built, or if the British section of the route leading to it is not fully developed, the worthwhileness of the schemes in northern France and Benelux will have reduced validity, because the prospective utilization may fall short of what is necessary to justify the investments. The British commitment to a third London airport, as an infrastructure duplicating the potential railway, has created an obstacle preventing British Governments from developing an active interest in the railways' potential contribution to the overall plan. Ministers who neglect the railway but insist on the new airport, and yet fail to recognize the implications of what they are doing, must face a charge of hypocrisy if they simultaneously claim to care about the environment.

Paris and London have somewhat similar problems, though the solutions for Paris are rather less easy. All of Britain's major conurbations, together with Paris, Brussels, Amsterdam and Cologne, are within 400 miles of London. Marseille, the Mediterranean and Toulouse are 450 to 650 miles from Paris, even with the help of the new Paris–Lyon route. Some important destinations within France will be more than four, and up to seven, hours' train journey from Paris, even after the greatest practicable rail improvement. But it will still be in the interest of Paris, just as of London, to keep the growth of its air traffic within the capacity of two major airports for as long as possible; to develop the railways to the maximum for journeys, short and medium, by day and night, within France and to England, Benelux, Germany and Italy; and to develop the French regional airports as reliefs for Paris, for inter-regional and international journeys, with a view to stemming the growth of Paris air traffic.

Believing that saturation of both air space and the roads was likely to arise, if the current trends in transport continue in the 1980s, the West German Government began in 1969 a study in depth of the potential of high-speed, high-output surface transport (Hochleistungsschnellbahn, or HSB). A draft report of the study was presented to the Minister in December 1971, but has not yet been published. It indicates that a huge increase of rail traffic, as distinct from other modes, could be achieved, attracting passengers by 'travel time, frequency of service and comfort'. Dr Leber argued for a common European effort for the development of a common high-speed transport system 'within a European framework'.[1]

A thorough cost-benefit study of future transport needs in West Germany, carried out in the Battelle-Institut on behalf of the Ministry and published in 1972, found in favour of heavy investment in German railways rather than airports for domestic passenger transport. Although the scope of this inquiry was limited to West Germany, some of the findings are relevant for the future of air and railway services in Western Europe as a whole. No such inquiry preceded the decision to build a new airport for London; there should be some advantage in paying some attention to the Battelle-Institut's findings. These findings gave support to the German Railways' plan to bring 1,200 miles of route up to high capability by 1985. The plan includes the upgrading of some 800 miles of existing two-track route (including quadrupling the track) and the building of several wholly new sections, amounting to 500 miles in all. The total cost is put at £1,200 million at 1972 prices.

The estimate of 1985 as the date for completion is important. Current discussion[2] of the rather similar work to be done in southern England, France and Benelux, in order to give the railway system an ability to divert the mass traffic from air, has tended to assume a more leisurely time scale. But the need for decision and action is urgent, if we are to avoid the error of building new airport infrastructures in response to apparent short-term needs and without any overall plan.

In France it is argued that a third Paris airport, at a location still to be decided, should be handling 5 million passengers in 1985 and 65 million in 1990 (in addition to 25 million at Orly and 50 million at Roissy by that date).[3] Yet a third of the Paris airports' traffic in 1970 was short-haul and another one-third was in the middle range of distance over which rail could make a substantial contribution.

If a Channel tunnel is built, all the major cities in England and southern Scotland, together with a continental area with a total

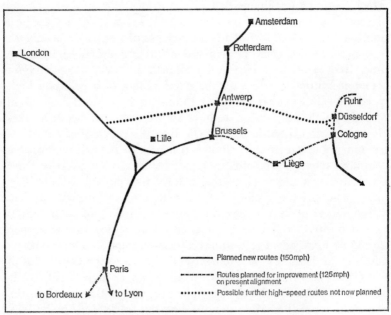

The European short-haul high-speed railway plans

population of 50 million, in Paris and northern France, all of Belgium and Holland, and the near part of Germany which includes Cologne, Bonn and the Ruhr, will be able to be reached from central London just about as quickly by train as by air (other than VTOL), taking into account the total travel-time in each case.

It is not necessary to undertake an expensive survey to know that the door-to-door journey-time by air between points in major cities, well served by existing forms of air transport, is from two to four hours longer than the time occupied by the flight.[4] If one of the terminal points is a town not served by a nearby airport, the overall journey-time is longer still.

People in a hurry can reduce their overall journey-time by using their own cars or taxis at one end (at great expense), and by being met at the other end by friends or business associates or taxis (mostly paid for out of business expenses deducted from tax, or thus from the public revenue). If they do this they also add to the congestion on the roads leading to the airport. If many do this, either they cause hopeless delays to each other or more new roads must be built to accommodate them – and even the next new roads may create a spiral of congestion. With railways the journey-times to and from terminal stations are not negligible; but given the flexibility of railways we should also remember that (subject to limits which have to be examined) the heavier the traffic, the greater the scope for providing a proportion of trains stopping at intermediate stations close to the passengers' points of starting or finishing their journeys. Such arrangements can reduce the journey-time for numerous small categories of travellers, and reduce the city-centre traffic problems. On major routes up to 300 or 400 miles with heavy traffic, high-speed trains should soon be better than aircraft on every count.

But the short-haul movement is only half the story. Roskill took no account at all of the potential transfer to rail of the travellers to places between 400 and 1,000 miles from London. Much of this is holiday traffic, to the Alps and the Mediterranean, and the railway could be a serious competitor. An overnight train journey of up to 12 or 14 hours, in adequate sleeping accommodation and without interruptions, involves no more loss of daytime than an air journey performed wholly by day. Also, many of those who travel by air between London and Zürich, Geneva, Nice, etc., have very long compulsory surface journeys at the other end: bus to town-terminal, possibly taxi to railway station, then a train or bus-ride of up to 3 hours to Lucerne or Interlaken or the upper Rhône Valley or St Raphael or Menton. This means 6 or 7 hours in all, taking up most of a day, much of it spent drearily waiting. If the 6 or 7 hours are during the night, the next day is spoiled by exhaustion. A journey of 8 to 14 hours in a through night-train with adequate sleeping accommodation would seem a better choice.

Table 5 shows the distances from London by rail, through the Channel tunnel, of the main European destinations, together with estimated minimum journey-times which might come into effect by stages in 1975–85, given sufficient investment and the traffic to justify it. They assume no delays at frontiers, but they should, by 1985, be cautious enough to provide for appropriate stops, and for some obstacles to continuous high speed which could not be eliminated. They also assume that trains from England would circle Paris much more quickly than they can already, and that the projected new lines in northern France and Benelux, and from Paris to Lyon, would be completed.

Although the British and main continental railways have promised that trains will be carrying passengers at well over 100 mph average speeds by 1978, they have not promised that such a performance will be the norm, even on a few major trunk routes. But a few super-fast trains on a route, interspersed with others which travel more slowly, might well be more nuisance than they were worth. They could be run only on tracks which were used far below their full capacity. If railways are to compete really effectively with air by 1985 it will not be enough to have a few super-fast trains. The whole service on the major routes must be brought up to the maxi-

TABLE 5

Distances from London – Victoria (through Channel tunnel) by rail and achievable door-to-door times, allowing for stops, around 1985: some examples (door-to-door time distinguished only for short journeys)

| | | Hours | | | | | Hours | |
| | | Train time | Door-to-door | | | | Train time | Door-to-door |
	Miles					Miles		
Short haul								
Paris	290	2½	3–3½	Amsterdam	375	3–4	3½–4½
Brussels	250	2¼	2½–3	Cologne	395	3½–4½	4–5
Middle distance,								
mainly business or foreign visitors to Britain								
Frankfurt	535	5	6	Lyon	550	5	5½
Milan	810	9	10	Geneva	600	6	6½–7
W. Germany	360–900	4–12		Copenhagen	850	12	(including ferry)
Holiday destinations								
S. France	800–950	8–12		Switzerland	650–800	7–12	
N. Italy	700–1,000	8–14		Austria	800–1,000	10–14	

mum standard, and this will require a big effort in building enough new rolling-stock to do the work, and in equipping the major routes to accommodate some mix of stopping and non-stop trains. The volume of the investment needed should be estimated and made public, in Britain and on the Continent, so that the comparison with the air option can be openly discussed; either option would need a

Rail journeys from London, 1980–85 estimates (drawn to time scale)

heavy commitment of public money and the rail option would require joint action by European governments.

Instead, all we have had from the British Government is endorsement of the DTI Working Party's statement that the effect of high-speed rail travel through a Channel tunnel on the demand for air travel from London airports is 'not expected to be large'.[5] In fact the size of the reduction must depend on decisions about the level of investment in the railways on both sides of the Channel, and the case for large investment needs to be discussed in terms of the alternative. The basic question is not even asked.

The minimum overall journey-time by air can be put at $2\frac{1}{2}$ to 5 hours for people using nearby airports at both ends, but when long surface journeys to or from airports are involved the time rises to 8 hours or more, possibly involving a night on the way. The minimum of $2\frac{1}{2}$ hours could be reduced for some types of cross-country trip, but very rarely for a journey which involves a conurbation of the size of London or surface journeys as long and time-consuming as those imposed by London conditions.

8

The rail–air comparison

One broad question must come before all the others, so broad and simple that it is neither economic nor political, but cultural or mythological. Surely, it may be said, a return to conventional railways is absurd, because it is against the very logic of human history. We have had horses, carts, carriages, canal boats, railways, motor cars, aeroplanes. All human history in the technological age has shown a progression from one device to another. Railways have had their day. They are finished, superseded by road vehicles and aeroplanes except for a few special tasks like carrying coal and urban commuters. Air travel is the next stage after railways for carrying people for 200 miles or more; we can't just turn back the pages and put this transport back on to the railways again. Just as human evolution moves on from bows and arrows to guns to nuclear devices as weapons of war, so it moves on in other matters too, including means of transport.

This objection is not on a high intellectual level, but it is important nevertheless, because most people would probably subscribe to it. It is supported by innumerable slogans, often repeated : prosperity depends on a healthy aircraft industry, the aircraft industry must grow, the conquest of the air is man's greatest achievement yet. Railways may be loved by a few antiquarians and (in theory) by nearly all environmental planners, but they have no substantial defenders. No wonder; most people's experience of them is pretty wretched, partly through the fault of the people who have run them these last 30 years.

Argument based on a vague conception of human destiny is not always sound. Technological progress does not move in a single unchanging line. Inter-city roads were outdated by 1860, but they came back again with the motor car. Long-runway aeroplanes look like being nearer the end of their useful life-span than the beginning.

In transport, vehicles and the tracks they use are partners depending on each other, and as technology finds new types of vehicles for one form of track or another, so the validity of the whole transport mode may change. Modern civilization is learning to be sceptical of the balance between the benefits and costs of the motor car, and of the aeroplane too. A substitute is not to be despised because it looks old and half-discarded. Those who scorn railways now may be no more progressive than their grandfathers who scoffed at horse-less carriages in 1900.

It would be plain stupid to settle for conventional aeroplanes rather than railway trains for journeys on which the two are still viable alternatives, just because the aeroplane has been a symbol of progress (with overtones of national prestige) to the generation now aged 40 to 70.

The jet aircraft is perhaps the greatest of man's technological achievements, and its provision of the ability to travel over long distances, with a high degree of safety and comfort, is a great benefit, not at all to be despised.

It is criticized mainly because of its noise, but this objection needs to be put in the perspective of other sources of noise. One of today's noisy planes, carrying 100 people 300 miles, causes a lot of man-units of annoyance to people on the ground per passenger-mile provided. The planes of the near future, carrying more people less noisily, will carry a much less heavy penalty per unit of service provided : the longer the flight the less the penalty. On this score we might on rational grounds be readier to accept long flights than short ones, and to prefer alternative means of transport for the shorter journeys if these are acceptable. The British Airports Authority's system of charging much higher landing and take-off fees for long-distance flights has disadvantages from this point of view.

For the 1980s the aeroplane's noisiness is not so serious a defect as its shape and its demands on space, including space for access to it.

Because of the aeroplane's shape, every airport, even one for VTOL/STOL, requires vast space, including provision for aircraft to be moved away from the loading-spaces to storage-spaces when not in use, even overnight. Railway trains have similar needs but they are more modest. Given the shape of a train, good station-design can quite easily ensure that the distance from the last local-access vehicle used, whether bus, taxi, private car or train, is small, though it must be admitted that the design of most existing railway stations, and of means of access to them, does not exploit this potential advantage to the full.

Advocacy of the new railways, as the main medium of public transport in Europe in the 1980s, in balanced partnership (or fair competition, if you prefer it) with the old and now familiar long-runway aeroplane, and later with VTOL, is not an attempt to reverse the trend associated with Lord Beeching's period as Chairman of British Rail. Beeching hastened British Rail's contraction; its work-force is now half what it was in 1950, and so is its passenger route-mileage. The contraction has been faster in Britain than in West Germany, where huge deficits still result from a generous supply of small-scale operations. But the Beeching rationalization was aimed at positively developing the railway's activity for the job which it can do well : carrying passengers on major routes with heavy traffic. The business well named as Inter-City has dramatically increased its profitability in the past five years, with a two per cent rise in passengers for every one per cent reduction in journey-time.[1]

Journeys terminating at London are peculiarly suitable for railways, because the population of the area both limits the accessibility of airports and provides a large demand for travel radiating in many directions. This does not imply that the railway is preferable to the aeroplane even for some quite short inter-regional journeys, where the volume of demand is too small to justify fast train services on heavily used routes. There should in the 1980s be many links for which small aeroplanes will be suitable, particularly those which join populations small enough to allow easy access to local airports. Newcastle–Blackpool is an obvious air or road link, and the same is true of Scotland north of the Glasgow–Aberdeen line (though it may well be desirable to retain the railways on social grounds).

Most contemporary defenders of the environment wish to see the railways gain traffic, and particularly freight traffic, from the roads. One argument for a switch from road to rail is based on the unpleasantness and danger of road transport; another concentrates on the congestion of the roads together with the colossal environmental damage and expenditure of resources involved in the attempt to alleviate that congestion by new road-building. Road transport is even now nastier than air transport, and the relative advantage of air over road will be increased in the future as aeroplanes become less noisy. But the railways' potential as a carrier of traffic which *might* go by road or rail depends on the railways' general efficiency, which depends in its turn on the level of investment in them. The distribution of investments between air and rail, with which the next chapters will be immediately concerned, will affect the distribution of freight and passenger traffic between rail and road. We are always brought back inexorably to the need to plan transport as a whole, and to the absurdity of the London airport decision in isolation; investment in London airports is indeed one part of a pattern of which even freight transport within Great Britain is another part.

In 1962 almost 40 per cent of all road freight carriage in Great Britain was on hauls of over 99 miles: 13 billion ton-miles out of 33·6 billion.[2] For a large proportion even of the freight movements of over 100 miles the railway cannot be a suitable mode, even with heavy investment. But there is still a heavy and increasing volume of traffic being carried by road along trunk routes over 300 miles or more, even involving cross-Channel ferry journeys at huge expense. The very large and heavy road vehicles involved cause much more than their fair share of annoyance and danger to the public, and provision for their movement probably accounts for road costs in excess of their contribution towards those costs. (This question has never been satisfactorily resolved.)

It may well be that not more than 10 per cent of the total ton-miles of freight traffic of the future, now likely to go by road, would be diverted to rail, even if the railways received investments great enough to make them adequate. But it would be the most offensive part of the road traffic, and the relief to the road system would be of immense environmental benefit. On the other hand, it might be difficult to justify the rail investment that would be needed in order to make this diversion feasible, unless the railways were also heavily developed for passenger use, with long-distance freight traffic using track mainly at night. And that passenger-development would only be justified if the railways received a large part of the future passenger load which is now conventionally assigned to air.

The London airports' freight business is already substantial in terms of value. It has increased rapidly in the last few years and is expected to increase further (the load handled at Heathrow, Gatwick and Stansted in 1971 amounted to 370,000 tons, plus 36,000 tons of mail). Diversion to improved rail services of much of their expected short-haul freight would produce a slight but welcome reduction in road-freight traffic feeding the airports.

Public opinion concerned with the quality of life is unanimous in its urgent concern to put on to the railways as much freight movement as practicable. Any study of the problem tends to indicate that the scope for transfer is limited, simply because much of the freight carried by road could not efficiently be carried by rail. However, in West Germany, with its great similarity with Great Britain, the railways currently provide more ton-miles of freight than the roads, while Britain resembles Italy in that road freight is three times as great as rail freight.[3] Comparison with France is not very useful as greater distances are inherently more favourable to rail, but Britain and Italy share an extreme position, and that position brings the highest environmental costs. The Netherlands and Belgium are also scarcely comparable, but the low contribution of rail in the Netherlands partly reflects Dutch government policy before 1971. A more integrative approach was an issue in the election of that year, and there are now positive plans.[4]

The rest of this chapter will attempt to list a number of headings under which the air–rail comparison might usefully be considered in the context of a Western European transport plan, without which London's airport requirements cannot be meaningfully assessed.

The potential capacity of railways
The first question deals quite simply with practical possibilities. Would it be technically possible, by the 1980s, for the railways to carry a rapidly increasing additional load at adequate speeds, in adequate comfort, and without loss of safety? Could British Rail carry 30 million people between London and the tunnel at over 100 mph by 1985, and perhaps 40 million by 1990? Could French railways carry a similar number between Paris and Lyon? There seems good reason to believe that the answer would be a conditional affirmative, subject to the necessary investment. The new Tokaido line in Japan, on which construction work began in 1959, carried 44 million passengers at such standards in 1966 and has amply justified itself, and railway technology has made great advances since it was conceived. For our case, the investment needed would be far more than the railways could find from their normal sources, but transport-investment funds now earmarked for the new airport need

to be weighed against equivalent funds which optimum rail development would need, with attention to the total economic and environmental outcomes, as well as the narrowly financial.

Comparative costs

What would be the cost, capital and current, of transporting a given number of people over middle distances, mainly 200 to 1,200 miles, by train as compared with air? The question should eventually be answered in terms of a whole series of possible distributions between rail and air, so as to provide for an assessment of total costs on a series of assumptions, and thus of the differences between successive steps. Chapter 9 sets up a model, assuming one particular distribution, a transfer of about 20 million London–Europe passengers to rail by 1985, and likely associated generation of new rail traffic.

This single model, making rather arbitrary assignments in the major travel markets on the basis of modified Roskill projections, should be useful as a guide and suggest questions for detailed examination.

Then we must introduce more sophistication, providing for that bane of all transport systems, seasonally fluctuating demand. It would be unwise to be influenced at the beginning by the very low rates now charged for some charter flights, including holiday package tours. The railway could play that game too, and perhaps more easily in the long run than air-operators below 1,000 miles.

These calculations can then be used to produce estimates of unit costs, of prices to be charged to travellers, as individuals or as members of groups, some at standard rates, some at reduced rates or on package deals.

Taking this into account, what would be the marginal cost of carrying a given number of additional passengers by rail over each major route? What would be the total cost, first on each route and then on all the routes together? How would these costs compare with the marginal and total costs involved in moving the same people by air?

Some elements in the cost-comparison can be identified quite easily. There are three main headings:

Track or airports. In the case of railways additional improvements and some additional maintenance would be involved. A greatly increased load on railways would demand a Channel tunnel and heavy expenditure on its link with London. For Britain these costs should be considered in relation to the share in airport and airport access costs involved in providing for an equivalent amount of traffic. Similar calculations should be made with respect to the railway systems in France and Belgium, and to a smaller extent those in Holland, Germany and Italy.

Improvements to access points (i.e. stations and airports) and access routes. Stations are now the railways' weakest point. Their inadequacy discourages rail travel. Much is being spent now; on the whole it is not the quantity of provision within a station that is inadequate, but the quality. Increased traffic might in many cases be accommodated within existing space and structure, but might both require and justify improvement of quality and design.

If the air traffic between London and Europe were to increase at the rate officially projected, heavy investment would be needed, not only in Maplin airport but in other European airports, to cope with this increase. In addition to the investment in airports, vast resources would have to be spent on improving the communication between airports and city-centres and other final destinations.

Large expenditure on some airports and on means of access to them will be needed in any case. The argument of this book is that, as *part* of the projected air market could go by rail instead, we ought to look at the comparison in cost between rail and air for that part of the market which could use either mode. Thus, in relation to airports and stations, we need to compare the cost of the *additional* work on airports, and access to airports (including city terminals) which would be needed if these travellers went by air, as compared with the cost of the additional work that would be needed at railway stations to make it practicable for them to go by rail, including local roads, car parks and bus-provision.

Vehicles. The next item for comparison is that between the vehicles, taking into account initial cost and rate of depreciation, in relation to capacity in terms of passenger-miles per day. Here we do have some material to serve as a guide. A modern long-runway subsonic jet aircraft costs around £20,000 per seat. In European conditions, putting together the short and medium hauls, we could reasonably expect the average aircraft to fly 800,000 to 1,000,000 miles per year and the average high-speed train to run 200,000 to 250,000 miles with passengers. If the train cost £1,500 a seat (including its traction units), its output per £1 initial cost would

101

be three to four times that of the aircraft, assuming the same effective life for each. However, past experience suggests that the expected life of the train should be up to twice as long as that of the aircraft.

Passenger operating costs. The main items for comparison here would be wages and salaries, fuel or electricity, and maintenance of vehicles. With both rail and air these costs are rather closely related to the number of seat-miles provided, though there are many items which do not vary much with load and thus tend to reduce marginal costs. Operating expenditure per passenger-mile by British Rail in 1970 amounted to under $1\frac{1}{2}$ pence, compared with $2\frac{1}{2}$ pence for BEA, though most of the railway's output was in unfavourable conditions, with commuter surges and much under-utilization of capacity, such as would not occur on the new trunk routes of 1985.

Consequential capital costs. The railways would need further investments in order to accommodate dense high-speed passenger traffic on the main trunk routes. On most of the trunk-line system separate tracks would be needed to accommodate the new fast trains as well as slow-moving freight and local passenger traffic. On some routes, still used at moderate levels of density, careful time-tabling would achieve the necessary result – e.g. Paris to Bordeaux, Preston to Glasgow – but high-speed trains could only go if all the other trains could go reasonably fast too. But the re-equipment expenditures needed to achieve this would yield a return on their own account, and the increased use of the infrastructure through the addition of the traffic transferred from air could be expected to increase the return on the whole investment.

Freight movement

The future distribution of passenger traffic between air and rail must also have repercussions on freight traffic, and thus also in the long run on the distribution of freight between rail and road. In some degree the distribution of passenger traffic between road and rail is also likely to be involved, with further environmental consequences. How would the railways' ability as freight-carriers be affected by the heavy investment envisaged?

The potential long-term usefulness of investment in conventional airports

Today's London airport-planning is based on provision for aircraft of currently conventional types requiring long runways. Meanwhile new types of aircraft are being developed, requiring only short runways. An airport remote from a town, as Maplin is from London, wastes their potential. Even apart from any thought of a switch of travellers to railways, are not the plans for development of today's long-runway airports excessive in relation to the probable level of demand for conventional runway space in the 1990s, by which time perhaps only long-distance planes will require airport facilities of the type currently provided? How then do the prospects of VTOL/STOL affect the viability of today's plans for the future of airports?

The social and environmental consequences of decisions now to be made

If rail passenger-movement in Europe were to develop more than is now envisaged, and air movement less, what would be the social and environmental consequences? More air movement means more noise, affecting huge areas, a little more pollution, more land used for airports and for access to them, more movement of surface-vehicles going to them, and consequently more disturbance to vast numbers of people in the airport zones and along the access routes. More movement by rail involves some comparable evils, but probably on a much more restricted scale.

Passenger preference between modes of transport

Is there really an absolute preference for travel by air? If there is now, will the magic have become stale by the 1980s? What proportion of people will by that time be ready to prefer a convenient train to an inconvenient aeroplane at the same price? Or a train of equal convenience at a lower price? We can be sure that the quality of station-access and car parking are key factors. A close study of Japanese experience would give useful guidance.

International co-operation

Could European governments all agree at the same time on the measures necessary for putting the major load of passenger-transport eggs into the railway basket? The prospects seem quite good; a British contribution would encourage railway-oriented plans now contemplated, and regarded with more enthusiasm on the continent than railways have been regarded by British Governments. But British co-operation is needed and active promotion from Britain would be enormously influential. A proposal for an all-European railway corporation would probably be unrealistic, as much the greater part of passenger and freight movement is and will remain within existing national boundaries. We could not rely wholly on EEC arrangements, because the Swiss railway system is at the heart of the whole European system, and Swiss participation, no less than that of the railways of the EEC countries, would be necessary both in making assessments and in taking action to develop the European railway system.

The internal administrative obstacles
Would the short-term and parochial railway budgetary requirements cause the national managements to become deadlocked in arguments about allocation of costs and resources among themselves? It is easy to foresee difficulties on this account, and also in relation to detailed pricing patterns. There is plenty of evidence to suggest that there might be formidable difficulties, but that evidence, derived from a study of current behaviour of railway managements (e.g. over the sale of the land of disused tracks), is merely a response to narrowly-based financial demands of national governments.

Industrial consequences
What would be the effects on British and other European industry of a slow-down in the expected increase of demand for aerospace equipment, and a huge increase in that for rail equipment? It looks as though the outcome might well be very advantageous. The rail equipment would be wholly manufactured in Europe, including Britain; it is likely that a greater proportion of the air equipment would have to be imported. When we think of the scope for exporting railway equipment from the basis of a really vigorous new British and Eurpean railway equipment industry, the usual calculations about the current and hoped-for exports of aircraft seem misplaced, particularly when we consider British imports of aircraft from America. A reduction in London's air traffic through a switch of some passengers to rail would cut the demand for Lockheed Tristars or European airbuses, but would not stifle it. The gain in the sale of the products of revitalized or new railway workshops could well be greater. This is speculation, but the question deserves to be asked.

9

The scope for future diversions
from London airports

It was suggested in Chapter 8 that the London airports might be relieved of almost half of their projected load by about 1985–90 by two factors which the Roskill and DTI projections did not take into account: the application of a rational plan for use of airports, and the development of the railways' new potential. This chapter will show in detail how this estimate was reached, following as far as practicable the nine headings used in Chapter 8. It will take the DTI Working Party's unrevised figure of 88 million travellers (21·8 million long-haul, 2·7 million Irish, 50·7 million European and 12·8 million domestic) in 1985, and look in some detail at the prospects of London's airports losing travellers in each of these markets. Account will be taken of the DTI Working Party's revisions for 1980, though for 1985 we can deal only with their implications. The revisions did not affect the European market.

The exercise will involve some very simple calculations which have a speculative element that is essentially no greater than that involved in the projections which Roskill used for the argument that the new airport would be needed by 1980.

It should be remembered that the figure of 88 million is higher than most of the projections which Roskill received. According to them this figure would not be reached before about 1988. If that is so, the argument of this book is strengthened.

Only published statistics will be used. The British Airports Authority's annual Reports give the numbers of passengers and aircraft movements for the main national origins and destinations. These figures relate to the Authority's airports (in the London area, Heathrow, Gatwick and Stansted). The BAA also gives a global figure for Luton, distinguishing the small domestic traffic there from the much larger international traffic.

Nearly all international scheduled traffic in 1970–1 used Heathrow, and 98 per cent of the passengers using Heathrow were on scheduled services. At Gatwick 80 per cent were on non-scheduled flights, and at Stansted 98 per cent.

At the three BAA airports together a fifth of all passengers were on non-scheduled flights. Although the non-scheduled proportion of international passengers is not given, it can reasonably be assumed to be about 23 per cent compared with 12 per cent ten years ago. The non-scheduled total has increased its share steadily during the past ten years; in the last two years shown it rose by over 65 per cent, while scheduled rose by under 25 per cent. This development is of some importance, because non-scheduled traffic may be less firmly attached to London-area airports than scheduled.

The Board of Trade's paper, *Passengers at London Airports* (1970), reports the findings of the survey made in the autumn of 1968, and produces reasonably hard information about the starting and finishing points of passengers at London airports in that year, including Luton.

The second group of sources to be used here is taken from the Roskill Report and the DTI Working Party's *Report on Traffic and Capacity at Heathrow*, published in 1971. Here we find projections of passengers in future years, up to 1980, 1985, etc., divided with less detail than in the BOT's paper. These figures are of course speculative because they relate to the future, and the Working Party admits that beyond 1980 its figures are mathematical extrapolations. Even the 1980 figures were drastically revised for the North American and domestic markets.

The DTI Working Party's long-term projections, tabulated on p. 37 of the Report, give three possible figures, 'lower', 'most likely' and 'higher', for each of five markets, year by year, up to 1985. The five markets are North America, other long-haul, Europe, Irish Republic and Domestic.

The choice of these sub-divisions suggests that little attention was being paid to any possibility that demand at London airports might alter as a result of changes in the pattern of travel. If we are to have a picture of future demand at London airports we need to divide the European and domestic markets into sections which correspond with the scope for transfer to rail. Improved railway services are unlikely to affect the Channel Islands or Northern Irish sections of the domestic market, but they are very likely to have an immense effect on the Northern English section, where the absolute number of air travellers can be expected to rise for a few years and then to decline sharply between 1978 and 1985, as the new railway capacity is progressively introduced. The same is true of the large sections for Paris and Brussels, assuming construction of the Channel tunnel.

Rather similar considerations apply, in different degrees, to the Scottish section of the domestic market, and to the Dutch and near-Germany sections of the European market, and to the European sections in the 400 to 1,000-miles ring.

The Board of Trade's *Passengers at London Airports* is a little more useful, because it divides the markets by national destinations, though the benefits of this division arise from chance rather than from intention. The Roskill Commission did not seek any further details relevant to degrees of 'railability' of sections of the market.

For the whole of the European and long-haul markets some break-down according to points of origin and destination within Britain, and according to business and non-business, British or foreign residence, would have been helpful for any survey of the scope for transfer from London-area airports to other British regional airports.

It would not be fair to criticize these documents for not specifically taking into account the possible effect of improved telecommunications in reducing business travel, or the effects of crowding at holiday resorts on leisure travel; but it is fair to observe that the whole apparatus of calculation, as published, however valid as a statistical exercise, has failed to take into account the effects of possible (or even likely) changes in the whole pattern of travel. The figures are thus valid only on the assumption that nothing is done to make possible a change in that pattern; to this extent the whole body of figures is fundamentally deficient. The proper function of a full enquiry would have been to determine how the pattern might be changed, and then to evaluate the effects of possible changes.

However, the projections have been regarded as valid for the calculations which have led the Government to accept that a third airport will be needed by 1980, and by the same token they are no less valid (as overall figures) for calculations of the amount of possible reduction through diversion to the railways. From the distribution between national origins and destinations, we shall calculate

107

TABLE 6—*Origin and destination of traffic, 1970–1*

	Air Transport Movements (000's)					
	Heathrow	Gatwick	Prestwick	Stansted	Total	Per cent of Total
DOMESTIC						
UK	37·4	6·8	4·1	0·2	48·5	15·2
Channel Isles	6·5	5·0	—	0·4	11·9	3·7
	43·9	11·8	4·1	0·6	60·4	18·9
EUROPE (excluding domestic)						
Eire	12·7	0·2	—	0·1	13·0	4·1
France	24·0	3·1	0·1	0·1	27·3	8·5
Benelux	23·0	3·7	0·1	0·3	27·1	8·5
West Germany	25·0	3·4	1·2	0·8	30·4	9·5
Scandinavia	9·6	1·3	0·5	0·4	11·8	3·7
Spain	9·9	11·2	—	1·4	22·5	7·0
Italy	11·2	4·5	0·1	0·4	16·2	5·1
Switzerland	12·1	2·1	—	0·3	14·5	4·5
Eastern Europe	4·3	1·4	0·2	0·1	6·0	1·9
Rest of Europe	14·4	3·3	0·1	0·2	18·0	5·6
Total	146·2	34·2	2·3	4·1	186·8	58·4
EUROPE (including domestic)	190·1	46·0	6·4	4·7	247·2	77·3
AFRICA						
North Africa	2·1	2·6	—	0·1	4·8	1·5
East, West and Cntral Africa	3·5	1·2	—	0·2	4·9	1·5
South Africa	2·2	—	—	—	2·2	0·7
Total	7·8	3·8	—	0·3	11·9	3·7
ASIA						
Middle East	6·6	0·3	—	0·1	7·0	2·2
India, Pakistan, Ceylon	3·1	—	—	—	3·1	1·0
Japan	2·8	—	—	—	2·8	0·9
Rest of Asia	1·0	0·3	—	0·2	1·5	0·5
Total	13·5	0·6	—	0·3	14·4	4·6
AUSTRALASIA	3·7	0·2	—	—	3·9	1·2
NORTH AMERICA						
Canada	4·1	1·6	2·2	0·1	8·0	2·5
USA	24·3	1·8	3·7	0·7	30·5	9·5
Total	28·4	3·4	5·9	0·8	38·5	12·0
CENTRAL AND SOUTH AMERICA						
Central America and Caribbean	1·9	0·2	—	0·1	2·2	0·7
South America	1·2	0·4	0·1	—	1·7	0·5
Total	3·1	0·6	0·1	0·1	3·9	1·2
Grand Total	246·6	54·4	12·4	6·2	319·8	100·0

Terminal Passengers (000's)						Cargo (000's Short tons)					
Heathrow	Gatwick	Prestwick	Stansted	Total	Per cent of Total	Heathrow	Gatwick	Prestwick	Stansted	Total	Per cent of Total
2,462	285	29	6	2,782	13·8	17·0	4·2	1·7	0·6	23·5	5·5
329	162	—	16	507	2·5	4·7	5·3	—	0·1	10·1	2·3
2,791	447	29	22	3,289	16·3	21·7	9·5	1·7	0·7	33·6	7·8
938	17	1	—	956	4·7	13·1	0·1	—	0·4	13·6	3·2
1,644	201	1	7	1,853	9·2	30·9	0·8	0·1	0·4	32·2	7·5
1,376	137	1	14	1,528	7·6	32·7	2·6	0·1	2·0	37·4	8·7
1,228	190	2	37	1,457	7·2	49·3	2·3	1·4	0·6	53·6	12·5
532	87	1	32	652	3·2	9·5	0·2	1·1	0·2	11·0	2·6
553	972	3	141	1,669	8·3	6·8	—	—	0·5	8·1	1·9
569	366	8	34	977	4·8	17·4	0·5	—	0·4	18·3	4·3
684	171	—	26	831	4·4	9·0	0·1	—	—	9·1	2·1
194	107	2	9	312	1·6	2·6	1·3	—	—	3·9	0·9
880	272	—	11	1,163	5·8	13·8	1·7	0·1	1·4	17·0	3·9
8,598	2,521	19	311	11,449	56·8	185·1	10·4	2·8	5·9	204·2	47·6
11,389	2,968	48	333	14,738	73·1	206·8	19·9	4·5	6·6	327·8	55·4
124	198	—	11	333	1·6	1·5	2·8	—	0·6	4·9	1·1
222	58	—	6	286	1·4	8·1	9·1	—	2·4	19·6	4·6
191	—	—	—	191	1·0	5·8	0·1	—	—	5·9	1·4
537	256	—	17	810	4·0	15·4	12·0	—	3·0	30·4	7·1
337	13	—	1	351	1·8	16·6	2·0	—	0·9	19·5	4·6
184	3	—	—	187	0·9	7·7	0·1	—	0·1	7·9	1·8
158	—	—	—	158	0·8	5·5	—	—	—	5·5	1·3
65	27	—	10	102	0·5	2·7	0·7	—	0·6	4·0	0·9
744	43	—	11	798	4·0	32·5	2·8	—	1·6	36·9	8·6
257	23	1	—	281	1·4	10·9	0·1	—	—	11·0	2·5
380	219	148	11	758	3·8	10·6	0·3	1·9	0·3	13·1	3·1
1,961	265	126	117	2,469	12·2	82·5	0·3	9·0	0·1	91·9	21·4
2,341	484	274	128	3,227	16·0	93·1	0·6	10·9	0·4	105·0	24·5
164	30	1	11	206	1·0	2·8	0·8	—	—	3·6	0·8
78	21	3	3	105	0·5	3·8	0·8	0·1	—	4·7	1·1
242	51	4	14	311	1·5	6·6	1·6	0·1	—	8·3	1·9
15,510	3,824	327	503	20,164	100·0	365·3	37·0	15·5	11·6	429·4	100·0

TABLE 7

The British Airports Authority: major passenger traffic flows, 1970–1

		Passengers	Percentage of total	Percentage change on 1969–70
DOMESTIC ROUTES				
Heathrow	Glasgow	631,242	22·6	−3·0
	Belfast	450,886	16·2	+1·3
	Edinburgh	419,794	15·0	−3·0
	Manchester	329,791	11·8	+0·1
	Channel Isles	328,722	11·8	−0·5
	Newcastle	217,259	7·8	+4·8
	All other routes	413,352	14·8	−2·0
	Total	2,791,046	100·0	−1·0
Gatwick	Channel Isles	161,539	36·1	−9·8
	Glasgow	120,245	26·9	+17·0
	Belfast	75,557	16·9	+40·5
	Edinburgh	81,776	18·3	+62·8
	All other routes	7,856	1·8	−55·9
	Total	446,973	100·0	+10·8
INTERNATIONAL ROUTES				
Heathrow	Paris	1,478,424	11·6	+6·9
	J F Kennedy	839,490	6·6	+12·3
	Dublin	754,189	6·0	+9·5
	Amsterdam	753,122	5·9	+10·4
	Brussels	422,605	3·3	+11·4
	Frankfurt	352,464	2·8	+19·7
	Zurich	344,718	2·7	+4·8
	Geneva	279,515	2·2	+4·5
	Copenhagen	267,685	2·1	+7·5
	San Francisco	204,612	1·6	+35·0
	Malta	200,303	1·6	−21·6
	All other routes	6,822,000	—	—
	Total	12,719,127	100·0	+9·8
Gatwick	Palma	437,893	13·0	+10·6
	Toronto	121,091	3·6	+7·7
	Munich	119,918	3·6	+144·9
	Ibiza	112,339	3·3	+116·3
	New York	109,177	3·2	+0·9
	Gerona	104,180	3·1	−27·8
	Alicante	102,081	3·0	−10·6
	All other routes	2,270,373	67·2	+31·3
	Total	3,377,052	100·0	+24·9
Stansted	Gerona	81,183	16·9	Not available
	All other routes	398,872	83·1	Not available
	Total	480,055	100·0	
Prestwick	Toronto	112,944	37·8	+4·1
	New York	68,196	22·8	−12·1
	All other routes	117,535	39·4	+28·2
	Total	298,675	100·0	+7·6

the distributions according to distance. The 1969 BOT figures, helped by the BAA 1970–1 Report, will be used for a forward calculation by distance-zones to 1985. In the past five years traffic to the more remote European destinations has increased faster than that to nearer places, but no detailed projections are available. In fact the relative rates of increase of the European market in the various distance-ranges cannot well be predicted, but some discussion of this problem and its consequences will be necessary.

None of the published statistics are really adequate. The 1968 figures may be 'hard' figures, but they are not divided according to distance from London of points of origin or destination. However, they do divide the passengers according to national origins and destinations, and when we examine these figures in detail, together with airline timetables and the BAA's 'major flow' statistics, showing traffics for Heathrow–Paris, etc., we can even now produce a pattern of travel according to distance which is unlikely to be significantly wrong.

The table on p. 37 of the DTI Report gives projections for each of the main markets, year by year, up to 1985. The figures for North America in the original projections were later revised sharply upwards, in the light of buoyant demand in 1968–70, influenced by new cheap charter fares. Revised figures are given in a table on p. 106 of the Report, up to 1980 only. The revision should be treated with scepticism, as it reflects short-term changes.

TABLE 8

DTI projections of terminal passenger movements at London
airports according to major origin/destination groups
(millions of passengers)

	North America	Other long-haul	Irish Republic	European	Domestic (incl. N. Ireland and Channel Isles)	Total
1968 actual	1·9	1·0	0·8	8·4	3·1	15·2
1980 first projection	8·0	4·6	2·0	30·6	9·0	54·2
1980 revised	11·0	4·6	2·0	30·6	7·8	55·0
1985 first projection	13·4	8·4	2·7	50·7	12·8	88·0

Although we have argued that the travel-market ought to be looked at as a whole, we must now look, as far as we can, at the

111

possible implication for the London airports' load of the various practicable transfers which have been examined above. The main object is to suggest the questions that might usefully be asked, rather than to produce authoritative answers. However, tentative figures will be entered, on the basis of assumptions which will be explained, and a range of variations will be suggested.

We may usefully divide the projected London airports' load in 1985 into two roughly equal parts, non-railable and railable. The non-railable market includes a majority of people terminating their journeys in the South-East and a minority outside it; we want to suggest proportions and members who might use regional airports instead of London. The potentially railable market includes a few who might use direct air services at regional airports, a few who might travel by through-train services; the majority would terminate in the South-East, and we shall need to divide them according to degree of 'railability', which depends mainly on the distance from London of the European terminal-point. There are some 'border-line' zones, notably central Italy, Yugoslavia and possibly northern Spain.

We should now look at the passenger loads and their likely evolution, taking three main groups of markets one by one: first, the main routes for which rail will be wholly irrelevant in 1985, namely long-haul together with all Ireland and the Channel Isles; secondly, traffic with the European continent, allowing for some of it to be non-railable; thirdly, the domestic traffic within Great Britain.

The North American section accounts for more than half of the total outside Europe. If the traffic grows at the rate projected during the next few years it is likely that by 1985 super-jumbos, with perhaps 1,000 seats, will have been developed and in service on this major trunk route. At the very least, most of the London–North America traffic will use aircraft of 350-passenger capacity. Thus, for this part of the market the Roskill projection of persons per aircraft (150 by 1980) is probably too low. It would apparently be reasonable to assume 200 to 250 persons per aircraft on the North American traffic by 1985, and 180 in the other long-haul traffic. The figures might possibly have to be revised downwards if a significant number of small SST aircraft were employed on these routes, but in view of their cost their number is likely to very small. (There is not the slightest reason why an expensive luxury such as supersonic travel should be subsidized by state money derived from the general

LONG-HAUL AND OTHER NON-RAILABLE MARKETS

TABLE 9

DTI projections of non-railable terminal passenger demand at London airports, 1980, 1981 and 1985, excluding European continent (adapted from DTI Working Party Report)

	1968	1980 revised	1985
North America	1·9	11·0	13·4*
Other long haul	1·0	4·6	8·4
Irish Republic	0·8	2·0	2·7
Belfast	0·4	1·0	1·5
Channel Islands	0·5	1·2	1·7
Total	4·6	19·8	27·7*

* No revised figure for 1985 is given. If we carry the DTI's 1980 revision forward, the North American total goes to 18 million, and the overall total to 32 million.

public; indeed, under any system of progressive indirect taxation, it should be heavily taxed. And it would be hard to find any good reason why overall transport planning should be distorted in order to provide for it.)

In 1970 North American traffic at all London airports had risen to 2·75 million passengers, involving 32,000 aircraft movements.[1] The DTI's projections for 1980 began with a figure of 8 million passengers, later raised to 11 million. The figure of 13·4 million for 1985 is unrevised, so we have to decide whether to accept it or to revise it upwards in its turn. If we leave it at 13·4 million we have perhaps 50,000 aircraft movements; if we revise it upwards to 18 million passengers we have 70,000 aircraft movements, assuming larger average loads per aircraft in the latter case. If the traffic increased at the higher rate, the likelihood of an increase in aircraft size and persons per aircraft would be all the greater. A hundred flights a day from London to North America would provide travellers with a slightly wider range of direct-flight destinations than fifty, but the advantage would not be enormously significant, even for consumers' convenience.

Roskill's terms of reference did not invite the Commissioners to ask how far the existing British regional airports might play a role as 'national' airports. This omission (discussed in Chapter 3) is highly relevant for the projected increases in the North American traffic, assuming better rail services within Britain.

In 1970 there was quite heavy traffic between Prestwick and North America, and some from Manchester. Prestwick passengers were 12 per cent of the total from BAA airports, but the London airports handled 80 per cent of the total.

By 1985 four main categories of transatlantic passengers might use British regional airports instead of London: first, British non-south-eastern residents; second, American holiday-makers wishing to travel round Britain; third, American businessmen with destinations away from London; fourth, holiday-makers, either way, more interested in low cost. The fourth group overlaps the second. If the total Britain–North America market rose to 18 million passengers by 1985, these first three groups would surely be likely to account for half of it rather than a third, leaving 9 to 12 million preferring a terminal point in London. But even those with London terminal points would not all need to use London airports.

We hardly need a full-blown national airports policy to see that Liverpool might well take a quarter or a third of this London–North America traffic away from London. All the figures are rather artificial, but if 12 million passengers on the North American route terminated in London in 1985, 3 to 5 million might well use Liverpool, in addition to the 6 million or so who would terminate away from London, and who might be distributed between Liverpool and other regional airports.

A combination of spontaneous and induced transfers of North American traffic from London airports to British regional airports could reasonably be expected to reduce the London load in 1985 to a level below that envisaged by the DTI's Working Party in 1980; if the 1985 total for Great Britain–North America were 18 million, London would not be likely to need to handle more than 8 to 10 million. With an average load per aircraft of 250 passengers they would still require 50 flights a day each way – more than enough to provide a reasonable variety of American destinations.

For long East–West journeys frequency of services brings few benefits. The clock determines the most acceptable departure times. Half a million passengers a year on a route could be dealt with by one 1,000-seater aircraft. If there were 8 million using London, half of them on three main trunk routes (New York, Chicago and California), there would be work for eight 1,000-seaters. Liverpool or Manchester to New York services might add a further two to six. As British North Atlantic traffic is only a small part of the world total on major long trunk routes, the total growth now foreseen would probably justify development of very large aircraft; there would be work for 300 of them worldwide. If the growth has been over-estimated, and the total passenger load is less, the case for these monsters will be weaker, but the problem of accommodating the traffic will be reduced in its turn. At any rate, the London–North America traffic should be capable of being handled by no more than 40,000 aircraft movements a year at London airports by 1985. If a fairly high proportion of super-jumbos were in use, a reduction to even 30,000 a year might well be achieved and sustained.

The long-haul traffic on routes other than North America is spread more widely. The DTI Working Party's figure is 8·4 million passengers in 1985, three-fifths of the first estimate for North America, or less than half of the assumed upwards revision. There would be some scope for regional transfer, but less than that for North America; and there would be few routes justifying the use of aircraft with more than 500 seats. Even so, the London total could very reasonably be cut to 7 million, and the number of London aircraft movements put at 40,000 to 50,000 in 1985.[2]

In 1970 the London airports dealt with almost 33,000 aircraft movements on North American routes and just over 33,000 on other inter-continental routes. Even if the total number of passengers increases at the predicted rate, these figures could probably be held below 50,000 for each group in 1985, without significant detriment to any travellers.

Traffic with Ireland and the Channel Islands is unlikely to shift from air to sea. It is not heavy, but the DTI puts it as almost 7 million passengers in 1985, about 8 per cent of the total. The British terminal points in these markets are widely distributed; no London airport is good for people terminating outside the South-East.

These routes are already fairly well served by British regional airports, so there may be limited scope for spontaneous regional transfer.

In the case of the Channel Islands there were in 1971 around 50 scheduled flights a week outwards from Southampton, with direct rail connection from London. By 1985 all the London–Channel Islands traffic could well be transferred to Southampton – or, failing this, to another southern airport – as could some of the Irish traffic. Given adequate rail-connection a proportion of the travellers between London and Dublin or Belfast might use Birmingham or even Liverpool, though an incentive such as differential airport charges might be needed.

These two small transfers are marginal to the main argument. They are unlikely to be necessary, but they could be a useful small reserve in case a gamble on deferment of the new London airport went awry. Without the transfers, these two small groups would probably demand about 30,000 aircraft movements in 1985, assuming a small average load of 100 persons per aircraft. The transfers could, on that assumption, bring the figure down to 15,000 or 20,000 aircraft movements, or less if the transfers were more drastic.

THE EUROPEAN MARKET

We now turn to the biggest element in the demand projected for 1980 and 1985; traffic with Europe. Here the published information is of limited value. The DTI projected about 50 million air journeys by 1985, and we have also a breakdown of the 1968 journeys by national destinations. But it is inadequate to project air journeys for this market in isolation from journeys by rail. What we need is a projection of total public transport journeys out of which we could make a series of models, assuming different distributions between air and rail and assuming different levels of quality of service, including price, which would in their turn affect the distribution. We also need to study the effect of the timing of railway improvements on the evaluation of market shares.

Another set of projections has been used in connection with the Channel tunnel. The GLC's *Channel Tunnel London Passenger Terminal: A Document for Consultation*, published in November 1972, quotes some estimates derived from railway sources. At one point it suggests that, if the tunnel were in use by 1978, the railway would take 70 per cent of the Anglo-European traffic if high-speed trains were available, but 55 per cent if they were not. The meaning of 'Anglo-European' is not defined. Figure 3 of the Document indicates that the annual London–Paris passenger load by rail would reach 10 million in 1985–6 if the journey-time were by then cut to 3 hours. It does not estimate the numbers assuming a 2½-hour London–Paris journey by that date. The DoE's Green Paper on the Channel Tunnel does not even raise the question of differences in the rate of transfer to rail arising from different journey-times.

But one of the options available is precisely to complete the planned new rail routes from London to Paris, Brussels and Amsterdam by 1985, together with Paris–Lyon (which, according to French projections, will be needed long before then, even without the addition of heavy through traffic from London).[3]

As our immediate purpose is to ask what proportion and what number of London–Europe passengers, officially assigned to air, might be taken out of the London airports' load, we shall work with the figures on which these official estimates were based.

We may start with the 1968 annual estimate for Europe, by country of origin or destination:[4]

TABLE 10

BOT estimates of passengers between London airports and European destinations, 1968 (000's)

	Heathrow	Other airports	Total	Approx. percentage of total to Europe
France	1,095	175	1,264	15½
Benelux	890	439	1,329	16½
W. Germany	795	78	873	11
Switzerland and Austria	512	129	641	8
Scandanavia	404	88	492	6
Italy	528	304	832	10
Iberia	971	1,110	2,081	26
Rest of Europe	469	130	599	7
Total Europe			8,111	100

Unfortunately the published reports of the Board of Trade, Department of Trade and Industry and Roskill Commission did not ask the questions which need to be asked in order to establish the numbers of travellers in the European markets who might use rail instead of air. The 1973 Channel Tunnel Green Paper's neglect of these questions may have been deliberate, in defence of Maplin.

117

Lacking proper information, we must make the best use we can of the poor tools that we can find.

Assuming a Channel tunnel and adequate rail services, the markets might usefully be divided as follows:

1. *Up to 300 miles.* Rail much cheaper and more convenient than air, and quicker except for that tiny minority who either have a final terminal point close to one of the airports and private car transport, or private cars or taxis at both ends (unless there are so many that they block each other).

2. *300–400 miles.* Rail much cheaper and more convenient, and about equal in time consumed, with the same few exceptions as above.

3. *400–1,000 miles.* In some degree this is a single market; all journeys in it will be capable of being done by rail by night with no more expenditure of usable time than by air. The cost by rail will vary upwards from below half the air cost according to the degree of comfort.

Rail travel by day becomes less competitive in time consumed above 400 miles. For many journeys in the 400–700 mile range it is closely competitive with air in time consumed, because rail stations can be more easily accessible than airports to final destinations. A large proportion of journeys in this range are likely to be for business (central France, West Germany and Switzerland) and it is reasonable to expect that about half of the business travellers would prefer air. Above 700 miles cheapness is the main rail-advantage, but there will be a larger proportion of holiday journeys, for which price tends to be an important factor in determining preference between modes.

4. *1,000–1,200 miles.* This small slice is rather difficult to assess. The main markets are middle Italy and much of Yugoslavia and Austria, with mainly holiday travel by British residents, though attractive train services might well bring foreign tourists from these areas to Britain. Day rail journeys are scarcely feasible; night journeys within 12 or 13 hours would be acceptable and feasible assuming that the night trains were able to profit from fast running on the new tracks which are now planned. Most of the journeys in this range, as far as Rome, should be able to benefit from these new facilities.

5. *1,200–1,500 miles.* The main markets are southern Italy and part of Yugoslavia. Even with the help of high-speed lines for part

118

of the way, the journey-times would exceed 12 hours. But the advantages of price and convenience should enable the railway to win part of the traffic, if it is worth their while to try. It probably is worth while.

We had better assume the traffic with Spain to be non-railable. It might conceivably be worth while to build new standard-gauge routes from the French border to Barcelona, in which case the railway could enter the mass market for travel to the Costa Brava.

In the absence of any detailed analysis of this market we may begin by putting forward an estimate of the possible percentage distribution of passengers beyond 400 miles in four distance-groups, showing business and non-business separately.

	400–700 miles	700–1,000 miles	1,000–1,200 miles	1,200–1,500 miles
Business				
Rail–day	0	0	0	5
Rail–night	25	15	5	0
Air	25	15	15	10
Total	50	30	20	10
Non-business				
Rail–day	20	20	10	0
Rail–night	20	40	40	20
Air	10	10	30	80
Total	50	70	80	90
	100	100	100	100

This estimate of a likely distribution between rail and air is based on a reasonable assessment of probability, but speculative. The speculative element could have been reduced if Roskill had been provided with information about the current split between rail and air in a number of markets which could have served as a guide. The information could have been refined to show the proportions of business and non-business travellers using air or rail both ways, or rail one way, air the other. The current split on the routes between Paris and Marseille, Paris and Nice, Hamburg and Munich would serve as quite useful guides to the likely split on journeys which can be accomplished by rail in seven to ten hours.

In all probability much of the information is already available, but has not been produced for demonstration to the public. It is quite an important piece of evidence, and without it the Roskill Report was not really complete. Even without the benefit of this piece of evidence, it can reasonably be claimed that the guesswork allocations made above are inherently less speculative (because based on a recognition of the probable consequences of new circumstances) than the projections of the DTI Working Party. The latter simply used the past trends as a basis from which to predict future trends, without allowing for changes in trend which could be expected to arise from possible changes of circumstances. For the European market the Government has the power to act in such a way as to affect the circumstances. The Working Party's figures assume that it will take no such action. A Government concerned to make intelligent decisions would wish to be informed of the likely consequences of its choices between options open to it.

The BAA Report for 1970–1 shows that 32 per cent of all aircraft movements were to or from points in the UK, France and Benelux, and a further 20 per cent to points in Europe within railable distance. By putting the figures in the main table together with the major traffic flow figures on p. 120 of the Report, we see that the percentages of aircraft movements in significant markets were approximately as follows:

		Approximate percentages of total aircraft movements at BAA London airports 1970–1*
1. Under 300 miles (railable in under 3 hours by 1985)		14
Northern England	5	
Paris	7	
Brussels	2	
2. 300–400 miles (railable in under 5 hours by 1985)		14
Scotland	7	
Benelux (except Brussels)	5	
Cologne–Düsseldorf	2	
3. 400–1,000 miles (railable in 4 to 12 hours by 1985)		18
France (except Paris)	1	
W. Germany (except near parts)	7·5	
North Italy	3·5	
Switzerland	4·5	
Denmark	1·5	

* In order to obtain these figures, use has been made of p. 54 of the BAA Report for 1970–1, which shows 1·69 million passengers between Heathrow or Gatwick and Paris, 0·9 million for Amsterdam, and 0·4 million for Brussels.

If the Channel tunnel is built and the railways' potential fully developed a considerable proportion of this traffic will be transferred to rail. If all transferred to rail, the London airports could lose almost half of their load to rail and no new airport would be needed until 1990 (though in that case we should probably need a second Channel tunnel by then). But our concern is with reasonable probabilities, so we shall now try to estimate the lower and upper percentages in each market which might be expected to transfer to rail by 1985.

At this point we should also introduce an allowance for the probability that the short-distance markets' share of the total will decline in the next two decades.

TABLE 11

The scope for transfer to rail of London airports' projected 1985 load

Market defined by distance and likely rail-journey time in 1985	Market's share of all aircraft movements at BAA London airports (per cent)			Range of percentage of market likely to transfer to rail by 1985		Percentage of all aircraft movements likely to be transferred to rail by 1985	
	1970–1 actual	1985 New projection		Lower	Upper	Lower	Upper
		Lower	Upper				
Under 2½ hours	15·5	13	15	70	90	10	12
2½–4 hours	14	12	14	50	75	6	9
4–12 hours	18	16	18	25	75	4	12
Over 12 hours, Europe only	17	20	22	5	15	1	3
Total						21	36

It seems highly likely that, on the basis of these calculations, a load equivalent to between 20 and 40 per cent of all passenger movements, at London airports, assumed in the Roskill and DTI projections, would be eliminated through transfer of passengers to rail around 1982. There would be a corresponding reduction in aircraft movements.

As soon as we begin to think of country-by-country projections, we are again aware of the speculative nature of the whole exercise – and this goes for the original projections on which Roskill was based. Exchange rates, political developments and other factors may greatly alter anything that is now foreseen.

Again, if we extrapolate all trends of the past fifteen years, including numbers of visitors to the main holiday localities, the rate of building new accommodation, industrial development, and the overcrowding, pressure on resources, and pollution of water, air and ecology that result, we may find that some of the holiday areas will have lost the qualities which now make them attractive. The projected rates of expansion of holiday traffic may be absolutely unattainable, if they involve a combination of factors which are completely unrealistic.

This depressing caveat is introduced as a reminder that the projections of future travel may be too high rather than too low, but the argument here will not rely on these doubts. Our present concern is with DTI's projected traffic between London airports and Europe, amounting to 50·7 million passengers in 1985. This is $6\frac{1}{3}$ times as great as the estimate for the year 1968 given by *Passengers at London Airports* and $4\frac{1}{2}$ times as great as the London–Europe total (12·4 million) in the year 1970–1 which we may derive from the BAA'S Report.

Passengers at London Airports gives international figures only by national destinations, without distinguishing the travellers according to distance within national markets. The BAA Annual Report does make this distinction to a limited extent; its list of 'major flows' is quite useful for our purpose; however, it gives only a single figure for Luton's international traffic, so that we have to make our own guesses about it. The danger of error is very slight.

In an attempt to find out how many of the 1985 London–Europe travellers might transfer to rail, we shall now take the BAA's figures for 1970–1 and assign them to distance groups so as to determine the proportion and number who might be regarded as potentially railable.

The BAA's total for the traffic between its three London airports and Europe (excluding British Isles) comes to 10,474,000. Luton's international traffic is shown as 1,924,000. Assuming most of the Luton traffic to be with Europe, the 1970–1 total is a little over 12 million. The DTI's 1985 total is 50·7 million. We shall therefore multiply each of the markets in 1970–1 by approximately $4\frac{1}{4}$ to give us a figure for 1985.

The main objection to this procedure is that it assumes that each market will multiple at the same rate. In fact it seems rather likely that the longer-distance markets, particularly that involving British holiday-makers' travel to the Eastern Mediterranean and the Black Sea, may increase faster than the norm (perhaps mainly at the expense of Benelux). However, all the figures are speculative, including the DTI's projections from which they start, and the assumption of equal growth is no more speculative than the main projection.

We begin, then, by looking at the 1970–1 BAA figures and identifying those national markets which could be accessible by train within about 12 hours according to the time and distance map in Chapter 7, p. 93. When there is doubt we shall err on the side of caution. The estimate of 75 per cent for Italy is rather cautious; so is the estimate of 15 per cent for the rest of Europe, when we remember that it includes Austria (most of which is potentially railable), the nearer parts of Spain and three Eastern European countries.

At this stage we are not trying to estimate the number who might be expected to transfer to rail, but only the number within the 12-hour rail ring; the estimate of reasonably foreseeable transfers to rail will come at the later stage of the argument.

The total of all passengers at the three BAA London airports was 19,837,000. Together with Luton the total was approximately 21·8 million.[5] Thus the potentially railable European total of about 8 million was about 38 per cent of the overall BAA total, including domestic journeys, and 36 per cent of the total including Luton.

We may next estimate the numbers and proportions of the potentially railable passengers in three distance-categories: (1) below 300 miles (rail preferable to air on every count for almost all passengers); (2) 300–400 miles (rail slightly slower than air for most passengers, but cheaper and more convenient and reliable); (3) 400–1,200 miles (rail slower, but cheaper).

A few of these figures require some explanation. Some are estimates, assisted by other sources of information. Wherever an estimate has had to be made it has been cautious, putting the short-distance figure too low rather than too high. This is because it is important not to spoil the argument for transfer to rail by over-estimating the numbers in the transferable groups.

(a) *France.* In the French figure the estimate of 85 per cent under 300 miles reflects the Paris percentage among all traffic with France. The BAA Report shows that of the 1·85 million passengers between

TABLE 12

Terminal passengers at London-area airports, on European routes,
1970–1, by country of origin and destination, showing proportions and
numbers who could be within 12 hours of London by rail and thus
potentially railable

British terminal	Foreign terminal	Terminal passengers (000's)	Passengers assumed to be potentially railable percentage	No. (000's)
	France	1,852	100	1,852
	Benelux	1,527	100	1,527
	W. Germany	1,455	100	1,455
3 BAA London Airports: Heathrow, Gatwick and Stansted	Copenhagen (Heathrow only)	268	100	268
	Other Scandinavia	383	0	0
	Italy	969	80	775
	Switzerland	881	100	881
	Other Europe	3,139	20	628
Luton	All foreign destinations	1,924	33	608
	Approx.	12,300	Approx.	8,200

Source: BAA Report 1970–1, pp. 118–19 (Prestwick figures omitted). The Heathrow-Copenhagen figure is taken from p. 120, Luton from p. 125. The approximate figures allow for a slight reduction in the Luton totals to take account of Luton passengers going outside Europe.

Heathrow, Gatwick and Stansted and France, 1·48 million were Heathrow–Paris. The 200,000 Gatwick–France passengers included the scheduled Paris service via Le Touquet. Thus London–Paris must have been at least 85 per cent of all London–France air traffic, excluding Luton. French statistics suggest that it was more like 90 per cent. Our estimate of 85 per cent is almost certainly over-cautious.

(*b*) *Benelux.* London–Brussels traffic was 0·42 million, or 27 per cent of all London–Benelux. Amsterdam was 52 per cent. Of the remainder the greater part was with Rotterdam, a little with Ostend. An estimate of one-third of the total below 300 miles is unlikely to be far wrong. For all the rest of Benelux, rail would be between an hour quicker and an hour slower than air.

(*c*) *West Germany.* The West German figure of 25 per cent below 400 miles refers to Cologne–Düsseldorf. These two airports had 30 per cent of all BEA–Lufthansa scheduled flights between Heathrow and West Germany in 1970, but neither is included in the BAA Report's list of foreign airports handling over 200,000 passengers to or from Heathrow. These airports serve the Ruhr area. London–Dortmund would be about 440 miles by rail through the Channel tunnel, but as Dortmund passengers would have to use Düsseldorf or Cologne airport if they went by air, rail would have a distinct advantage. The 20 per cent over 700 miles for West Germany is mainly Munich.

(d) *Italy.* It is assumed that Rome would be railable within 12 hours, but that 20 per cent of the Italian traffic would be for places south of Rome, including Sicily and Sardinia.

(e) *Other Europe.* Only 20 per cent of this is assigned to the railable column. The total includes Austria and assumes a small railable traffic with northern Spain near the French border, and

TABLE 13

Estimated percentage of passengers using London airports in various time and distance groups, 1970–1

Country of origin/ destination	National total	Group 1 (up to 3 hours) under 300 miles		Group 2 (3 to 4 hours): 300–400 miles		Group 3 (4 to 7 hours): 400–700 miles		Group 4 (7 to 13 hours): 700–1,200 miles	
		%	No.	%	No.	%	No.	%	No.
France	1,852	85	1,576(a)			15	276		
Benelux	1,527	33	510(b)	67	1,017				
W. Germany	1,455			25	355(c)	55	800	20	300
Copenhagen	267							100	267
Other Scandinavia	383							10	33
Italy	969							80	775(d)
Switzerland	881					100	881		
Other Europe	3,139							20	620(e)
Totals in distance groups	9,370		2,086		1,372		1,957		1,915
Estimated Luton traffic						8	250	25	470
Total all airports rounded up	12,400		2,100		1,400		2,200		2,400

similarly with parts of Eastern Germany, Czechoslovakia and Yugoslavia.

(*f*) *Luton traffic* (as of 1970). All of this is assumed to be on charter flights, mainly to Spain. The figure of one-third potentially railable is a rough estimate.

We may now use round figures, both for the sake of simplicity and in order to remind ourselves that all calculations relating to the future must be inexact.

The 1970–1 total within the potentially railable ring amounts to 8·3 million, or two-thirds of the total between all London airports (including Luton) and Europe (12·4 million, allowing for a small percentage of Luton flights to be outside Europe). The European railable total is about 40 per cent of the total Heathrow traffic – and we have not yet dealt with British domestic traffic, all of which is highly railable.

This book does not argue that all the railable passengers should or would go by rail, or that each section of the European market will retain a constant share of the total. Our concern is with what might reasonably be expected to happen, so we have next to consider what proportion of the total traffic might be potentially railable, and what the proportion of this potentially railable traffic which might reasonably be expected to choose to go by rail, given the attractive rail-option that it is reasonable to assume. Roskill's single figure of 5·5 million divertable to rail for Paris and Benelux in 1980 might well be acceptable for that year (and useful for holding the demand for London airport travel at bay in 1980–1), but Roskill did not look at the realistically possible further transfers in 1980–5. Our next step is, unlike Roskill, to start with the maximum proportions who might transfer to rail and to try to arrive at a realistic-looking transfer rate for 1985.

The plan will be to take the boxes in Table 13 and apply the principles of p. 119 to each of them. A few particular explanations may be useful.

Table 13 gave us ten groups of travellers in distance groups for a series of national destinations. Each should be studied in turn in the light of the general principles.

(*a*) France below 300 miles. This is almost all to Paris, though a little is to places north of Paris, and this is even more eligible for rail. London–Paris amounted to 14 per cent of all London–Europe air traffic in 1970–1.

126

As rail would be quicker for almost all London–Paris passengers, as well as cheaper and more convenient, we might expect 85 per cent to transfer to rail, virtually all by day.

(*b*) France above 300 miles. This is mainly non-business traffic. Sixty per cent might transfer to rail (40 per cent by night, 20 per cent by day).

(*c*) Benelux below 300 miles. As with France, but in this case 90 per cent might transfer to rail, because of the easy rail connections between London and parts of Belgium other than Brussels. Virtually all the rail traffic would go by day. British Railways have put the time for London–Brussels at $2\frac{1}{4}$ hours.[6] Some local traffic between London and Belgium might continue to use Ostend or a replacement airport.

(*d*) Other Benelux. Many people on London–Amsterdam business journeys might well still wish to travel by air to save an hour or so; so might a few of the numerous non-business travellers. We might suggest that 70 per cent would transfer to rail (50 per cent by day, 20 per cent by night).

(*e*) West Germany, Group 1 (300–400 miles). Similar to Netherlands traffic, but with a bigger proportion on business. Sixty per cent transfer to rail (20 per cent by night, 40 per cent by day).

(*f*) West Germany. Group 2 (400–700 miles). A fairly large part of the non-business travellers might transfer to rail by day, others by night; and night trains might take nearly half of the business travellers. Sixty per cent transfer to rail (30 per cent by night, 30 per cent by day).

(*g*) West Germany, Group 3 (over 700 miles). Mixed business and non-business from both ends. Sixty per cent transfer to rail (50 per cent by night, 10 per cent by day).

(*h*) Italy. Rail by day would attract few travellers, but night trains would serve many others well. Sixty per cent transfer to rail (55 per cent by night, 5 per cent by day).

(*i*) Switzerland. Mixed business and non-business. Sixty per cent transfer to rail (40 per cent by night, 20 per cent by day).

(*j*) Other Europe within 12 hours of rail travel. Fifty per cent transfer to rail, all by night.

(*k*) Luton traffic within 12 hours by rail. All holiday-makers, to whom the cheapness of rail would be very important. Eighty per cent transfer to rail.

It should be noted again that this discussion refers only to the passengers on journeys for which rail would be favourable.

Table 14 gives us 42 per cent of the projected London–Europe air traffic in 1985 transferring to rail, out of a total of 70 per cent who might conceivably be expected to transfer. In other words, it assumes that three-fifths of the passengers who could transfer to rail,

TABLE 14

Approximate estimate of travellers assigned to air who might reasonably be expected to transfer to rail in 1985, distinguishing those likely to travel by day and by night

Market	Total assigned air passengers eligible for transfer to rail		Proportion and numbers of railable passengers estimated as likely to transfer to rail in 1985.					
			Total		By day		By night	
	1970 000's	1985 000's	%	000's	%	000's	%	000's
France (under 300 miles; generally quicker by rail)	1,576	6,600	88	5,700	85	5,500	3	200
Other France (over 300 miles)	276	1,200	67	800	27	320	40	480
Benelux (under 300 miles; generally quicker by rail)	510	2,200	88	2,000	88	2,000		
Other Benelux (300–400+ miles; slightly slower by rail)	1,017	4,200	70	2,800	50	2,100	20	600
W. Germany (Cologne–Ruhr)	355	1,500	60	900	40	600	20	300
W. Germany (mid) (400–700 miles)	800	3,400	60	2,100	20	700	40	1,400
W. Germany (over 700 miles)	300	1,200	60	700	—	—	60	700
Denmark	300	1,300	50	650	—	—	50	650
Other Scandinavia	360	1,400	—	—	—	—	—	—
Italy	775	3,250	50	1,600	10	300	40	1,300
Switzerland	881	3,750	60	2,250	20	750	40	1,500
BAA Other Europe	620	2,600	50	1,300	—	—	50	1,300
Luton traffic	720	3,000	40	750	—	—	40	750
Total (approx.)	8,400	35,800		21,500		12,250		9,200

without loss of more than one hour of usable time, would in fact transfer.

Given the types of rail services that can reasonably be envisaged, subject to adequate investment, the proportion transferring spontaneously might well be higher in practice. Much would depend on the relative price and quality of air and rail services. It seems fair to make the following assumptions; that standard rail fares for day travel, basic and 'luxury' (first class) would be one-half of the standard air fares for the equivalent journeys; that the train seats would be rather more comfortable than those in aircraft; and that the charge for overnight accommodation in trains would vary downwards from a basic maximum of a fare equal to the air fare for a room for single occupancy. It should be assumed that by either rail or air a proportion of the passengers would pay similarly reduced rates for their transport, whether on 'package tours' or on other reduced-rate systems.

The most likely source of error in the calculation made above is its assumption that all markets would increase at the same rate. During the 1960s the Iberian market increased much faster than any other major European market. Since 1970 there has been a new and energetic boom in the market for travel further afield still, with an exploding number of British holiday-makers travelling to the Eastern Mediterranean and the Black Sea. It is quite likely that these markets will continue to expand faster than others, and they are for the most part non-railable. British holiday-makers' traffic with the Costa Brava and the Spanish Atlantic coast might conceivably find rail-plus-bus preferable to air-plus-bus; and for the remoter parts of the Balearic Islands rail-plus-hovercraft might be preferable to air-plus-bus or other local transport. This point is quite important, because Palma itself could not absorb a quadrupling of its 1970 peak tourist-load, nor could its airport. We have not assumed any transfer to rail for Spanish traffic, but such an assumption might well be realistic; its feasibility can be borne in mind to set against the possibility that our earlier estimates may have underestimated the remoter destinations' share of the total European market.

Up to this point we have found that it should be quite reasonable to expect that out of the 50 million London airport passengers expected for 1985, rather more than 21 million might be expected to transfer to rail. This leaves almost 30 million still travelling by air; this level of transfer to rail alone, according to the Roskill argument, still allows about four years' deferment of a new London airport.

Let us next look at the almost 30 million still travelling by air in 1985. Of these about 14 million are opting for air, though they might quite reasonably have gone by rail instead. Another 15 million are on journeys too long for rail to be convenient (except for the few who doggedly prefer to see the country and have time to spare, or for whom price is very important).

Of the first group, those who opt for air in spite of its high cost, a fairly large proportion might well be business travellers. Out of the 14 million it might be expected that two-thirds would have British terminal points in the South-East, and that these would prefer to use a London airport. The remaining one-third, amounting to 5 million, might be expected to have their British terminal points outside the South-East. If they all used non-south-eastern airports the collective load for all British provincial airports together would amount to fifty 250-seat planes a day each way at 60 per cent load factor, or one hundred 120-seat planes on a similar basis. It seems reasonable to assume that at least 80 per cent of these passengers would have British terminal points fairly convenient for one among nine British airports (one of which, Manchester, would have three times the load of any other single one).

There would not be 200 daily links to cover every route, though Birmingham and Manchester could serve several, being more convenient than London for over half the range of British terminal points outside the South-East.

For some of these travellers to or from British regions through-trains, mainly overnight, would be the best solution.

A not unreasonable distribution of these 5 million passengers to or from the British regions might be as follows:

Air via a London airport: 2 million.

Air via a British non-London airport: 1·5 million.

Rail: 1·5 million.

This still does not take account of the regional travellers assigned spontaneously to British regional airports from their own development in Roskill's accepted transfer to them. They amount to 3·5 million for all routes world-wide in 1980, and thus about 6 million in 1985. But 2 million of these might be expected to transfer back to rail, along with a further 2 million of those who could be assigned to regional airports from their own spontaneous growth.

Next, our new calculations assume the DTI's 50 million London–Europe projection to include 15 million on non-railable routes. These are mainly British holiday-makers going to Iberia, the Eastern Mediterranean and Southern Italy. After allowing for Roskill's regional transfer (Report, Appendix 6, para. 21; cf. above, p. 62), we might assume that 6 million of these would terminate in British regions, but that 4 million could be better served, for their chosen destinations, by a British regional airport than by London.

We are still left with 11 million passengers in 1985 between the South-East and non-railable points in Europe. For perhaps a tenth of these a South Hampshire or Exeter airport would be as good a British terminal as any of the existing London-area airports. For half of the remainder, it would involve about an hour's extra journey. Development of a relief airport to take 3 or 4 million passengers out of the London load on these routes by 1985 might be a possibility, but one which should perhaps be given relatively low priority or kept in reserve. Any role for such an airport for London passengers should be combined with a role as a regional airport.

TABLE 15

Practicable redistribution of DTI's 50 million London–Europe passengers, 1985

A. *Journeys below 1,000–1,200 miles*
Transfer to rail from London: 21 million
Transfer to regional airports: 1·5 million
Transfer to through rail services for regions: 1·5 million
Air via London airports (SE passengers): 9 million
Air via London airports (non-SE passengers): 2 million

B. *Longer journeys*
Spontaneous transfer to regional airports: 4 million
Using London airports: 8 million
Possibly induced transfer to non-London airports: 3 million
The number still using London airports comes to 19 millions, or, if induced transfer is avoided, 22 million

At this rate the number of passengers a year between London airports and continental Europe would be 60 to 75 per cent greater in 1985 than in 1970. To take account of error we might widen the range, and say 50 to 100 per cent greater. But by 1985 the average number of persons per aircraft on these routes is likely to be more than double the 1970 load. On our estimate of 19 million London–Europe passengers, allowing for induced transfer to non-south-eastern airports, and assuming 140 persons per aircraft, we have about 140,000 aircraft movements a year in this market in 1985. With no induced transfer the figure rises to some 180,000. If we then allow for 20 per cent optimistic error, the figure rises to 225,000.

If we add these figures to the 100,000 long-distance aircraft movements, and say 25,000 for non-transferred Irish and Channel Islands traffic, we have a probable total of below 300,000 aircraft movements in 1985, with a higher figure, not very likely to be required, of 350,000. This is to be set beside the estimate of a total capacity by 1980 of 475,000 movements (about 300,000 at Heathrow without overload, 110,000 at Gatwick and 54,000 at Luton). We have not yet counted the traffic within Great Britain, but we are as yet a long way short of filling Heathrow and Gatwick; we have reduced the load below the figure for 1971, giving that alleviation to local inhabitants which ministers oddly implied that they would gain through the opening of Maplin.

THE BRITISH DOMESTIC MARKET

Main routes
The domestic component of the projected total load at London airports, in 1980 and 1985, deserves close study because there is obvious scope for transfer to rail of traffic with northern England and Scotland.

Both Roskill and the DTI Working Party's *Report on Traffic and Capacity at Heathrow* made some allowance for the ability of improved railway services to attract part of the growing traffic in this market, but the allowances are not fully worked out or justified by any detailed consideration of the likely effects of future improvement to rail services.[7] The inadequacy of the figures makes them difficult to work with.

The DTI Working Party's projection of a 'most likely' total of 88 million London airport terminal passengers in 1985 includes 12·8 million on domestic routes.[8] After deducting 1·5 million for Belfast and 1·7 million for the Channel Islands (because they are non-railable), we have 9·6 million between London and places within Great Britain. This amounts to about 12 per cent of the total load, or almost two years' expected growth of total air traffic.

The DTI's first figure for 1980 (9 million domestic) was later revised downwards to 7·8 million,[9] because of slower traffic-growth in 1969, but the revision was not carried forward to 1985.

In fact, the distribution of the domestic traffic between air and rail will depend on the relative door-to-door time and on price, and to a smaller extent on some other factors. The Northern English air traffic may actually decline and the Scottish remain static.

The DTI's figure of nearly 10 million London–Great Britain passengers for 1985 is four times the total in 1968. The actual figure for 1968 amounted to about 1·5 million passengers terminating at London and 0·84 million transferring at London airports to or from international flights. It is worth quoting the detailed figures from *Passengers at London Airports*, adapted by separating them into two main routes corresponding with the two main rail trunk-routes:

TABLE 16

British domestic air passengers, 1968

	BOT's annual estimate of passengers terminating London in 1968 (millions)			Passengers transferring at London airports between domestic and international flights, 1968 (millions)
	Heathrow	Other airports	Total	
NW route				
Birmingham	0·013	—	0·013	0·046
Manchester	0·148	0·006	0·154	0·127
Liverpool	0·077	—	0·077	0·048
Glasgow	0·418	0·054	0·472	0·104
Prestwick	0·072	0·005	0·077	
Total NW route			0·793	0·325
NE route				
Leeds	0·057	—	0·057	0·041
Newcastle	0·136		0·136	0·042
Teesside	0·099	0·009	0·109	
Edinburgh	0·328	0·043	0·371	0·098
Aberdeen	0·047	—	0·047	0·011
Total NE route			0·719	0·513

Source: BOT, *Passengers at London Airports* (1970), Cols. 1 and 2 of Table 8; Col. 4 of Table 12.

We may now further divide these passengers into four categories, to England and to Scotland and in each case terminating or not terminating at London. It is worth distinguishing England from Scotland, because the journeys within England could (like those to Paris and Brussels) almost all be accomplished more quickly door-to-door by train than by air by 1985.[10] For journeys to Scotland the door-to-door time will in many cases be slightly longer by rail than by air (as for London to Holland or Cologne–Ruhr), though the exact incidence of shorter and longer times will vary with journey times between house-door and airport or railway station.

For the English routes we may begin with one piece of evidence. In 1965, when rail electrification was completed, the rail journey-time between Manchester and London was cut from $3\frac{1}{2}$–4 hours to $2\frac{1}{2}$–3 hours. Total air traffic on this route dropped at once from 500,000 passengers a year to about 300,000, and remained at about 300,000 for the next five years. Meanwhile, rail traffic increased steadily. In 1970 it was calculated that rail was carrying 50 per cent of the London–Manchester travel market, or 1·6 million passengers a year (compared with 9 per cent by air, 4 per cent by bus and 38 per cent by car).[11]

Any projections of air traffic on the inland routes north of London must be speculative, as the speeding-up of the rail services can be on a scale without precedent. The effects on the split between rail and air are likely to be greater than those of the rail-time reduction already achieved for London–Manchester. The experience on that particular route, following the railway electrification, may be a guide to what may be expected for London–Tyne-Tees; the effects on shorter routes will probably be more drastic, those on the Scottish routes rather less so. As general extrapolations are of no value, we may usefully discuss the London–Manchester prospects as a guide to the probable prospects for the rest of the system, always assuming that the railways receive investments sufficient to enable them to realize their potential.

Between now and 1985 the rail journey-time may be reduced from $2\frac{1}{2}$–3 hours to $1\frac{1}{2}$–2 hours. The door-to-door air journey-time is likely to increase rather than to decrease. The road journey-time was reduced in 1970–2 by the opening of new stretches of motorway. These stretches meant that the motorway was complete, but carrying an increasing load. Travel by it is more likely to deteriorate than to improve in 1973–85. The conditions of road travel, including travel by motorway, are likely to become steadily more disagreeable and dangerous as the volume of traffic increases.[12]

The London–Manchester air market in 1970 was divided about equally between terminating and interlining passengers. As there is real scope for (*a*) improvement in rail services and (*b*) more direct air services to and from Manchester, the airlines' share of both parts of the London–Manchester market could be expected to decline. The actual numbers travelling by air might decline.

The London–Manchester rail service could be expected to gain more traffic from air and road with each increase in speed, and then to become more flexible and cheaper, in terms of vehicle and current operating costs per unit, with each successive increment in traffic. In 1972 trains ran about once an hour in the morning and evening periods, every two hours in the middle of the day. There were 14 trains a day taking under 3 hours, for nearly 2 million rail passengers a year. Every train stopped at least twice *en route*.

Road and air projections suggest that the total London–Manchester passenger market should double or treble by 1985. If rail then maintained its share at 50 per cent, the rail load would amount to $3\frac{1}{2}$ or 5 million passengers a year. In this case an increase to (say) 35 trains a day would make possible a more flexible service. There could be a few non-stop trains and a much better service for intermediate points. Both factors would tend, in various degrees, further to increase rail's attractiveness in relation to air and private car. If an increase in the rail traffic resulted in a decrease in unit costs, and hence in price in real terms, as well as improved accessibility and door-to-door timing, rail could attract further traffic from the roads. Rail's share would be likely then to rise to more than 50 per cent. If rail gained two-thirds of the air-share and of the bus-share (bringing its total to 60 per cent), it would be well placed for gaining more of the private cars' share. The private car traffic could well drop from 38 per cent to 25 or 30 per cent; but if rail carried about two-thirds of the total load rather than one-half (that is, 5 to $6\frac{1}{2}$ million passengers rather than $3\frac{1}{2}$ to 5 million), there would be scope for a further improvement in the rail service.

On these assumptions it would be surprising if air travel between London and Manchester were to increase at all. Even for many of the people making international air journeys to or from Lancashire, and obliged to go to or from London to find a plane to Kuwait, a rail journey via London or Watford would be preferable to an inconveniently timed local flight.

This discussion has concerned only London–Manchester. Very

similar considerations would apply for all the other routes between London and northern England, divided mainly between the North-West and North-East routes, the first group to Birmingham, Lancashire and Glasgow, the second to Yorkshire, Tyne-Tees and eastern Scotland (though the latter might, according to British Rail's 1965 plan, be reached from the west route and Carlisle).

For journeys between London and Edinburgh and Glasgow the door-to-door journey will probably be up to an hour quicker by air than by rail even in 1985. The time differences will be important, at least for some business travellers, particularly those wishing to go there and back for a meeting within a day. Rail overnight will still be a reasonable option, but it can hardly be improved in timing or price. Passengers' current choices between air and overnight train are unlikely to change much; there might be a slight tendency for more people to prefer rail over-night if better vehicles, track and train-control could give a smoother ride.

The main scope for switch to rail is on the day journeys, and the potential level of switch will depend heavily on the amount of reduction in rail journey-time below four hours. In 1970 the total London–Glasgow market was put at 1·7 million: 29 per cent rail, 41 per cent air, 18 per cent bus and 12 per cent car. This was with a rail journey-time of over six hours, and no more than five day-trains each way per day, together with three over-night. For an annual load of 0·5 million passengers the provision looks generous. Rail suffered quite severely from the competition of buses, whose only advantage to travellers was cheapness. The long-distance bus has advantages in accessibility to people ending their journeys away from big cities, but none for long inter-city journeys.

If the London–Glasgow market should treble to say 5 million travellers in 1985, and the air-share fell to 20 per cent, or 1 million instead of 0·7 million now, and rail carried 60 per cent, the rail load of 3 million, nearly all by day, would justify some 15 to 25 trains a day each way, justifying non-stop trains at the busiest times as well as others giving good access to various points *en route* without much loss of time. Such a distribution ought not to be unrealistic, in view of the reductions in unit costs and real price reductions that might ensue.

London to Edinburgh is virtually the same distance; the air market on this route in 1970 was nearly four-fifths that of London–Glasgow. In general these markets were similar and are likely to remain so. For Aberdeen and other places north of Glasgow and Edinburgh, air is likely to lose little of its share of the market, because the rail journey-time is unlikely to be brought below six or seven hours; but in 1970 under 60,000 people went by air between London and northern Scotland. Even a quadrupling of air travel would leave the figure below 0·3 million.

For the whole of this domestic market it would seem likely that the greater the increase in the next two decades the greater the share that is likely to use rail, provided that the potential of the railway is adequately developed. But the greater the number of rail travellers, the more it will be worth investing in the railways' infrastructure by building overpasses to eliminate level rail junctions and undertaking other works to reduce possible sources of delay. We start with a favourable situation in that there is already quadruple track on the two main routes for long distances north of London. Some work might be needed to enable the eastern route to accommodate 25 or 30 million express-train passengers a year as far as Doncaster, in addition to freight (and there are several alternative routes, all now underutilized, to relieve the load on the two main routes if their total load approaches saturation).

It would seem reasonable to work out a series of options under which, whatever the increase in total domestic passenger-travel, the load by air between conventional London airports and places in England and Scotland could be kept below 3 million, or even 2 million, in 1985, and remain static for some years thereafter.

The reduction of the London airports' load through this particular rationalization of traffic would not in itself remove the need for a third airport, but it would be a useful addition to the other reliefs which have been discussed.

British domestic interline passengers
The existing domestic air services between London and the British cities do not serve terminal passengers only. Table 12 of *Passengers at London Airports* shows that in 1968 one-quarter of the air travellers on these routes (nearly 700,000) were not terminating at London but changing at London airports to or from international flights. As one would expect, these 'interline' passengers were a particularly large proportion of the air travellers on routes to places near London. Of a total of 57,200 air passengers between London and Birmingham, 46,300, or 80·9 per cent, used these flights as part of inter-

national journeys. On the Manchester, Liverpool and Leeds routes the interline passengers were nearly as numerous as those terminating at London. The proportion fell to around 20 per cent in the case of the air travellers between London and Scotland. There were also a few people transferring at London to Channel Islands services.

If the number of air services between London and these major British cities were actually reduced, it would seem at first sight that there would be a consequent real deterioration in the provision for these travellers between British regions and foreign destinations. We should bear in mind that if total movement between these regions and distant points increases, as is expected, there will be increased scope for the provision of direct flights. These will take care of a proportion of the travellers. For the remainder the alternatives seem to be as follows:

(*a*) Assuming air travel within Britain, high probability of a need to travel between Maplin and Heathrow or Gatwick, through London: more than 60 miles by surface transport, and high probability of a long wait for a connection.

(*b*) Assuming frequent rail services, the alternative provision of a connection by rail could well be much better for the individual traveller.

Substitution of greatly improved rail-bus links to airports would probably give a better service to the majority of travellers, provided that the railway service was developed to a great enough extent. However, there would still be some who would find the air link more convenient, particularly if there were no third airport so that Heathrow continued as the main London airport.

We have here a good illustration of the dilemma which faces us. Assuming we build Maplin airport, we have the following options for dealing with interline passengers:

1. Keep Heathrow and Gatwick also in operation. In this case the majority of interline passengers would have appalling inter-airport journeys. Adequate roads between the airports could be provided, but would not justify high priority in the national road programme merely to serve this purpose. Even by continuous motorway Heathrow–Maplin would take $1\frac{1}{2}$ hours, allowing for inevitable terminal delays. At least 3 hours between plane-times would be required. Without special provision the time would be 4 hours or more, in line with BEA's estimate and Roskill.

2. Abolish Heathrow and Gatwick altogether, and have all air

movements at Maplin. This would solve the interline problem, and the idea seems attractive to people who would like to free London of aircraft noise. But on the current projections of future air traffic this seems unlikely ever to be realized. (Cf. above, p. 30.)

There is no ideal solution. Assuming no third London airport, but substantial railway development, we might foresee the following pattern :

1. The increased total traffic would justify more direct flights from British regional airports.

2. Travellers between British regions and places not served directly from them (e.g. most of Africa) could choose for the British end of their journey between domestic air service, if convenient, and vastly improved rail services.

With virtually all domestic public transport traffic on major routes concentrated on rail, the services could be frequent and flexible as well as fast. At least two-thirds of the British population outside the South-East live in areas which could become conveniently accessible to Heathrow by air or road without going into London. With Heathrow passengers twice their present number (as they are planned to be by 1980, even if Maplin is built), the rail-bus connections which have already been established can be improved (currently via Watford, Reading and Woking). The road connections are all designated as 'strategy routes', to be motorways or other dual carriageways by 1985,[13] so the concentration of London's major air traffic at Heathrow would, from this point of view, be preferable to its distribution between Heathrow and Maplin.

REVISED DISTRIBUTION OF AIR TRAFFIC SUMMARIZED

It remains to set out in a single table the revised distribution of the 83 to 88 million passengers whom the DTI's Working Party assumed to be using London airports in 1985, according to the categories which we have used for this chapter. It is unfortunate that the rather precise figures for the domestic and long-haul markets are here added together with the round figures for Europe. The former are taken directly from the DTI's projections, which are relatively exact; the latter, not being part of a time-series, are rounded off. Not all of the transfers would need to be carried out in order to maintain the London airports' ability to deal with the remaining load. Some of the rates of transfer could probably be raised.

TABLE 17

Practicable overall redistribution of passengers for 1985

Market	DTI London airport total	Revised totals millions of passengers		
		London airports	Other airports	Rail
N. America	13·4+	10·0—	3·4+	—
Other long-haul	8·4	7·0	1·4	—
Irish Republic	2·7	1·0	1·7	—
Northern Ireland	1·5	1·0	0·5	—
Channel Isles	1·7	0·7	1·0	—
EEC, Switzerland, Austria and Scandinavia	31·7	10·0	1·5	20·7
Iberia and rest of Europe	19·0	14·0	3·0	2·0
GB internal	9·6	2·4	—	7·2
	88·0	47·0	12·5	30·0

By adding together all the transfers away from London airports we are left with a total of about 46 million passengers still using them in 1985. This is well below the number of 60 million which they will be required to carry in the last year before Maplin comes into use, if it is built; indeed it is below the number which Sir Peter Masefield expected them to be carrying in 1985, even *with* Maplin in use.

From Table 18 we may now go on to estimate the aircraft movements at London airports required to deal with the reduced future passenger load.

The figure of 320,000 in Table 18 is well below the expected capacity of Heathrow and Gatwick alone in 1980. We are then left with a considerable margin to play with, in case it should be impracticable or undesirable to bring all the transfers into operation, at the rates assumed, by 1985.

It does seem not unreasonable to argue that, on the currently accepted projections, the number of air movements at London airports could be kept below the currently accepted figure for 1980 until about 1990. Maplin could thus well be deferred until 1990, by which time further growth might well be checked by transfer to VTOL/STOL using another new airport nearer to the central area.

140

Many questions still remain to be asked : if the transfers were achieved, what would be the effect on the quality of transport, by rail and air? How would the transfers be achieved? And what about the cost, in economic and financial terms?

The likely evolution of traffic and airport capacity under this scheme can best be illustrated by reproducing the two figures of Appendix 7 of the Roskill Report, and adding new dotted lines to indicate how the new scheme might affect the position (p. 142).

Roskill's figures show the number of aircraft movements overtaking the maximum capacity of all airports in the early 1980s. The new line superimposed shows the number of aircraft movements in 1980–5, assuming the Channel tunnel to be already open in 1980, and beginning to make an impact on the traffic from that date. The heavy dotted line shows the London aircraft movements assuming a moderate rate of regional transfer as well.

We assume that the railway works necessary to give high-standard services would be complete by 1985, but that the transfer to rail would be phased in 1980–5; this would allow for the full potential capacity of rail to be not quite ready by 1980.

The total air movements in 1985 are well within the capacity of Heathrow and Gatwick combined. There is no overload at Heathrow and no need for a further runway at Gatwick. Luton and Stansted could both be abandoned, if that was desired (though it

TABLE 18

Passengers and aircraft movements at London airports,
1985, assuming practicable diversions and aircraft size at various levels

Market	Millions of passengers	Passenger load per aircraft	Thousands of aircraft movements	Average no. of London flights per day each way
N. America	10	200	50	70
Other long-haul	7	140	50	70
Irish Republic	1·5	100	15	20
N. Ireland	1	150	7	10
Channel Isles	0·7	100	7	10
EEC, Switzerland, Scandanavia	10	150	70	100
Iberia/rest of Europe	14·7	150	100	140
GB internal	2·4	120	20	20
	47		320	

could well be useful at this time to keep their runways and facilities as reserves); also, Luton is rather well placed for freight operations and for South Midlands passengers, and it might well be used moderately for these purposes. There is a considerable margin, in case some of the transfers should be impracticable at the level or timing envisaged, and the margin should be wide enough to cover the period up to 1990. We have the probability that in 1985–90 increasing average capacity per aircraft will reduce the demand for runway space in relation to number of passengers; also in that period the spiral of regional transfer will continue to move upwards, if total air travel increases. For the 1990s there are many uncertainties, many options that it would be advantageous to keep open, but which will be closed through the commitment to Maplin.

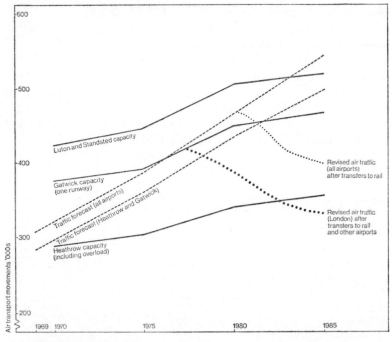

Adapted Roskill graph showing traffic movements at London airports to 1985. Congestion costs at Heathrow and Gatwick, assuming no diversion of traffic, first exceed postponement cost of the third London airport in 1982. Congestion costs at all airports first exceed postponement costs in 1983

10

The switch to rail and the quality of transport

Volume of air services and rail alternatives

It may be objected that, if a large proportion of the passengers in the early 1980s switch to rail, the numbers travelling by air to the main European destinations will be too small to justify any viable air services at all. It may then be claimed that travellers will be deprived of a reasonable density of air services at times spread through the day; that the air operators will be ruined, and that they will not be able to revise their schedules. It may be said that if the total passenger load is reduced, large aircraft will be unsuitable, so that, with the airlines compelled to use smaller aircraft, the number of air movements will be increased again, until it invalidates the main argument of Chapter 4. Roskill thought of this.[1]

Let us look at the implications in some detail. We may begin by putting the revised projections of air passengers in 1985, country by country, beside the actual numbers in 1968.

200,000 passengers a year on a route would require one 500-seat train each way per day or two 250-seat flights, assuming 55 per cent average seat occupation in either case. This applies at least to regular scheduled services. For a route including some charter trips the frequency of the scheduled services would be reduced.

We may begin by observing that a 50 per cent increase in passengers at London airports alone can hardly be called running the service down. All the same, the downward revision would lead to some reduction in the frequency of some air services if large aircraft were used.

If the air traffic between London and Paris fell by 1985 to half

143

the present load, and average aircraft size were doubled, there would be a need for about 10 London–Paris flights a day, instead of 35 to 40 now from Heathrow alone. If the rail service, in $2\frac{1}{2}$ hours by non-stop train, took 5 million from the implied official projections of air traffic, it would be likely to take 2 or 3 million in addition by projection from the present surface traffic, together with new traffic generated by this new and attractive service.[2] With 40 or 50 trains a day each way (one train each way per 200,000 annual passengers both ways), this service would make nonsense of Mr Noble's observations about infrequent trains – and the demand could be expected to grow after 1985, unless the official air-traffic projections are wrong.

The London–Brussels air service might well fade away. The door-to-door journey would after all be slower, for almost all travellers, by conventional aircraft than by rail. But Table 19 gives us 8 million

TABLE 19

Potential redistribution of officially projected air passengers to and from London airports, 1985 (national totals assumed from DTI continental projections with equal increase in each market)

| | 1968 (millions) | 1985 (millions) | 1985 totals after transfers to rail or other airports (millions) | | | |
			London airports	Other airports	Total air	Diverted from air to rail
France	1·25	7·8	1·3	0·1	1·3	6·5
Benelux	1·3	6·4	1·6	—	1·6	4·8
W. Germany	0·9	6·1	2·4	—	2·4	3·7
Switzerland/ Austria	0·65	3·7	1·5	—	1·5	2·2
Italy	0·8	5·0	2·5	0·8	3·3	1·6
Norway/Sweden	0·3	1·4	1·0	0·4	1·4	—
Copenhagen	0·2	1·3	0·6	0·1	0·7	0·6
Iberia/Rest of Europe	2·7	19·0	10·4	7·2	17·8	2·0
	8·1	50·7	21·3	8·6	30·0	21·4

passengers a year to Brussels and beyond, to other Benelux destinations and Germany – enough for 40 trains a day each way. This is before adding continuing surface and generated traffic, which might be put at 2 million more. The provision of public transport between London and Benelux would be better on this pattern than any that could be given through the projected massive growth of the conventional air services, and there would be scope for a good variety of permutations with stopping and non-stopping trains. Out of 40 daily trains on the route there might be 20 non-stop trains to Brussels and 5 non-stop to Amsterdam. If route development should permit a three-hour timing on the Amsterdam service, there could be further transfers from air and generation of new traffic. Extensive route development would be necessary, but would also be likely to produce the traffic to justify the expenditure, particularly when we take into account the additional traffic from Paris to Amsterdam, the rest of Benelux and North Germany.

At first sight the number of day passengers by rail to be expected on routes above 400 miles, to much of Germany, Switzerland and central France, would seem to be too small to justify a frequent service. However, there would also be intermediate traffic on these routes and this would change the picture.

With long-distance overnight rail services, travellers are interested in convenient times for departure and arrival. Many of the overnight rail passengers might well travel in non-scheduled package-holiday trains; even so, the pattern envisaged would be likely to justify at least 30 or 40 scheduled trains out of London each evening before we add the British regional services. This would justify a choice between at least two departure times to each of the major groups of destinations.

On the air side, likely to be of interest mainly to business travellers, Amsterdam–Rotterdam would go down to 8 or 10 air services a day each way – hardly a serious deprivation when backed by a cheaper rail alternative, which would be frequent, almost equally fast, and far more flexible.

West Germany would go down to about 24 London air services a day each way, instead of the 23 in 1971, Switzerland to 15. Italy would have twice the present number of air passengers from London and about the same number of flights, assuming large aircraft to be used. At least there would still be room for a morning and an evening flight each way on the main business routes for major European cities.

Many of the people who now fly from Heathrow to Geneva, Frankfurt, etc., have long and tiresome surface journeys at both ends, so that some 800-mile overall journey-times (e.g. Bristol–Montreux) could be the same by day-train as by air. Any slight deprivation suffered by midday city-to-city passengers would in any case continue only until VTOL began to provide them with a service far better than they could ever get from conventional aircraft.

The effects on railway systems

The potential role of railways in European transport depends on the level of investment in them, and on its timing. On most major routes in Britain, France, Germany and Italy some passenger trains are now operating at start-to-stop average speeds of 70 to 80 mph. If the railways are to become preferable to airlines for distances of 200 to 400 miles, the rail timings must be improved; the difference between 100 mph and 130 mph average speeds would have an important effect for journeys between 300 and 400 miles. But an average of 130 mph over a 400-mile journey would be difficult to achieve with more than one stop *en route*, and non-stop trains could usefully be operated over such distances only if the total passenger traffic was heavy enough to justify them (not just two or three trains a day, but a full service).

On the London–Paris route the market should be big enough to justify an intensive service from the time of the completion of the system, which should preferably be complete on land at the same time as the opening of the Channel tunnel. The new London–Paris load would be quickly added to the intra-continental traffic.

The existing Paris–Lille section looks likely to approach saturation by some date in the 1980s, given the heavy and mixed load of traffic to be accommodated on two tracks. Two new tracks, preferably on a new alignment, will be desirable, but the investment would be unlikely to bring in a reasonable return from French domestic and other intra-continental traffic alone. Most big new items of transport infrastructure tend to start with excessive spare capacity. In this case the tunnel and the railway routes together, by diverting massive traffic rather suddenly from air, would be exceptionally well placed for a rapid build-up of traffic.

The capacity of a route, or of a track, depends heavily on the homogeneity of the traffic using it. The highest output can obviously be achieved by a track used only by trains which travel at exactly this same speed and stop, if at all, at the same places. London underground tracks regularly accommodate up to 30 trains per hour at rush hours. A track used only by high-speed trains, such as London–Paris, could deal with at least 18 trains an hour, perhaps

20, provided that they went at the same speed and stopped at the same places. At 150 mph this would give an interval of $7\frac{1}{2}$ to 8 miles between trains; if the distance required to stop from 150 mph were below two miles, sophisticated train-control might conceivably increase the capacity beyond 18 trains per hour. An assumption of 250 trains a day would leave a margin and time for daily maintenance work. If freight trains travelled more slowly than passenger trains, they would need to be grouped. If the track were being used to capacity there would, in the extreme case, be room only for one period of the day for the passage of freight trains. However, that difficulty would disappear completely if overnight passenger and freight trains travelled at the same speeds; and except through the Channel tunnel itself a full development of railways would provide at least two tracks in each direction, either separated or together, on each of the main long-distance routes which might be subject to heavy loads.

Any mixture of traffic on a track reduces its capacity and tends to increase unit costs on a major route when infrastructure costs are taken into account. But a considerable mixture is necessary if the railway is to exploit its potential flexibility, as it must do if it is to attract future traffic from the roads. On many major routes this means that there must be at least two tracks in each direction, not necessarily within the same permanent way. A route with four tracks has more than twice the capacity of one with two tracks if the traffic is not homogeneous.

The existing substantial spare capacity on the major routes north of London is due partly to the policy of reducing the mix, partly to the fact that the main route is already quadruple for a considerable distance, partly to the existence of additional routes in such profusion that some long-distance freight traffic can be diverted to them.

Within France only one major route, Paris–Lyon, is approaching saturation on the basis of projections of existing traffic. The building of the projected new route, cutting the Paris–Lyon journey from the present $3\frac{3}{4}$–$4\frac{1}{4}$ hours to 2 hours, would have the effect of transferring from air to rail almost the whole of the projected Paris–Lyon air traffic, and it would attract some traffic which would otherwise go by road. It would have similar effects on traffic between Paris and the fast-developing area south of Lyon (the Rhône Valley, Marseille and the Mediterranean), where there is already one route on each side of the Rhône. The capacity of these two routes together will depend on the level of investment, which in its turn must be decided in the light of projections of future traffic.

On the whole of this section of French Railways south of Paris the potential load from Britain and Benelux is a substantial factor in any calculations, and that load depends heavily on the investment in new complementary routes within this northern area.

All the Western European countries share one technical problem. Almost all the main railway trunk routes have only two tracks, and many of them will be overloaded at various dates between 1975 and 1985. Normal growth of traffic would demand quadrupling, and a need to accommodate high-speed traffic makes quadrupling all the more urgent. Some of the existing routes are unfavourable for widening to quadruple track, because of existing land-use and frequent curves which would restrict the speed even of trains built on the Advanced Passenger Train tilting design (and the APT is a British development). Hence the plans to relieve some of the existing system (Paris–Lyon, Cologne–Frankfurt, etc.) by building completely new routes for the main long-distance through-traffic.

With respect to some of the routes there is at present uncertainty whether the likely rate of increase of total traffic will be swift enough to avoid new deficits on routes which are likely soon to become too heavily occupied to be able to provide a really good service without the heavy investment of quadrupling. It is here that the prospective British traffic through a Channel tunnel becomes of prime importance, and this traffic can only become important if there is appropriate investment within Britain too, so as to provide unrestricted high-speed movement to and through London.

The addition of some 30 million passengers a year to and from London by 1985 would give the continental railways a significant addition to their loads, probably about 15 billion passenger miles a year spread over 9,000 route miles, all on trunk routes and concentrated unevenly, though the additions would be heaviest on sections best able to accommodate them. The British addition amounts to some 20 per cent of the total passenger mileage in the EEC countries' railway systems in 1971 (over 22 billion each in France and West Germany, and 20 billion in Italy, compared with 19 billion in Britain).

From the French end of the Channel tunnel the new traffic would soon divide into two arteries, one towards Paris, one towards

Brussels, with possibly a third between these two. The line towards Paris would have to cater for passengers terminating at Paris, and for those continuing further south, including some to Italy or Switzerland, and conceivably some to Spain. The potential addition of this large new traffic from England would immensely strengthen the case for the already planned construction of a wholly new conventional clearway railway-line between northern Paris and Lille, adapted for steady speeds above 150 mph, and also for the further new 250-mile ultra-fast Paris–Lyon line. Without these developments the railways could scarcely be expected to play a full part in the transport map. If London–Paris traffic rose to 5 million diverted from air plus 3 million continuing by surface or newly generated, traffic between Benelux and Paris and beyond could be expected to rise too. Rail already carries almost 90 per cent of the public transport traffic between Paris and Brussels, although ordinary trains average below 70 mph, while Trans-Europe expresses, first class only, average over 80 mph.

The addition of all this traffic between Britain or Lille–Benelux and places south of Paris would presumably justify investment in a through-Paris rail link on such a scale as to ensure that Paris was no longer a barrier to rapid through-communication. There is already a through-Paris link, the *petite ceinture* line, but in its present state it is very slow. It could be developed. Its main use would be for trains travelling through the night, not only from London, northern France and Benelux, but from the British Midlands too.

Although the vehicle costs and operating costs per passenger are relatively high for overnight trains providing adequate comfort, the additional use of infrastructure during the night, when it would otherwise be under-used, is an argument in its favour. Overnight traffic would be important on all the lines going south of Paris. Trains going right through would not in general compete for space with Parisian trains. The existing route via Dijon would benefit from traffic to Switzerland and beyond and be useful for freight.

South and east of the Mâcon–Lyon area the main artery divides, with important branches towards Switzerland (via Geneva), Italy (via Mont Cenis–Turin) and Grenoble, while the main line continues southwards until it divides east to the Côte d'Azur and west to the newly developed Languedoc–Roussillon holiday area and northeast Spain. Some investment on the branches might well be desirable.

The second main artery from the Channel tunnel towards Brussels would soon divide, one branch to Holland, North Germany and Copenhagen, one to Cologne and thence in several directions, most of them carrying heavy traffic already but capable of being adapted to carry far more. The new traffic from Britain would be only a small addition to the German railways' load (perhaps 0·5 billion passenger miles a year diverted from air), but there would be a generated addition, raising the load on the main arteries by over 10 per cent. With associated rail traffic from France the addition would be greater.

Possibly a third artery, between these two, would go from Lille to Strasburg and Basel, eventually to serve eastern France, southern Germany, eastern Switzerland, western Austria, north-eastern Italy and Yugoslavia. This Lille–Basel line is at present little used by long-distance passenger traffic, though it is already electrified as a major freight route. No special plans have been announced for large new investments here, and the volume of traffic would probably not justify it. Even so, if it served destinations in Switzerland and western Austria within 8 to 12 hours, at rather unambitious speeds, it would provide reasonable overnight journey-times. In this case the best route to Milan would probably be via the Paris–Lyon route, diverting through the Rhône Valley and the Simplon Tunnel, or via Turin.

The key to the system is an irregular four-spoked wheel on the map, with a long flat hub with its eastern end at Brussels, and the spokes ending at London, Amsterdam, Paris and Cologne–Ruhr. With a few small branches the whole system amounts to rather less than 1,000 route-miles. If we add the traffic from Paris to Benelux and Germany, we seem to have a projection of not less than 30 million passengers a year, each travelling between 200 and 400 miles. If we put the average journey at 250 miles, we have $7\frac{1}{2}$ billion passenger-miles, to which we might add 5 billion more on account of passengers, not yet counted, travelling beyond the end of one of the spokes. A potential 12 billion passenger-miles on a 1,000-mile system represents an intensity of use 15 times the average achieved on the whole existing British railway system, and 20 times that now operating in France and West Germany.

One minor point: the volume of traffic would seem likely to justify an extension of this network by the building of one or two sections of route by-passing Brussels, for the benefit of through traffic between London or Paris and Holland or Germany. This would relieve pressure on the lines through Brussels. Some existing little-used routes might perhaps serve as a basis for these new developments, lowering the cost of construction. This addition to the continental plan would allow a substantial shortening of the longer journey-times. If Amsterdam and Cologne were thus brought within three hours of London by rail, the rate of transfer to rail on these routes would probably be further increased and the London airports' load correspondingly reduced. The increased rail load, including that on the Paris route, would probably justify the investment in addition to that already envisaged for the continental railways.

All this demands that the highest standard of speed should be universal for passenger trains on the main trunk-routes, not reserved to a few supplementary-fare Trans-Europe expresses. The mixture of ordinary trains and a few faster prestige trains, now favoured in France, Germany and Italy, is practicable only on tracks which are less than optimally occupied. The task of providing a mix of stopping and non-stop trains would present problems enough (except on four track routes) to make the luxury of prestige fast trains difficult to accommodate. Heavy occupation brings such great economies that it should be worth aiming at a complete service of high-speed trains. There is thus a problem of heavy investment in new rolling-stock over a short period, but this needs to be compared with the air investment involved in the alternative. The adoption as a norm of speeds above those of today's Trans-Europe expresses should be practicable and economically advantageous.

It has to be admitted that continental railwaymen seem until now to have concentrated their attentions rather heavily on prestige trains – much more so than the British. There may be a case for keeping this kind of thing going, where it is practicable, but a universally high standard of speed along the main trunk routes, with high occupation of the tracks, would seem to have more to recommend it.

It may be that there are some people who are more ready to travel by train if they pay extra for privileges reserved to a few (the popularity of the few English Pullman trains supports this rather contemptible psychology). There are even some people who will pay £6 extra to sit in a first-class aeroplane seat for an hour, and others who will not bother to sit in one for nothing when it is available in a cut-rate night-flight.

All this does not imply the introduction of a universal common standard of accommodation. If there is to be no room for a few trains which travel faster than the others, it will still be perfectly possible to provide special facilities and equipment, both luxurious and useful, on some or all of the trains which travel at the new normal speeds. Secretaries, dictating-machines, radio-telephones, gourmet restaurants, boudoirs, hairdressing-salons, super-drawing-rooms, the whole gamut of prestigious attractions, can be provided without the slightest difficulty within the new system, if such things are commercially justifiable. They could be provided on some or most or all of the trains, and there would still be room for some complete prestige trains with special names. But as track occupation becomes heavier and nearer to the economically optimum use of the infrastructure, so it becomes more difficult to accommodate differential running-speeds.

As far as concerns the traffic from Britain using the French system south of Lyon, the German system south of Cologne, and through Switzerland and northern Italy, very high standards of speed over the routes as a whole are not so important. The traffic coming from Britain will be mainly by night, and the scheme of this book does not depend absolutely on very fast running by overnight trains. It does not matter much whether an all-night journey takes 8 or 12 hours, provided that it is comfortable, and almost all the traffic expected to transfer from air to overnight trains is to places within 1,000 miles of London. It should be easy to fit in the traffic from London with the rest on the various routes involved, particularly after the major improvements which the national railway systems are likely to want to make for their own developments.

Another question concerns the pricing of sleeping-car accommodation in overnight trains. This is quite important, because the argument of this book requires that about 40 per cent of the future travellers transferring from air to train should make their rail journeys by night. To make the night trains really competitive with air the railways need to provide single-berth sleeping-car space at a price no greater than the air fare plus the cost of local journeys to and from the airports. In 1972 British Rail just succeeded in doing this but French Railways did not.

In British Rail sleeping cars a standard supplement is charged: about £2 above second-class fare for travel in a two-berth compartment, or £3 above first-class fare for a single compartment. On the continent the charges are much higher. The normal rate for a place in a six-berth couchette is a little more than £1 flat rate above the standard second-class fare. Coaches of British loading-gauge are not big enough to accommodate six-berth couchette compartments. They could accommodate four-berth compartments, and did so until a few years ago. In France and in the rest of the continent, couchette arrangements are relatively uncivilized but bearable to holiday-makers, and charged for at moderate rates slightly below the rates charged in Britain for two-berth sleeping cars; these are also cheaper than air travel.

The couchette system, an ordinary compartment with folding upper berths, could well be used on night trains between Britain and the continent; it allows passengers to lie down without necessarily reducing the number of persons to a coach. (The new continental standard also provides for six-seat compartments for day-use.)

A good deal of hard thinking would be needed to make the system work. There are several factors unfavourable to overnight operation.

1. Passenger-carrying capabilities are relatively low if comfort is high. Assuming the use of rolling-stock suitable for the existing British loading-gauge, the carrying capacity of a normal sized railway-coach is roughly as follows:

(*a*) Seating for daytime use – 48–64.

(*b*) 4-berth couchettes – 32.

(*c*) 2-berth sleepers (convertible to 1-berth) – 22–24.

(*d*) 1-berth sleepers (convertible to 2-berth) – 11–12.

(With the continental loading-gauge it is possible to build coaches of 50 per cent greater capacity.)

2. The initial cost of a sleeping-car is higher than that of a day-coach of similar size.

3. Fully-equipped sleepers are not very suitable for daytime use. Each vehicle is in effect restricted to one journey in each 24-hour period, except that couchette-cars can be used with ordinary seating by day.

4. Cleaning and maintenance involve fairly heavy costs and these operations are inescapably labour-intensive.

5. Most overnight travellers want to arrive, particularly at a city destination, between 7.30 and 9.30 in the morning. Later arrival should be acceptable to leisure travellers, but any overnight train has a rather limited flexibility.

On the other hand, there are some counterbalancing factors which could reduce the cost per coach and justify a reduced allocation of specific costs for night operations.

1. Overnight train travellers do not want their journeys to take less than 8 hours, and in general they do not much care if it takes 12 hours. Most overnight trains could travel more slowly and the journey-timings assumed above have allowed for this. Trains could be heavier, with more coaches to a train. A newly-built London terminal could be provided with long enough platforms (the main continental stations already have them).

2. Overnight trains would be using an infrastructure which would be under-used without them. Eight million night passengers with average journey of 700 miles would involve 5,000 million passenger-miles on the continent, mainly concentrated on 3,000 miles of major trunk routes, already reasonably prosperous but needing more business. Nearly half of the total would travel on some 1,000 miles of French railways; it should be in France's interests to agree to a constructive price-structure if the alternative was to lose the whole of this market – and that might well be the price of failure.

The time scale for the improvement of the railway routes envisaged by this study is much more urgent than that assumed by current official thinking. The GLC's 1972 paper on the London rail terminal does not envisage a $2\frac{3}{4}$-hour train service from London to Paris until about 1995, though a few months earlier Mr Marsh put the date at 1978. The slower time scale would affect the route to Benelux and Germany.

Such delay in exploiting the railways' new potential would sustain the demand for air travel in the 1980s and would make it less easy to dispense with a third London airport at that time. But one major reason for Britain's lack of enthusiasm, in 1971–3, for large investment in railway routes has been that the building of Maplin airport will absorb so much in the way of construction resources that it is difficult to push the two schemes through at a high tempo together. The financial implications of the simultaneous development are damaging too. But if the airport takes priority and the railways fail to realize their fully competitive capacity as European carriers by the 1980s, the relative timing of the two schemes may well turn out to have been wrong, with the growth of rail traffic stunted just at the time when it might have been progressing.

Although most of the new work on railway systems would have to be done in France and Belgium, a major share of responsibility for timing falls on the British Government. Without the Channel tunnel there is no point in the heavy investment in northern France and Belgium, and as late as August 1972 British official attitudes to the tunnel were lukewarm (see Chapter 11, p. 167) and showed no sign of interest in the broader railway development of which the tunnel must be a part.

THE QUALITY OF TRANSPORT IN BRITAIN AFTER THE SWITCH TO RAIL

The choice between rail and air within Britain is simpler than for Europe as a whole, but it has similar long-term implications. The Roskill Commissioners had no opportunity, within their terms of reference, for considering the future of the inland component of the London airports' load in the framework of a plan for transport as a whole. Ministers' speeches, and other indications of the direction of official thinking, such as Mr Barnes' evidence which is reproduced in Appendix 1, show no sign of long-term thinking on this question. On the contrary, their whole direction positively suggests an assumption that the pattern of transport will develop incrementally from previous trends. The only indications of a positive approach to change are to be found in the current plans of those local authorities which are beginning to seek ways of promoting public transport, rather than the motor car, as the best means of approaching a solution to urban traffic and planning.

The DTI's Heathrow Working Party estimates of traffic at London airports up to 1985[3] (and even its reduced estimates for 1980)[4] apparently assume that the airlines will increase their share of a growing inter-city passenger market within Great Britain. There is no demonstration that such a development is either likely or desirable. Indeed it seems unlikely to be fulfilled, simply because the rail alternative will become more attractive, even if there is no substantial new investment in the rail infrastructure. If there is to be substantial new rail investment, the plausibility of the Working Party's assumption is reduced still further. But there is a need for serious examination of the level of rail investment that would be desirable in comparison with alternative investments, not only in airports but also in roads.

Movement of people between any two points on a major trunk route, say 200 miles apart, is nowadays divided between air, rail, bus and private car. Established operators of the first three (public transport) modes tend to wish at least to maintain their respective shares of the market, and if possible to increase them. Government action or inaction, in relation to investment on the infrastructure of any of the modes, will affect the future division between the modes of transport, and so no single estimate of the future load on any of the modes can have any unconditional validity.

Any government has several sources of motivation which conflict with one another. There is not so much pressure from the producers of air transport to promote the whole aerospace industry, both manufacturing and operating, but a long-established harmony between both sections and the Government, which values the benefits which the industry produces in national prestige and in foreign-currency earnings. Rather similarly, some governmental orientation towards roads is fostered not just by private car operators, or by the AA and RAC, or the road hauliers' organization, but by the Government's admiration of the foreign-currency earnings of the whole automobile-manufacturing industry.

The British Railways Board is itself not well placed to advocate a wholesale commitment to railways. It may be that railways would be highly profitable if there were some new pruning of little-used branch-lines and an energetic development of the main routes which rail is well adapted to serve. We are not quite clear how far branch-pruning would damage the main routes. But commitment to railways is supported by obvious and well-known environmental arguments, and by a public opinion which has so amply shown its consciousness of these arguments that it is unnecessary to quote from the mass of letters to newspapers, leading articles and other comment. Virtually all of this public comment is in favour of rail as distinct from road; the rail–air split tends to be left undiscussed, because its significance is less obvious, its impact on road–rail not perceived.

Harold Wilson does report that late in 1965 he had it in mind to institute a new and broad survey of future transport needs. He was 'impressed by Dr Beeching's vision for the future and his plans to ensure that the new streamlined rail system should get the traffic necessary to make it viable and relieve road congestion at the same time.' He wanted to put Lord Beeching in charge of the survey, but gave up the plan because 'certain Cabinet colleagues, road-conscious, regarded Beeching as an enemy of road transport.' Wilson's comment is highly significant and worth quoting : 'It was an occasion when I yielded to sectional Cabinet pressure and, looking back on it, I was wrong.'[5]

Wilson reverts to this topic only to refer, several times, to the Transport Act of 1969, which sought to integrate road and rail transport. But there was no consciously integrated plan for investment in the infrastructures of transport, based on assessments more thorough than any that have been made yet, and including the air component of the national transport system. In so far as part of the transport systems within Britain involves movements which terminate overseas, no survey would be adequate if it neglected the overseas element.

Any such survey would, if it were honest, have to recognize that its answers must include a large speculative element, which no amount of technique could remove. This book cannot produce definite answers, but it is possible, without the apparatus of a large and expensive survey, to identify a number of factors which would seem to give indications with a reasonable chance of being valid.

It seems likely that the public transport between London and northern England, and probably southern Scotland too, can best be promoted by a policy of developing the railways, even at the expense of the air routes. This is simply because the main railway trunk-routes are under-utilized now; if their traffic were substantially increased the quality of their service would be improved, and quality here includes not only running speed but (more important) frequency and flexibility of service, combined with a reduction of unit costs.

Let us begin by assuming that 7 million passengers a year, now assigned to air on routes from London to northern England and southern Scotland, in 1985, might go by rail instead. In this case the additional load on the two main rail trunk-routes, with their branches (West Midlands, Lancashire, Leeds and perhaps Sheffield) would amount to approximately 2 billion passenger-miles, with a prospect of a steady increase after 1985. This 'interchangeable' load is equal to about one-tenth of the total passenger-miles carried by British Railways in 1970; its incidence is entirely on about 1,000 miles of route, with much the greatest part of the additional load falling on the sections nearest to London, which already have at least four tracks.

A very frequent and fast service of trains, some non-stop and some stopping at one or two or three places *en route*, would probably provide a better overall public transport system than a combination of fewer trains and more air flights. But the flexibility of the train service (by which we mean ability to run some stopping trains at established sub-centres like Stockport, or at new suburban collecting-points, well served by the road system), would be likely to attract a significant number of passengers who would otherwise travel by private car.

It would be difficult to quantify the possible switch from car to train; even an expensive survey would produce unreliable forecasts. But we can be sure that, of the 38 per cent of London–Manchester passengers estimated to have travelled by car in 1970,[6] some only just decided on car instead of train.

The choice between train and car is obviously influenced by several factors; overall journey-time, price, convenience, amenity and habit. The availability of a public service at a time when it is wanted is quite an important factor in any personal decision.

An improvement in the rail service in any of these factors would divert some travellers from car to rail. A big improvement in all these factors would divert quite a large number. The railway could probably not attract many three- or four-person groups having a car available and wishing to go with all their impedimenta from one private house to another. But the present car loads do not all consist of such three- or four-person groups; they include some solitary business travellers, who are highly eligible for transfer to rail. For many of these, and for many two-person parties, congestion and parking problems at the far end of the journey are likely to produce new reasons for not going by car. The conditions of travel by road throughout the journey are likely to deteriorate in the next few years. The M1 is not far short of saturation (though that is not a precise concept). By 1985, on the normal assumptions about the growth of the economy and of mobility, this road will be, to say the least, very unpleasant, and possibly less fast than in 1973. The need for duplication will present itself well before 1985. But any additional road-building will be both expensive and damaging to the environment. It will also be opposed, on respectable grounds. Any deferment of new road-building, made possible by increased rail transport, should be credited to the cost of the rail alternative (and not only the money-cost of the road should be counted).

It seems likely that, in order to enable the railway system to accommodate a vastly increased passenger load on the trunk routes, large investments in the freight side of the railways would be necessary, including an accelerated replacement of much of the existing stock of wagons. It may be somewhat unrealistic to claim that the railways can greatly increase their share of freight-carryings nationally. But there is scope for an increase on the trunk routes. Even here, there may be a danger of conflict between increased freight and passenger loads, though investment in the railways could well be designed specifically to deal with this conflict. Even the two most important northern routes will be free of fast-moving passenger trains for about ten hours each night.

Articulate public opinion is intensely troubled by road freight-transport. The greatest practicable transfer to rail demands not only good trunk routes but better loading facilities, reducing the need for road transport through town streets between factory and rail loading-point. But investment in the trunk routes would seem likely to be justified as part of a whole process; the split of passenger travel between rail and air is relevant to this much broader objective.

11

The Channel Tunnel

On 16 August 1972 the British and French Governments announced the inception of 'the next phase of studies into the Channel tunnel', a year's work expected to cost £4 million. This came after the conclusion of preliminary investigations which had cost £1 million; it was 'expected that a decision whether or not to undertake further work leading up to actual construction would be taken as soon as possible after the results of the studies were available.' According to *The Times* report, French ministry spokesmen described this decision as 'a decisive step in the realization of the tunnel', while 'in London it was emphasized that there was no commitment beyond the next study phase.' The French Government's attitude was much the more positive of the two.

As matters stood in autumn 1972, it seemed reasonably certain that a road tunnel was technically impossible and a bridge too costly; but it should be technically feasible to build a railway tunnel and to complete the work within five years of its inception. Little had been released of the results of the preliminary studies, but according to the *Financial Times* the latest estimate of the construction cost was £366 million at 1972 prices, not taking into account interest charges. Press reports did not indicate whether this figure included car-terminal stations or car-transporter wagons; the cost of these (£22 million) was included in the total capital cost of £137·7 million estimated in 1962.[1]

A road tunnel under 20 miles of sea was impossible because it could not be ventilated, and no solution to this problem was in sight. A bridge was possible, but ruled out by cost; taking charges on capital and current costs into account, any given number of road vehicles could be ferried across the Channel more cheaply by being carried on railway wagons through a railway tunnel. Apart from this, it would scarcely be worth running the risk that sooner or later a ship would hit the bridge.

Another possible device has been described in several publications. This would provide for a fixed link of which about half the length would be under water, half above it. The two tunnel sections would each be about six miles long. The tube containing them would rise up on a causeway in the middle of the Channel, where the water is shallow. The two tunnel sections would be short enough to allow for adequate ventilation, as in the Mont Blanc road tunnel, which is six miles long; shipping could pass unimpeded along the two wide channels which would be left free of obstruction. However, this would still be a more expensive way of getting road vehicles across the Channel than by carrying them on ordinary but suitably designed railway wagons through a fully submerged tunnel.

For these reasons the survey in 1971–3 concentrated on an ordinary rail tunnel; a similar tunnel is already being built in Japan. But all public discussion was bedevilled by the general assumption that the conveying of road vehicles across the Channel would be a major part of the tunnel's function.

The idea of building a Channel tunnel is more than a hundred years old; for the last twenty it has been discussed mainly as a means of taking cars between Folkestone and Calais. The discussions of 1970–2 assumed a substantial load of conventional railway traffic, but up to the end of 1972 the 'shuttle-service' for cars continued to be an important part of its expected function.

Much of the public comment favourable to the tunnel has been based on vague 'political' arguments about the symbolic value of a fixed link with Europe. We shall not be concerned with these arguments here. Much of the unfavourable comment has been based on well-justified scepticism about the usefulness of the car-carrying function, particularly as the existing sea-crossings are perfectly adequate and capable of substantial development. By hovercraft they are as quick road-to-road as the rail shuttle would be; by ship they are more pleasant. It will be argued here that the car-carrying shuttle-service would be of little value and probably ought to be abandoned. The other role, which predominated from 1860 to the 1930s, was as a conveyer of through-trains, for passengers and freight. That role has now re-emerged as the major one to be considered because its nature has been transformed by the railways' new capabilities.

The car-carrying role does not overlap with Maplin's, but is of doubtful value. The sea-crossing by ship, and now also by hovercraft, has improved beyond all recognition since 1963, and is still improving. Sea Ferry operators claim that they can carry road vehicles more cheaply than a tunnel could. A train 600 yards long could carry 700 persons and their 260 cars from a terminal near Folkestone to Sangatte (near Calais). Loading and unloading would take quite a long time. The car-passengers' road-to-road time would be a little over an hour (the same as by hovercraft, and an hour less than by conventional ferry). The train's output in a year would be restricted by fluctuating demand and by the terminal operations. The intensive-use car-loading bays would, according to the 1973 study, cost a third as much as the tunnel itself. They would disfigure the countryside.

A non-stop train 300 yards long, of the type that should be in mass service by the early 1980s, could carry 500 passengers between these points in twenty minutes, as part of a stretch of 100 miles within an hour. Its output in that hour would be ten times as great in terms of passenger-miles, being part of its $2\frac{1}{2}$-hour journey to Paris or Brussels; or it might be on its way to Frankfurt in 5 hours, to Milan in 8 or Rome in 12 by night or day. Such trains would perform a function which would compete with the aeroplane's.

No study of the tunnel's role or cost, no inquiry into its utility, can be of any use unless it takes into account its potential role as a replacement for a large volume of air-transport, and specifically as a justification for about five years' deferment of a new London airport. But the role in carrying public-transport passengers could be performed only if the railways on both sides of the Channel received sufficient investment to provide clearway running for very frequent non-stop trains averaging over 100 mph, and preferably maintaining their 150-mph capability throughout their inter-city journeys. So the role of the tunnel as a means of transit for public-transport trains cannot usefully be considered except as a part of a wider railway plan, co-ordinating the several national railway plans which are now at various stages of advancement.

Under the option which would involve maximum commitment to railways the tunnel's conventional railway traffic could build up rapidly to 30 million passengers a year. Assuming an average train capacity of 500 passengers, with realistic average load-factors, this would mean 150 passenger trains a day in each direction, or in practice rather less than this as a basic service, rising to a maximum

of 200 at peak periods. There would also be 20 to 40 freight trains,˙
though there would be few of them at peak periods.

The maximum capacity should probably be put at 250 trains
a day each way, so as to allow some margin for mishaps and some
time for daily maintenance work. As traffic could be expected to increase steadily, there would be no room for the Folkestone–Calais
car-carrying shuttle service in addition, particularly as its peaks
would probably be very sharp and would coincide with the peaks
of the conventional railway service.

However, there is still a demand among motorists for another
type of service, now wholly unsatisfied, but capable of interesting
development. This is for the relatively luxurious transport of cars
with their drivers and passengers by train over long distances between Britain and the continent. Some of the cross-Channel motorists
would be well served by a facility for entrainment at some point on
the south-east edge of London, preferably at a place chosen for
being near a circular motorway; let us say, for the moment, Orpington. There would be great attractions in car-transporters over distances to points in Europe 500 to 800 miles away. In 1972 there
were some 38 car-sleeper trains a week during the summer in each
direction to and from Calais and Ostend. If non-business air travel
to Europe (or travel now assigned to air) is to multiply four times by
1985, it is reasonable to expect demand for car-sleeper travel to
multiply at least as much. This cannot be a cheap way of taking a
holiday, but it is a very comfortable and convenient way.

It now takes some 20 hours for a motorist to go from Surrey to
Avignon by driving to Dover, then ferry, then car-sleeper. The
scheme now envisaged would enable him to do the same journey in
10 hours. He could have dinner at home, go to bed in the train at
11 pm and be driving on a Spanish or Italian road the next morning. If air travel to these areas, with no improvement in service, is
to multiply with spreading affluence, then car-sleeper travel, thus
greatly improved, should multiply far more. It might attract some
travellers assigned to ordinary rail for the present model, and some
still left with air; and it might generate a new demand on its own
account.

Car-sleeper traffic between the British Midlands or North and
Europe could then be added to all this. A Birmingham or Manchester motorist finds the drive through London a greater obstacle
than a ferry-crossing. A facility for loading at some point such as

Rugby or Crewe (chosen for convenient motorway-access), with an overall journey of 12 or 14 hours from doorstep to a Provençal or Italian road, could create a big new market. There is no parallel experience to serve as a guide to the likely effect of so great an improvement in a service, particularly for people living in or travelling to points north of London.

Given adequate rail links through London, there could well be substantial car-transporter traffic, with accompanying passengers, terminating both north and west of London. With several terminal points and no colossal pressure of traffic at any of them, the terminal points could be quite simple. There are already a dozen in Britain and several dozen on the continent. With such a spread, some of the equipment could be used for carrying new cars from factories when not needed for peak-load work on the car-sleeper services, so the allocation of cost would be on a different basis from that assumed for the 1973 study's cross-Channel transporters.

At least it would seem that by 1985, assuming 20 million passengers a year through the tunnel transferred from London airport projections, and 10 million others, the tunnel would already have enough use to justify its building, but still enough spare capacity to accommodate the various types of traffic which could be expected to use it, except for shuttle-services across the Channel. These may usefully be summarized, along with the daily average number of trains in each direction for each group, assuming an average train load of 300 persons per train (though the number of trains for a given number of passengers would be reduced if trains of continental loading gauge increased the capacity per train):

1. Day passenger-trains terminating at London (average 80 to 100 each way per 24 hours).

2. Night trains terminating at London (average 30 to 50 each way per 24 hours).

3. Day trains to and from the British regions (possibly none specially for this purpose: they would probably serve London too, adding a further 20 to the estimate under (1).

4. Night trains to and from British regions (15 per 24 hours).

5. Passenger and car-carrying trains terminating in the London area, including 'Orpington', mostly by night (say 3 to 10).

6. Passenger and car-carrying trains terminating north or west of London, almost all by night (say 3 to 10).

7. Freight trains (up to 30 each way per 24 hours, but fewer at

the passenger peak-periods at summer weekends). The estimate of 5 million tons a year implies 7,000 tons a day each way; the number of trains implied is less than 30.

This gives a total of about 200 trains each way for passengers, including car-sleepers and a few daytime 'motor-rail' trains, spread over 18 hours in each 24-hour period, with perhaps 250 on peak weekend days towards 1990. Virtually no southbound passenger trains would pass through the tunnel between 2 and 8 am. and none northbound between 11 pm and 5 am. The slack times would allow for maintenance and for freight trains; some could be interspersed if necessary with overnight passenger trains. With further growth of traffic the tunnel would be approaching its maximum capacity not long after 1990, but by then some of the growth could well be diverted back to air, by the development of vertical and short take-off aircraft operating from new airports near town centres.

The view of the tunnel's function as that of merely ferrying cars across the Channel, a function with which many people still mainly associate it, has been severely attacked from several quarters, and with good reason. The objections are as follows:

1. The terminal points at Folkestone and Sangatte will be horribly disfiguring.

2. The traffic generated by them will be very heavy and concentrated, necessitating much expensive road-construction in Kent and in France, with some environment damage.

3. The sea-crossings for accompanied vehicles have been improved out of all recognition during the 1960s, with huge investment in ferry terminals and ships. A motorist can travel road-to-road by ferry in $2\frac{1}{4}$ hours, in conditions which are usually very pleasant, as compared with about $1\frac{1}{4}$ hours by the tunnel medium, in unpleasant conditions if he sits in the car.

4. The hovercraft has already begun to play a part in this market and may well develop much further. Its road-to-road time is potentially less than that of the tunnel transporter. Though less agreeable than an ordinary ship, it is more agreeable than the tunnel would be. In the long run its costs could turn out to be quite low.

5. The Channel ports are much concerned at the possible damage to their local economy through the loss of the ferry traffic. The big investment in ships and ferry terminals would become useless overnight.

Quite understandably, an opposition group has been formed. They fear that the tunnel would ruin the port of Dover, half of whose working population depend, directly or indirectly, on the seaborne trade, most of which the tunnel would destroy if it took enough cars to justify its building. People rightly hate the idea of vast and hideous new terminals near Folkestone and Calais, and the effect of all the traffic on the roads through Kent.

If a rail tunnel were bored under the Channel, with immediate cross-Channel transport of vehicles as its main function, there would be a sudden and catastrophic collapse in ferry business. The existing car-ferry terminals, built for heavy traffic, would be largely wasted. If however the tunnel came into use as a means of passage for ordinary passenger and freight-train traffic, with no facility for loading cars on the English side nearer than 'Orpington', only the existing ferry system for public-transport passengers would become useless overnight. But provision of this kind has remained at a minimal level through all the increase in total travel of the past 20 years. The train-ship-train provision between London and Paris is no faster now than it was 40 years ago, and the services are actually fewer. There has been hardly any investment, except for a few buildings on the quays to make the passengers' situation a little less ineligible; there is not much to lose anyway.

All this argument is of relatively minor importance, but it is not negligible. It is a minor support to the notion that the tunnel should be seen, from its opening, mainly as a public-transport conveyer for passengers and freight, and not mainly as an awkward and uncomfortable conveyer of cars between two terminals close to the tunnel entrances. Much more important is the tunnel's major contribution to maintaining the vitality of the whole railway system, with all the long-term effects that this would have, spreading outwards to the whole environment.

If the capital cost of the tunnel amounted to £550 million, and the charge on this were soon to be shared between freight and 30 to 35 million passengers a year, rising to a probable maximum (at capacity) of 50 million by 1990 or soon after, the investment would seem likely to be worth while, particularly in view of the low unit costs that could be expected from such intensive use. Any attempt to add shuttle-service cross-Channel car-ferry services would drastically reduce the potential return on the capital, provided the total load of conventional train-passengers, seasoned with a few in car-sleepers, rose rapidly after the opening of the tunnel. Given the projections of air passengers on routes between Britain and Europe, the market should be big enough to provide numbers of this order, but only if the railways on land were adequately developed.

On this basis, additional tracks would be required in the 1990s. Decisions on this matter could be left until after 1985. Additional fixed cross-Channel link facilities might by then conceivably take the form of a bridge-tunnel-causeway-tunnel-bridge, capable of accommodating cars driven normally, emerging on to a causeway in the mid-Channel shallow water. But this decision could be left open for ten or fifteen years yet.

A Green Paper on the Channel tunnel was published in March 1973.[2] This document was in the nature of an interim report, to provide a basis for 'informed discussion'; it gave promise of further information on some points later. Like the report of 1963 it did not suggest alternative roles for a tunnel. It assumed, without question, a tunnel for transporting cars and lorries across the Channel as well as through rail traffic, passenger and freight. But it did not discuss the interdependence, for rail traffic, of the tunnel and the railway-systems on both sides of the Channel; it made no reference to the effects of different levels of railway-investment on the railway-load.

Para 1.4 simply asserted that the tunnel 'might attract from air in 1980 some 2·7 million passengers . . . and would not affect significantly the level *at that time* [italics—P. B.] of aircraft movements at Maplin to all destinations'.

The figure of 2·7 million was just half of the maximum that Roskill had envisaged, and on which the Secretary of State for the Environment had relied in his speech introducing the Maplin Bill six weeks earlier.[3] Some explanation of the new figure for 1980 would not have been out of place. Instead of explaining it, the Green Paper went on, in another section (8.18), not merely to pretend (falsely) that there had been an explanation, but to distort even the assertion by pretending also that the lack of effect on demand for air travel from Maplin had been demonstrated, not just for 1980, but for an unspecified period thereafter.

The low estimate of transfer from air to rail in 1980 was indeed acceptable and immaterial; a full railway system could not be ready by 1980. But it is the period after 1980 that matters. The new railways could be ready by 1982 or 1987 to affect air travel much more significantly, and the exact date must depend on the exercise of choice by governments. But the Green Paper did not admit that any choice was available. It did not even mention the railways in France and Benelux. It did discuss the railway between London and the tunnel (para. 4.7–12) but only in terms of the difficulties of improving an existing route. By omitting all mention of really substantial investment in railways it excluded in advance any thought that the railway through the tunnel should be an important carrier of through passengers.

The promise that car-transport trains would run 'at least every four minutes at peak periods' suggested an assumption that passenger-traffic would be unimportant. Provided (*a*) that the minimum interval between trains was no more than two minutes, and (*b*) that additional tracks were to be provided for the car-transporters' acceleration and deceleration, to and from a maximum speed equal to the maximum permitted in the tunnel, there would be no problem. If these conditions were not fulfilled, then a high-frequency car-transporter service could be achieved only at the cost of obliging through trains to enter and leave the tunnel at slow speed, and run at the same rhythm as the car-transporters. It seems unlikely that a through train would lose less than 10 minutes, and it might lose 15. Such a delay, imposed to suit the convenience of the car-transporters, would constitute a breach of the Green Paper's promise of 'parity of treatment between the users of through rail services and the road vehicle ferry trains'. (Para. 4.2.)

Surely, then, the drafters of the Green Paper must have intended to provide acceleration and deceleration tracks. But if so, it should surely not have neglected to mention an item so important and expensive.

According to the Green Paper's estimates, revenues in 1980 and 1990 would be made up as follows:

	£ million (1972 prices)	
	1980	1990
Passengers	15–17	22 – 28
Car traffic	23–28	42 – 53
Freight	14–18	26 – 35
Miscellaneous	2– 3	3·5– 4·5
Total	£54–66	£93·5–120·5

It was not stated whether lorry revenue was included under car-traffic, freight or miscellaneous.

The number of rail passengers was estimated at 4·3 million to 5·8 million in 1980. Presumably the (unstated) estimates for later years must have been in the region of $5\frac{1}{2}$ to 7 million in 1985 and 7 to 10 million in 1990, so the revenue per passenger could be put at about £3. The average revenue from each car-plus-occupants appeared to be around £12 to £20 (1·2 to 2·1 million cars in 1980). Considering the space required by a car, the comparison indicates generous treatment of cars.

But out of the total cost of £366 million, £58 million was for the terminals; part of the £73 million for development, management and contingencies should be attributed to the terminals; and the whole (unmentioned) excess cost of building the running-tunnels with an extra-large diameter, to accommodate rail-wagons carrying big lorries (as compared with the cost of continental loading-gauge tunnels), should be attributed to the function of transporting cars and lorries. There was also the mystery of the acceleration tracks for car-transporters.

Thus, on the Green Paper's figures, the tunnel system for through rail traffic only would apparently cost around £250 million. But if there were say 30 million through rail-passengers in 1990 (25 million of them transferred from air) the revenue from them would, on the Green Paper's figures, be not less than £90 million, and the rail-freight revenue would be no less than the Green Paper's figure. There would also be some revenue from long-distance motor rail traffic.

Thus the revenue would in all probability be greater than the Green Paper's highest figure, in return for a much lower investment. Assuming the tunnel not to be a profit-making venture, the charge per passenger could thus be reduced by half, and the return would still be more adequate than that envisaged by the Green Paper's plan.

It was a pity that this product of the Department of the Environment did not envisage a tunnel as part of a new railway scheme, as a key link in Europe's transport system. However, it did produce statements (though not arguments) to satisfy the proponents of Maplin airport. It also satisfied the road-haulage interests by providing an extra-large tunnel to accommodate lorries loaded on wagons. It gave no figures whatever on which the worthwhileness of the provision could be evaluated, even in economic terms. Meanwhile it sought to placate the environmental lobbies, by suggesting that the through rail-freight provision would 'moderate the use of our roads by heavy lorries carrying Continental freight'. (4.12.) Why, then, the expensive provision for lorries through the tunnel?

On 2 May 1973 a new estimate, reported in *The Times*, put the cost at 'nearly £500 million', without allowing for interest charges, inflation or road and rail links, and on the same day Lord Harcourt, the Chairman of the Channel Tunnel Company, in a debate in the House of Lords, put the figure at £470 million in terms of January 1973, to which £189 million should be added for interest during construction. He also suggested a figure of £160 million to take account of probable inflation, but this was merely speculation.

The new figures did not affect the argument about dispensing with the car-transporting element in the Tunnel system. Even at this higher cost, the Tunnel would be likely to cost less than the railway-works on land which would be needed to provide a rail-service of better than Tokaido quality. What really needs to be examined for comparison is the escalation of the cost of Maplin Airport with its access-routes.

The quality of the Green Paper, with its omissions, obfuscations and inconsistencies, is relevant to the discussion of administrative behaviour and of the values which inform it, in Part Three of this book.

12

New rail investment in London
and the South-East

The London part of the rail-plan looks likely to raise the biggest difficulties, because several options are available. Any choice would have effects on London's traffic problems.

If 30 million passengers (two-thirds of them diverted from air) are to be carried between London and the Channel tunnel at high speeds, in 1985 or soon after, the new load on this small part of the railway system will rise to 2,200 million passenger miles a year, which is equal to 12 per cent of the total passenger mileage on the whole British railway system in 1970, with 9,000 miles of passenger routes.

A massive switch to rail would depend on two requirements: that frequent trains should have unimpeded high-speed passage through Kent and the southern suburbs, and that passengers should have good access to them in central London. The British Rail Chairman, Mr Marsh, has spoken of trains between London and Paris in $2\frac{3}{4}$ hours before 1980, and has accepted a fairly heavy passenger load. However, the figures used in the GLC's paper on the tunnel terminal, issued in November 1972, envisage a slower time scale for the introduction of trains at this speed. The timing of the investment is a matter for the Governments concerned.

Clearly, quite heavy investment would be necessary, both to provide acceptable and efficient terminal arrangements, and to accommodate the movement of trains. In estimating costs, there should be two distinct operations: first a purely financial assessment of the return to be expected in the investment, and secondly a full economic assessment of costs and benefits, taking account of the share in expenditure on airports that would be saved or added as part of the whole package. The economic assessment is part of a much wider examination, including operating costs by air and rail.

To give clear running at high speed all the way to London, it would be necessary to build at least two new tracks the whole way from the tunnel to London, partly by widening an existing permanent way, partly by building a wholly new route. The existing tracks on the route would have to be incorporated in the new system. In order to provide a clear run, all level junctions would have to be converted to flyovers or underpasses. Overhead electrification, by a system compatible with that in France, would be necessary, not only for two new tracks but for others (if any) forming part of the continental route. This would mean much work on bridges and tunnels.

Should the new route be converted to the continental loading gauge? Trains of British loading gauge can operate over all the continental main lines, with some minor design-adjustments, but vehicles of continental loading gauge are too big for normal British tunnels, bridges, etc. One advantage of the continental style is that the larger vehicles can accommodate more people, or the same number with more comfort, or a few more people with a little more comfort. If all the bridges and tunnels have to be altered to provide for overhead electrification, it would probably be as well to alter them to the continental loading gauge too. There would probably be some saving on operating costs, mainly because more sleeping-berths could be packed into the coaches. But this is a question for detailed analysis, taking into account the cost, including vehicle storage-areas and sidings.

In any case the continental loading gauge could not be extended into England beyond the London area. Through-trains to and from places beyond London, for ordinary passengers, car-sleepers and freight would clearly have to be of British loading gauge. Such through-trains together might be expected to account for about 25 per cent of the total using the lines through London and Kent.

The first 40 miles from the tunnel towards London should not present too much difficulty. The existing route is dead straight between Folkestone and Tonbridge. North-west of Tonbridge the problems become more awkward. By the end of 1972 the choice of a route was still open, with British Rail favouring a westerly sweep via Croydon into the existing West London line rather than development along the line of the shortest route via Orpington and southeast London.

The choice of a route for the thirty miles at the London end is linked with the choice of a site for a terminal and with the provision of a route for running through London to the rest of Britain. The through-London connection is immensely important for freight, both for regional considerations and in order to enable the railways to provide the best practicable service for long-haul traffic which might otherwise be driven to use the roads. Through passenger traffic to the regions, avoiding the need to change stations in London, is also an important consideration. The choice of site and the quality of the through-London route must have a major influence on the attractiveness of the railway and thus on its traffic.

In the consultative document published by the Greater London Council in November 1972 eleven possible sites were examined. The document concluded that only three deserved serious consideration : Victoria, White City (on the existing West London through route) and Surrey Docks.

The GLC preferred Surrey Docks 'because it would offer the strategic advantage of bringing a most valuable stimulus to eastern London.' This site is, however, bad for access from most of the rest of London; its choice would seriously reduce the attractiveness of the whole railway system.

White City (like one of the discarded sites, Kensington-Olympia) is on the existing West London line, a route which could easily be adapted. It would have the great advantage that it would provide through running to the main existing Western and Midland routes, so the line could be used for direct passenger, freight and car-carrying services between Birmingham, Manchester, Bristol, etc., and the continent.

The great objection to this is that a main station in the White City area would be too far from the City and Westminster, which in 1968 were the air travellers' main points of origin or destination within London (see BOT, *Passengers at London Airports*, 1970). However, existing underground connections reduce this disadvantage. The GLC's objection to the White City was that it could 'aggravate existing pressures and "overheating" in West London as regards employment and congestion generally, and for these reasons would not redound to the overall benefit of Londoners.'[1]

Victoria would clearly be very good for access and by a long way the most attractive to travellers. Its good public-transport connections would be an immense advantage; less vehicular traffic would be generated. But it would be 'difficult for the terminal to be operational by 1980.' Another objection was lack of land for further

development. Also, 'the area is currently subject to considerable demand for new activities on an already intensively used site.' On the
GLC map the use of Victoria would imply an approach to London
through a south-easterly route, not through Croydon.

Victoria is a 'dead-end' station, like all the existing main terminals
in London (as well as Paris, Milan, Rome, etc.). A 'through' type
of station, such as White City would be, is on the whole more
efficient, because it gives better utilization of the tracks approaching
a station, particularly when trains have separate locomotives or are
removed for cleaning, etc., between journeys. However, if trains
are of multiple-unit type or have traction units with drivers' compartments at each end, this disadvantage of the dead-end terminal
is greatly reduced, provided that trains can be cleaned, inspected
and prepared for the next journey quickly while waiting at the
terminal. Even so, if a train is not passed as fit to begin its next
scheduled journey, some difficult adaptations are required which
must be time-consuming. These problems are not discussed in the
GLC document.

The document did not discuss the possibility of using both Victoria and White City; indeed, it explicitly says that if Victoria were
the terminal, through-trains between the continent and the Midlands would have to go into Victoria and out again. This is evidently
not necessarily the case. If Victoria were the main terminal there
might well be room for through-trains to omit it and run directly on
to the West London line, stopping at a secondary station at White
City. This scheme would not be justifiable until the traffic built up
to a high level; its attractiveness provides a minor argument for a
really determined commitment to the railways for railable European
transport.

The GLC consultative document[2] foresees that, both in 1980–5
and 1995–2000, 26 per cent of all passengers through the Channel
tunnel will have points of origin or destination beyond the South-
East. Nearly 20 per cent would be on British routes served by the
West London line connection (for details, see below). If about a
fifth of the total Channel-tunnel load consisted of passengers going
through London, a second station specially for through traffic would
be a useful addition to a main Victoria terminal. Its additional use
by domestic and international passengers terminating in the western
part of London and the Home Counties (from both directions) would
both relieve Victoria and contribute to raising the total load at this

secondary station-terminal to a figure large enough to justify an adequate independent service. (Assuming 30 million London terminators a year, the total using the West London route in preference to Victoria could be put at around 10 million, of whom nearly half would terminate at London. The total implies an average of 50 trains a day each way, of which probably more than half would be night trains. There might be car-sleepers too.

If 30 million passengers a year ended their continental journeys at London, some of them would find a western station (White City) more convenient than Victoria; similarly a few domestic passengers would prefer this station to Euston. The problem is how many domestic routes would have enough passengers to justify this service. Birmingham could collect passengers from many parts of the Midlands and North. For overnight through services there would have to be some shunting of sleeping-cars between trains at this point.

Any through route would have heavy Channel-tunnel freight traffic, and this may be an argument in favour of giving only a secondary role to a passenger station on the through route, with Victoria as the principal passenger terminal.

A through-link with the northwards routes from King's Cross might be provided by a northwards branch from the tunnel line south of central London, into the existing Brixton–King's Cross route. In 1967 it was proposed to use this line for the railway service to Stansted airport. There were to be three trains an hour. A somewhat similar adaptation could presumably be considered for the through-link with the tunnel line. Its main use would probably be for freight, though some passenger trains might use it too. The traffic would probably not justify large expenditure on upgrading these few miles, but a slight time-penalty of perhaps 20 minutes would not be very serious. Most of the passenger trains involved would travel by night, and thus cause little interference with normal passenger-traffic in the area.

If Victoria were to be the major terminal the station would have to be rebuilt; but, as the GLC consultative document points out, it is proposed to rebuild the station in any case. The difficulty of providing additional platforms, and lines for the first four miles out of the station, while keeping the station operational, is cited as a serious objection, and there is a gloom about the prospect of completing the work in time. (This is a penalty imposed by our failure to look into the whole Channel tunnel question at the same time as the London airport question, beginning a few years earlier.)

However, if the problem can be treated in relation to London's rail transport as a whole, there are other developments which might be considered. The GLC document deals with the broad effect of the choice of site for a terminal, but it does not relate this possible change in the public-transport picture with the changes implied by other new developments with London Transport Railways, notably the Victoria and Fleet lines. The scale of work at Victoria Station could be vastly reduced if some of the suburban trains which now run into it could be diverted away from it altogether; at first sight such a simple and obvious solution would seem likely also to be good on transport grounds and to ease the pressure on the transport to and from Victoria and on the area near the station.

Simultaneous planning of the Channel terminal and of the Fleet Underground line could provide useful scope for rationalizing the railway system south of the Thames. The south end of the Victoria Line might also be adapted. If the two new tube-systems were integrated with the existing British Rail near-suburban routes, up to 50 or 60 trains an hour could be taken from the Southern Region routes to run into (and through) London as tube trains, greatly reducing the load now shared between Victoria and London Bridge–Cannon Street–Charing Cross.

Specifically, some short-distance suburban trains from British Rail tracks might become Victoria Line tube trains north of Brixton. In addition some which now run into either Victoria or Charing Cross might become Fleet Line trains north-west of New Cross-New Cross Gate. Some middle-distance trains now using Victoria might then be switched into the BR London Bridge–Charing Cross route. Much reconstruction would be necessary at Brixton, New Cross and New Cross Gate. A major replanning of the use of the BR system would be involved and various other diversions might also be considered.

With the main BR line west of New Cross–New Cross Gate and the London Bridge–Charing Cross terminals thus relieved of many short distance suburban trains, a large part of Victoria's middle-distance traffic might be diverted to these stations without increasing their present load. If Victoria thus became mainly a terminal for high-speed trains (including one or two per hour to Eastern Kent), the pressure on the station and its approaches would be relieved, and the need for fundamental reconstruction reduced, both at the station and for the first three or four miles south of it.

From a transport-planning angle these developments would not be revolutionary; they would correct the unbalanced shape of London's rail-transport Underground map. North of the Thames most local lines up to 15 miles from central London are part of the LT system; south of the river nearly all the suburban routes are funnelled into the Southern Region termini. This was not deliberately planned; it just happened this way. The existing system south of the river creates centres of congestion at the termini and decreases the proportion of passengers who can be transported without change of train to destinations in central London. Commuters from, say, Blackheath might lose five minutes because their trains, having become tubes north-east of New Cross, would stop more often, but taken as a whole they would probably find a reduction in average overall journey-time as well as an improvement in convenience. The subject seems to deserve detailed study and analysis.

There are two obvious practical difficulties: the adaptation of tube-type trains, with their smaller loading gauge, to platforms, etc., built for standard-sized BR trains, and the need to adapt the electric pick-up. These should not be very serious. Much more serious is the objection that tube-type trains provide less accommodation than BR trains. Tubes are limited by the length of platforms, and an overall extension of platforms would be very expensive.

The scheme would also prevent any eventual southward extension of the Victoria Line as such, because its southward extensions would already be running into the existing BR system. However, if the principle were accepted, it might be possible to bring the southern ends of the Bakerloo and Northern Lines into the project as well. The Bakerloo now ends rather wastefully at Elephant and Castle, though there are plans for extension. The Northern Line goes well out southwards as far as Morden, but the southernmost end is over-supplied with trains. The two middle sections of the Northern Line could afford to be fed by at least three more branches, either newly built or switched into it out of the BR near-suburban system.

The maximum number of near-suburban trains capable of being taken out of the BR Southern Region termini into the tube system would appear to be in the region of 90 to 120 – that is to say, the whole lot, excluding the south-western section which uses Waterloo.

Such a result would be desirable on its own account, if only because the use of dead-end stations in the central area of London by near-suburban trains is highly uneconomic. The same is not so true of longer-distance trains. If all the terminal platforms were available to be shared between trains to the exurbs, Sussex and outer Kent, and those going to the Channel tunnel, the need for substantial reconstruction on the rail-side of Victoria might be avoided. This might mean the diversion of Sussex travellers from Victoria to Charing Cross, but this would on the whole be to their advantage. If Charing Cross got two or more extra platforms at the expense of Villiers Street, only the most undiscriminating defenders of all that exists would complain.

The changes proposed here would not increase the load on the railway system in central London. They might slightly reduce it by enabling more passengers to avoid deviations from straight lines (caused by route changes at right-angles). They would reduce changes of train, and thus reduce crowding of stations below ground.

Much more important, the scheme would greatly reduce the present wasteful use of London's railway infrastructure by cutting out dead-end terminal operation by suburban trains. Every tube train terminating at Brixton, Elephant and Castle, New Cross or New Cross Gate occupies a platform, in a near-central area, un-economically, and in effect requires two tracks for a short period in its terminal movement.

Similar inefficient use of infrastructure is even more serious at the existing BR termini. Every BR train running in and out of a terminal uses its track while parked there for a considerable period, and each train's movement in or out of these dead-end terminals may deny to other trains the use of two, three, four or more tracks. This problem appears to be a major obstacle to the improvement of commuter services south of the Thames.

At present about 150 trains leave Victoria, Charing Cross, Cannon Street, London Bridge or Holborn Viaduct, on the central and south-eastern sections of BR, betwen 5 and 6 pm each weekday evening, and nearly two-thirds of these trains are local slow trains. More than 20 dead-end platforms at the termini are used to provide terminal facilities for this fairly small number of trains, and all these platforms occupy space within the innermost area of central London.

All LT lines accommodate a maximum frequency of 30 trains an hour on any one track. If we look at this solution in terms of the possible extension on LT systems into the BR network, there appears to be scope for greatly improved use of the whole infrastructure.

Even if a maximum of no more than 60 suburban trains could in practice be diverted in this way, with little new construction other than the necessary underpasses at four junction-points, there should be no great difficulty in providing the 8 or 10 platforms that would be needed to accommodate up to 15 Channel-tunnel trains an hour at Victoria. It might even be possible to dispense with a second deck for trains. Some widening of the station on its east side might be considered. (Objections to such slight environmental damage should be weighed against the damage to be caused, even within London, by the access routes to Maplin.)

The construction of a wholly new route, with at least one track in each direction, and partly in tunnel, for the high-speed Channel-tunnel trains, through at least ten miles of South London, must probably be accepted as a necessary condition of the viability of the tunnel route. If, in addition, some tunnel trains (passenger and freight) were to run through to the West London line via White City to Willesden (for the Midlands and North-West) and Western routes of British Rail, there would be a need for some flyover or underpass work in the area south of Victoria. But this would be small in relation to the total at stake, and this total ought to be measured against the benefits which could be obtained from the (minimum) five-year deferment of Maplin airport (plus its road and rail access routes) which a fully developed rail system through the Channel tunnel could justify.

An incidental advantage of the scheme might be a net increase of a (theoretical) maximum of 20 to 40 trains an hour serving the southern commuters. This addition would be subject to the constraints imposed by the capacity of the various existing BR rail routes between 3 and 15 miles from the centre of London; but routes in this section already exist in great profusion, in a network so intricate that most of the directions could be connected with any of the three tube lines. Some of these routes have four tracks and are thus capable of accommodating a heavy load of both stopping and non-stopping trains. BR and extended tube trains might need to share the same tracks in some cases, so there would be some need for adapting the design and the administration.

The suggestion put forward here may look wildly unrealistic. It claims to offer some advantages to London's own transport system, but the advantages are probably not great enough, on their own account, to justify the expenditure involved. But this is only in the short run, and even in the long run the scheme is put forward, not as an absolute but as a palliative to the disadvantages involved in trying to insert the Channel tunnel traffic into Victoria Station in addition to its existing and developing load of local traffic. Many other solutions could be suggested as alternatives; the new fast railway from the Channel tunnel might be put in a tunnel right under some part of Central London – perhaps running under Victoria and Paddington, and so out to the West and North from there, with deep stations under these two existing termini. But any solution of this kind would raise the problem of access to the stations from the existing public transport system and by private car and taxi.

One thing is certain. If the Channel tunnel railway is to play its part in attracting passengers there must be at least one really good access point in Central London, placed in such a way that up to 20 or even 30 million tunnel passengers a year can join or leave their trains at it. This means up to 40,000 per average day in each direction (and far more on a peak day), including a large number of passengers arriving or leaving by car or taxi. To add this load to the load of any existing terminal, without taking any measures to balance the increase by reducing the existing load, would bring a danger of severe congestion.

A thorough study of the effects on the pattern of journeys would demand detailed research, but *prima facie* it seems likely that there would be an overall net reduction in journey-times and a considerable reduction in time spent at stations. The one possible disadvantage to travellers would be an increase in the need to stand in trains, because vehicles passing through the central area must inescapably have ample doorway and circulation space at the cost of seating. But it is arguable that vehicles with maximum seating increase station delays and add to the discomfort of crowded conditions: fewer may have to stand but their sufferings are worse than in a more open plan, and their presence is disagreeable to the people who do have seats. Even on this count, an increase in the total provision of trains, and thus of space within them, made possible by this rationalization, would come near to eliminating any increase in passenger-minutes spent involuntarily standing in moving trains.

It seems likely that this slight loss would be compensated by other immediate gains.

The costs of railway reconstruction at Brixton, and possibly at Elephant and Castle, would have to be taken into account, but properly as part of the whole package, including the potential use of Victoria as a terminal for the Channel-tunnel railway at a greatly reduced cost in reconstruction on the 'rail side' of that station. The need for a second deck there would be obviated if the switching of BR trains into the tube system were substantial enough.

A rationalization of British Rail and London Transport routes south of the Thames appears not to have been revived when the Victoria Line was under consideration; the paper by Foster and Beesley on this project-appraisal does not raise the question.[3] But in view of the GLC's statutory function of considering and co-ordinating priorities for investment in all forms of transport in London, under the Transport (London) Act 1969, it would seem that it would be appropriate for the GLC to look at the Channel-tunnel terminal together with plans for local transport in London, and to bring together the whole group of items which might have been excluded from previous plans and when considered individually, on grounds of cost, but which, taken together, could add up to a useful combination of solutions to a combination of problems.

This chapter has wandered a long way from the third London airport. So did the Roskill Commission, for part of its exercise in comparing the costs of the possible airport sites. But for the sake of an examination of the alternatives to a third airport, it is necessary to try to see what those alternatives would imply. It is also useful to look for options which involve the smallest possible expenditure of resources and disturbance.

Under the Maplin scheme, with no diversion of any of the expected London air travellers, and assuming no growth of aircraft movements at the existing airports, Maplin's growing load will nearly all have to leave London by train from one terminal. It is not possible to see how it could be distributed among two or more terminals, unless Broad Street Station were used as a reserve terminal. Many people would be brought into London from the provinces to catch the train to the airport. The disturbance in London looks certain to be very much more severe than it would be if the prospective air travellers were redistributed in the way proposed here, with very few brought into London from outside the South-East, and with the people leaving London by train distributed between Victoria, White City and Euston (i.e. those going to America via Liverpool). The railway-works between London and the Channel look likely to be less disturbing and probably cheaper than those between London and Maplin with its appurtenances, and the 500 to 1,000 lane-miles of road which Maplin will demand would be avoided altogether; nothing specific would be required in exchange.

13

What about the costs?

No procedures, however sophisticated, can give us a wholly reliable answer to the economic questions raised by the theme of this book. In order to save the airport cost, it would be necessary for large resources to be spent at several British regional airports, and on the railways, permanent way and stations, signalling and rolling-stock. But once these investments had been made, there would be differential operating costs.

Conventional procedures may not be adequate for measuring these costs. A full proposal for even a method of dealing with the problem would need a book to itself. The best thing we can do at this stage is to identify the essential issues, in primitive terms; though in order to identify them it may be useful to include a reference to the first answers suggested by some of the evidence now available.

Avoiding the use of economists' terms, it would seem that there are two economic questions to be asked with reference to the two blocks of interchangeable traffic.

First, what we may call an economic assessment: what would be the cost in resources, measurable in money terms, of providing blocks of transport under option A or option B, without as yet considering who provides the services, or how much the users pay for them?

Secondly, what may crudely be called a financial assessment, for want of a better term: taking into account the sources of finance and the receipts to be expected from the users, how would the financial balances work out?

Having made these two distinct assessments, other considerations, such as environmental factors, should be taken into account in relation to the options. If option A turns out to cost more than option B, but option B is likely to have greater undesirable effects on groups of persons, or on the community at large, or (looking at it another way) on the environment, narrowly or broadly interpreted, what value ought to be set on these differential effects? As a consequence of this further assessment, would it be appropriate or just to make use of taxes or subsidies in relation to one mode or the other? At what rate, and why?

Next would come a stage of broadening, with examination of long-term implications, both social and economic (for example, a comparison of Essex with Merseyside as sites for the employment of 20,000 or 50,000 airport personnel, taking into account the effects on the need for housing, schools and other social capital, and on regional employment). There would be indirect effects on the distribution between road and rail, and on the cost of road-building and congestion on the roads. The financial aspects of these consequences should be assessed in their turn. The environmental effects are less easy to measure in terms of costs and benefits, but they should clearly be taken into account. There would also be a comparison of the effects on the consumption of energy and on measurable pollution, first direct, then indirect.

The degree of precision with which these consequences could be measured varies enormously. Some of the direct consequences could be assessed with considerable accuracy quite easily, and a first indication can be given even now without any sophisticated research. But the scope for error can be assessed in its turn. And with all these operations there is an advantage in publicity, both for what is being done and for what is being omitted.[1]

The transport costs under the available options fall into three headings: infrastructure, vehicles and current operations. For vehicle costs and operating costs some kind of comparison between the options can be made as a starting-point on the basis of simple calculations. For the infrastructure costs the comparison is more difficult and complex.

The railway option, in so far as it concerns Europe, depends on the readiness of continental Governments and railways to undertake the necessary works; but as their consequences depend heavily on British policy there is a need for collaboration between governments in this matter of common concern. By February 1973 the British Government had still not announced that it had sought or obtained such collaboration; it can be argued that any action undertaken should be made public, and where there is inaction the reasons for it should be given. Any of several types of administrative process could be employed, separately or together : inter-governmental consultation, the existing Union Internationale des Chemins de Fer; possibly the EEC could work in the field, though the exclusion of aviation from the treaty of Rome is an obstacle.

We may usefully begin by taking note of the Japanese finding that the cost per passenger mile of the Tokaido operations has been about one-fifth of what the same load would have cost if moved by air, taking all factors into account, including interest on the vehicles and on the construction costs of a complete new system through an exceptionally difficult terrain. This finding is not precisely valid for British and European conditions, but at least it is a useful indication of what can be achieved.

The British routes north of London differ from those southwards and on the Continent, in that apparently less investment on infrastructure would be needed to enable the British routes to accommodate a heavy load of high-speed trains. However, the costs of vehicles and of operations would be unlikely to be greatly different in these two areas. A first look at the small-scale domestic problem should be a useful start.

BRITISH DOMESTIC ROUTES

The accounts of BEA and the British Railways Board provide information from which some rough preliminary figures might be calculated.

Starting from DTI figures, out of about 6 million passengers apparently assigned to air in 1985 after Roskill's deductions, 3·5 million might go by rail instead. We are interested in the additional cost of carrying these 3·5 million passengers by rail or air in addition to those who would otherwise be carried; we are also interested in the average cost per passenger carried on the whole route, before and after the additions.

Any calculation of global costs is bound to be highly questionable for an operation such as this. However, as no calculations of any kind have been made public, we may here suggest some figures as a starting-point.

The vehicle costs are the least susceptible of error. As we are dealing in rough figures we may begin by assuming that, on the interchangeable domestic routes, 3·5 million passengers are equivalent to 1,000 million passenger miles, and that additional vehicles are provided in appropriate numbers to accommodate them. At

50-per-cent seat occupation by either mode[2] this could amount to 2,000 million seat miles in a year. We may legitimately assume that the vehicles, rail or air, would have been acquired new at the same dates, so the timing of the investment in them presents no problem.

A modern aircraft costs about £20,000 per seat, or rather more. BEA's planes in 1970 covered between 600,000 and 1,000,000 miles each;[3] those used for shorter journeys, such as those which might be transferred to rail, covered fewer miles per year than those equipped for longer flights.

The figures that have been published about the cost of an Advanced Passenger Train are hopelessly inadequate (e.g. £250,000 for a 'train', without any indication of the number of coaches or seats; the rate of production would also have an effect on the cost of each unit produced). However, we do know that a normal new passenger coach in 1972 (not APT type) costs rather less than £1,000 a seat second-class and rather over £1,000 first-class. If we put the cost of a new APT at £2,000 per seat, including the cost of its traction units at 1970 prices, we shall almost certainly not be underestimating, particularly as the rolling-stock we are envisaging would be produced in large quantities, with resultant economies of scale.

Allowing for days out of service the average running per unit of such rolling-stock, in 1985, might be put at 250,000 miles per year. Thus, even if we allow for aircraft seat occupation at 60 per cent, the train's annual output in miles per seat would seem likely to be at least a quarter as much as that of the aircraft, which would cost ten times as much. If we allow 10 per cent as an annual capital charge on the vehicles and 10 per cent for depreciation, the annual cost of the air vehicles for 2,000 million seat miles could be put at £10 million (0·5 pence per seat mile, almost 1 penny per passenger mile). On the same basis the annual cost of the rail vehicles for the same task would be £4 million (0·2 pence per seat mile or 0·4 pence per passenger mile).

Comparison of the current operating costs, excluding all interest charges, is more difficult. BEA's operating costs in 1970–1 amounted to 3 pence per passenger mile. Assuming that the downward trend in real costs for air operations continues,[4] we might put the cost per passenger mile in 1985 at 2 pence at 1970 prices. An increase in the total load would have rather small benefits; the marginal operating costs would not be much lower than the average costs.

The rail operating costs would apparently be very much less. In 1970 British Rail provided 19 billion passenger miles of transport. Their total operating costs, excluding all interest, amounted to £490 million. Half of their revenue came from passenger operations. If we put the passenger cost at £250 million, the cost per passenger mile was around 1·2 pence. However, this average cost was spread over the whole of British Rail's operations, including those on under-utilized routes and those in the suburbs, with highly uneconomic commuter surges and irregular use.

Operations on the 1,200 or so miles of British routes to which traffic might transfer from air would in general be in more favour-able conditions for low-cost operation than have ever been experi-enced by British or European railways anywhere. We could, for example, assume 250 to 300 pasengers per train, assuming the capa-city of a train to be between 500 and 700 passengers. This compares with 103 per loaded train-mile on the whole British system in 1970.

The British Railways Board's paper, *The Development of the Major Railway Trunk Routes*, published in 1965, estimated that at that time the route costs, excluding interest, per passenger/ton-mile would be 0·13 pence for a density of 20 million passenger/net ton-miles, compared with 0·57 pence for a density of 2·5 million, which was the density actually found on the system as a whole. The mar-ginal cost of each additional unit of traffic was estimated to fall steeply, until the average cost per unit fell to 0·07 pence for a density of 45 million passenger/ton-miles (which was assumed to be the maximum capacity of a four-track route).[5]

The 3·5 million passengers who might go by rail instead of by air would be using routes which would already be carrying loads of between 5 million and 30 million passenger/tons per mile per year, so it would seem reasonable to make a first suggestion that the average cost per passenger would be between a fifth and a half of the average over the whole BR system, and the marginal cost would be much less than this.

Even after allowing for additional rail costs caused by higher standards of service, such evidence as can be produced suggests that the operating costs of providing for the interchangeable part of the British domestic market by rail would be less than a quarter as much as by air. For the item of 1,000 million passenger miles under consideration it is not easy to suggest a figure.

If the average cost, for vehicles and current operations, were put at £30 million per year, by air, and £5 million to £10 million by rail, we should have at least a starting-point. In the case of rail the low marginal cost of the additional load would reduce the average cost on the whole operation.

The infrastructure costs to be assigned are even more elusive. Part of the cost of Maplin-plus-access should be assigned to the air operations, but the exact annual amount cannot easily be calculated. Here the timing of the investments, and of the return on them, complicates the problem very seriously. One crude device might be to take this domestic load of 3·5 million passengers as being equal to 10 per cent of the assumed 35 million by which the total projected load is expected to exceed the capacity of the existing airports in 1985, and to assign to this item 10 per cent of the cost (up to that date) of building Maplin-plus-access; but this would scarcely be an acceptable procedure except as a preliminary guide.

British Rail already has an infrastructure on the two main northern trunk routes which could accommodate a big load of high-speed trains. Every reduction in journey-time tends to increase rail's share of the market in relation to air, and also in relation to road, though, in the case of road, price is probably a more important factor than time. But even on these two trunk routes there are points at which reduction of journey-time together with an increase in load-demand investment in works, to remove possible causes of delay, is necessary.

A train capable of 150 mph could pass through Crewe 70 minutes after leaving London, provided that it was never obliged to reduce its speed. Assuming that it is physically possible to carry out works on this route which would remove all situations capable of causing permanent speed reductions, how much is it worth spending on such works? The question needs to be considered in relation to the effects on the distribution of transport between rail, road and air, which in its turn affects the cost of road congestion and the cost of road works to relieve congestion.

One partial approach might suggest that if an annual load, interchangeable between rail and air, can be carried by rail with operating and vehicle costs £20 million less than by air, it is worth investing up to £200 million in the railways to make the interchange possible. But this is not adequate; the calculation must be more sophisticated.

Table 14 (above, p. 128) suggested that, assuming a given quality of railway service, the passenger load that might be transferred from air to rail on journeys between London and Europe might amount in 1985 to 12 million short-journey passengers and 8 million over 400 miles. We may put this at 4 billion passenger miles on short journeys and 6 billion on longer journeys. All these journeys would be on heavily used routes. If the vehicle-plus-operating cost by rail amounted to 1 penny per passenger mile, for the short journeys the total for 1985 would amount to £40 million, as compared with a cost by air of £80 million at 2 pence per passenger mile. The 6 billion passenger miles on longer journeys would be mostly (but not all) at night and would have higher unit costs. If they averaged out at $1\frac{1}{2}$ pence they would cost £90 million, as compared with a cost by air of £120 million. But transfers from air to rail could take place on this scale only if there were very large investments in the key routes in France, Belgium and the Netherlands. If there were such investments, intra-European traffic would also be affected. Decisions on the key routes from Calais await a decision on the Channel tunnel, but the decisions on the tunnel and the railways ought to be taken together; they are interdependent. The fact that some other rail projects, further away from Calais, are already decided (e.g. Paris–Lyon) or going ahead (Rome–Florence) is relevant to the situation nearer Britain.

The comparison between the third London airport and the alternatives cannot be adequately discussed except on the basis of estimates of the comparative infrastructure costs. In the case of rail these would involve an appropriate part of the railway investments at least as far as Paris, Amsterdam and Germany. In the case of air they would involve an appropriate share of Maplin-plus-access, of a future (but probably avoidable) Paris airport in addition to Paris–Nord and Orly, with its access, and developments at other major airports in Europe.

What would the new rail-works cost? London–Maplin is estimated at less than £1 million a mile; the contract for the first 90 miles of Florence–Rome was let at £1·2 million a mile; new routes in Germany are estimated to cost rather more than this. We need about 800 miles of new route between London and Paris, Amsterdam and Germany. A total of 20 million London passengers transferred from air would cover some 6 billion passenger miles with the limits of the wheel which we have defined. Probably less than half of the infrastructure cost should be assigned to them, the rest to intra-European traffic transferred from air and generated traffic, and some to freight. If we put the total cost, including the tunnel, at £1,500 million, shared between passengers covering 15 billion passenger miles, the contribution of each passenger to the infra-structure cost, at 10 per cent per year, works out at a penny a mile.

We cannot make a comparison with the air infrastructure cost without more information, and furthermore the air infrastructure costs should be computed per passenger, not per passenger mile. If we put the cost of Maplin-plus-access at £600 million, by the time it is handling 30 million passengers, its infrastructure alone works out at 2 pence per passenger on the same basis. We have not yet taken the new Paris airport into account – nor escalation.

All this is a gross over-simplification; it cannot be taken as a proper estimate. But at least there is material to suggest that the rail solution should not be rejected because of higher cost. Even on a financial basis, with rail passengers paying on average half as much per mile as air passengers, the rail solution would not stand con-demned as less viable, in advance of a full study.

This is where we come to the difficulty about treating the addi-tional short-haul traffic within the near-Europe area in isolation. These rail improvements cannot in the long run be treated in isolation from the planned improvements south of Paris and beyond Cologne. If a large body of London's short-haul continental traffic went by rail instead of by air, the same routes would be used also by other traffic, also transferring from air, terminating beyond London, Paris and Cologne, and this ought also to be taken into account for any assessment of costs; so would the new traffic gener-ated by the improved rail services, and traffic likely to transfer from the roads both within the short-haul area and beyond its limits. Overall average costs would then become important too.

The West German internal transport problem may seem rather far-removed from the London airport, because only about 3 per cent of the potential journeys out of London in 1985 would be on short-haul routes to Germany, and 5 per cent of the journeys between

400 and 800 miles. However, the West German problem is shared by the Benelux countries and by most important French routes, and the German Transport Ministry has already made a thorough prognosis of the optimum distribution of future domestic traffic between air and rail. The major research project initiated in 1969 is not yet complete, but the first findings of the Battelle-Institut of Frankfurt, commissioned by the Ministry, were completed in 1972.[6]

In 1972 almost all the major West German trunk routes had only two tracks, and they serve more varied forms of freight and passenger traffic than British Rail.[7] Nearly all are approaching saturation.[8] The relatively light load of freight traffic on the roads brings important social and environmental benefits, but it contributes to the rather high unit cost of the rail transport. The same may be said of the generous continuing provision of stopping passenger-train services.

The tendency to overloading is accentuated by the provision of two levels of long-distance passenger trains. In general, minimum-stop trains have limited accommodation (with 100 to 250 seats per train), exclusively first-class with supplementary fare (so that each passenger pays 60 to 75 per cent above the basic fare). These trains travel faster than the normal long-distance trains; thus the loading of the track, already heavy because of the high volume of freight and local passenger traffic, is yet further increased by the conflict between the demands for track space made by at least two types of long-distance passenger trains.

Both passenger and freight traffic are increasing; the overloading already reduced efficiency in 1970–2. An increase in unpunctual running led to a slowing-down of schedules in 1972, thus reducing the attractiveness of the railway in comparison with its competitors.

The Battelle-Institut's research findings, using a large series of assumptions, suggest that on economic grounds it would be justifiable to expand the West German railway system by providing 1,300 miles of route with quadruple track. One-third of this total, or 500 miles, should be in the form of new two-track routes, separately located from the old, providing for through passenger and freight traffic.[9] The cost of new routes, including electrification and train-control systems, was put at between £1 million and £3 million per mile, and the total comes to £700 million. But contemporary thinking, in the light of difficulties encountered in Japan over repairs to the Tokaido system, even envisages the desirability of a third track in reserve, which would increase the cost. The other 800 miles of route would be quadrupled and otherwise improved on their existing alignment, at an estimated cost of £500 million. This scheme, involving a total investment of £1,250 million, is regarded as preferable to an alternative of substantial airport development for domestic services, and parallel development of the railways and airports is rejected because it would involve extravagant duplication of provision. With this heavy investment in the railways and no extension of the air network beyond the existing eleven main airports, air traffic would be expected to increase by 50 per cent in 1970–80, and first-class rail traffic by 60 per cent.

All this starts from an assumption that the market for travel by fast trains or by air is distinct from the mass travel market over such distances. The German study seems to assume that the super-fast rail travel will be available only by trains with small accommodation and high fares. Against this two points might be made.

If it is possible to run 600-seat fast trains, including accommodation at basic fares, such trains should be preferable to 'elite' trains; if the new routes are provided they should be used, and adequate use would imply the passage of the mass of long-distance passenger traffic. Provision of some passenger trains travelling at slower speeds would reduce the effective capacity of the routes. But provision of mass-passenger transport at high speeds could set in motion a spiral of increasing utilization and falling unit costs, leading to increasing utilization through transfer to rail of some of the travellers who would otherwise use their own cars. The scope for reducing journey-times above 100 miles by private car in West Germany is probably slight, except on relatively minor links not yet provided by the 3,000 miles of motorway network already in existence. The factors whereby potential car-users can be persuaded to use public transport are convenience, price and time, in that order. Convenience involves frequency of public services and acceptable access to the stations. The substantial saving of door-to-door journey-time that fast trains can provide, on journeys above 200 miles, is a useful starting-point waiting to be complemented by other factors. For non-business journeys price is an important factor. Provided that rail marginal costs would fall with increase of traffic on the newly enriched system, very large increases of passenger traffic could be expected to reduce overall unit costs.

The West German study is of slight immediate relevance to the

British–European transport problem. However, the whole conception of it would be valid for the travel market within Europe as a whole, including the British domestic market.

In the long run there is a costing exercise to be done for Western Europe as a whole, or at least for the EEC, Switzerland and Austria, covering public transport travel on journeys between roughly 150 and 1,200 miles. Separate sets of projections may exist for travel by air, rail and bus, each based on annual percentage increases expected in the light of the rates of increase in each mode observed in recent years. By putting together the projections for the separate modes we could obtain a single projection of public transport as a whole. There is no good reason why the total package should continue to be split among the available modes in the same way as in the past; environmental protection and conservation of resources tend to favour rail rather than the alternatives.

Within the total package two divisions might be made, first into distance groups, second into types of route, major and minor. Similar calculations might be made for freight traffic.

Having established the totals and sub-totals we could then estimate the total costs, operating, vehicle and infrastructure, assuming various distributions between the available modes.

On the passenger-side some proportion (maybe 10, 20, 30 or 40 per cent) is almost certain to go by rail, another proportion (maybe 10 or 20 per cent) is almost certain to go by air. In between there is a large load that is prospectively interchangeable between the two. Having fixed the proportions in these three groups we want to compare the costs of moving different proportions of the interchangeable group by air and by rail; with freight the main items to be compared are rail and road, with water as a significant element (environmentally preferable to all others) in parts of the area.

We have some rough data from which to start. On major routes with heavy traffic, rail operating costs are likely to be relatively low, and to fall with increasing loads. Both operating and vehicle costs on the main section of the package are likely to be lower by rail than by air. We know too that in order to enable the European railway system to carry a substantial part of the interchangeable section of the market in attractive conditions very big investments in infrastructure would be needed. But probably 3,000 miles of new double track would be needed, even to provide a minimum rail service south of Paris and Cologne. If these improvements were undertaken as separate operations, without a full-scale Channel tunnel railway system to produce ample through traffic, each separate piece would have spare capacity, producing diseconomies. The additional investment in infrastructure, needed to accommodate a large share of the interchangeable section of the package, might not be large in comparison with the additional investment in airports and their access routes that would be needed to accommodate the same load by air.

Separate calculations by each nationalized industry, in each of several countries, of the likely returns to given investment-options, are not alone enough. In the long run no one of these options can adequately be calculated in isolation from the European whole of which it is a part.

Advocacy of a full analysis of the comparisons might well be condemned as an unrealistic demand for utopian transformation of planning methods; yet such an analysis is both practicable and desirable; and Europe has available to it the contrasting lessons of American and Japanese experience.

Taking Europe as a whole, the additional rail investment, particularly in the London–Paris–Ruhr area, would be likely to produce a rather high return, because it would increase the return on the various plans which are either decided or contemplated outside the quadrilateral.

The next stage should be an analysis of the freight market, where once again there is a future load which can be seen as interchangeable between rail and road.

Until we know something more about the fundamental comparison between air and rail, and road and rail, for the interchangeable parts of the passenger and freight markets, in terms of resources needed, fragmentary costing exercises, calculating the likely financial return to particular schemes, are merely diversions from the essential task.

14

Further arguments and answers

This chapter will present some arguments, which have not emerged as yet, but which might be expected to be put against any questioning of the decision to build a third London airport. The most revolutionary part of this alternative programme involves exploitation of the new capacities of railways, and most of the arguments will be related to the new use of railways which has been advocated in earlier chapters.

Some of the arguments are claims that it is, in any case, disadvantageous to develop the railways at the expense of part, even a small part, of the airlines' future business; some arguments take up a few likely popular reactions.

These are all what we might call long-term arguments, whose validity has not changed with the passage of time. Each argument will be stated in italics, followed by a reply.

If these replies, together with the arguments of Parts One and Two of this book, are valid, they show only that the Government ought, in 1968, to have instituted inquiries with much wider terms of reference than those given to the Roskill Commission. Alternatively, they show that in 1971, confronted with the dreadful dilemma posed by Roskill's findings, the Government should have instituted a new inquiry into the timing of the need for the airport, with full consideration of the options that had been considered only partially and piecemeal.

But what about 1973? The developments of the past two years produce new arguments against a change of plan. Even if mistakes were made in 1968–71, is it not now too late to think about a remedy?

The last group of questions, relating to the position in 1973, will be discussed in the second section of this chapter.

1. *A synoptic review would be too difficult to organize, too slow and too costly, involving too many governments and railway managements.*

This difficulty is probably less great than it looks at first sight. Our European partners are less committed to air movement than we are. They already have their plans for railway development, and the insertion of a big new load of travellers to and from England into their principal routes would give added justification to plans already under consideration.

2. *Even if all these snags were disposed of, there would be great difficulty in securing agreement over the financial details, national shares of contributions and revenue, and so on.*

This pessimistic view assumes that greedy and suspicious haggling by short-sighted national interests among the European nations would frustrate the achievement of a solution beneficial to all together and to each severally. Such a fear is not groundless, in view of past experience. However,

(*a*) the European railway systems have succeeded in settling such problems among themselves reasonably well in the past;

(*b*) with so much to gain from a rail-based solution the French national interest would have strong grounds for helping it to work.

(*c*) Here is a real task for the EEC to tackle, and a British initiative such as this would be a sound and realistic contribution to collective European interests, material and symbolic. Banal but important issues like the pricing of sleeping-car accommodation ought to be capable of being dealt with sensibly.

3. *People want to go by air, and they will continue to want to do so. Why should they be forced to go by train instead?*

In terms of public opinion currently articulated, and demonstrated by the choices that people are making now, this argument seems quite impressive – if you forget that in providing a more eligible option for some people, you are not forcing them to use it.

That opinion is based on people's experience of the modes of travel that have been available until now, and these modes include not only the process of being conveyed for the main part of the journey, but the business of organizing the journey, finding out the timetable and the price, buying the ticket and reserving the seat. They also include the process of getting to and away from the train or aircraft, the quality and comfort of the station or airport facilities, and arrangements for dealing with baggage.

On all these counts air transport today is on the whole more eligible than rail transport. But there is no need for the objective difference in quality of service to continue. Public opinion is judging on the basis of a body of experience which is not a valid guide to the potential alternatives.

There is no question of forcing people to go by train. The scheme put forward in this book allows for a continuing air element in the short- and middle-distance travel pattern. For distances up to 400 miles the improved rail travel envisaged, being no slower than air, more convenient and less restless, and at half the price, should attract the share of the market envisaged. The advantages of overnight travel, expounded in Chapter 7, should similarly be attractive enough. With rail movement on this scale, the journey-ends should no longer have the uncivilized qualities that they have, regrettably, today.

If the calculation should turn out to be over-optimistic, further incentives to choose rail could be created by fiscal devices. It would be easy to justify a tax on take-off and landing at London airports. Such a tax would be a source of revenue akin to the present taxes on motoring in excess of the cost of the roads, and no less appropriate. There is nothing novel or remarkable about taxes with a regulatory purpose, or designed to secure a social objective. There is no need to doubt the potential effect of such a tax as an influence on the balance of demand; and given that air travellers impose some penalties on the rest of the community, such a tax is not merely justifiable but positively appropriate.

Private motorists pay about a penny per vehicle mile to the state over and above the cost of providing the roads, and there is nothing wrong with this. It is regularly argued that they should pay up to ten times this amount for travel in congested areas. We have not brought in road-pricing for urban roads, because the problems, including the cost, are so daunting. Air travel is at least as valid an object of taxation. If taxation is merely a neutral way of raising revenue, it would help to recoup past subsidies; if taxation has a social purpose, it is more valid still. An air-travel tax would be essentially 'progressive' (rather more so than a tax on motoring); it would reflect the damage that air travellers inflict on those not travelling; differential charges as between airports could be compared with urban road-pricing, but would be less difficult to impose effectively.

4 (*a*). *This whole scheme looks like a nasty piece of elitism. Just as technology and its associated affluence are putting air travel within reach of more and more people, this scheme would restrict the circle of people able to enjoy it.*

This radical line is really the same argument as the last, put in more emotive terms. It is based on false premises. Air travel would still be available on all the routes where it is available now, and its increase on routes to the southern Mediterranean would be unaffected. The British public, scattered through the country, would gain through the availability of more holiday flights from nearby airports. They would also have more options open to them for shorter journeys.

If, through heavy use, the railways could carry people to desirable destinations more cheaply, the effect would be to widen the circle of people able to travel, not to narrow it.

The scheme envisaged in this book, involving no new London airport, would indirectly put air travel to more remote, non-railable destinations within reach of more people, by reducing the overall average real cost of all air journeys. Maplin airport must be paid for. The right people to pay for it are the travellers through all London airports, and the Government's plan to charge higher rates to aircraft using Heathrow is a very proper device for spreading the charge. (In fact a large part of the cost of Maplin will be borne by the taxpayer for many years, but air travellers will have to bear a share which ought to be heavy.) If there were no new airport the air travellers would not have to bear this burden.

Travellers terminating in British regions would be particularly hard-hit by Maplin. They would have not only to contribute to the cost of its construction but suffer the cost, delay and inconvenience of journeys between a London airport and their terminal point.

If Maplin raises the cost per unit of travel, and the travellers ultimately pay the price, the number of people able to travel will be reduced. All would-be travellers will be asked to pay a contribution which will really be a tax to cover the cost of inefficient planning.

4 (*b*). *Well, then, if by not building the new London airport, we could have increased the number of people able and likely to travel,*

what is there in this for the environment? More travel means more environmental damage, so why encourage it?

This is the obverse of the 'elitist' argument. It brings us back to the great dilemma which faces contemporary society. Everyone wants more consumption, but most consumption damages the environment and uses resources which may become scarce. But if we have two options, either to consume 120 units at a cost of 80 units of environmental damage, or to consume 100 units at a cost of 100 units of environmental damage, we ought to choose the former. If the former choice is the sounder on economic grounds too, the reasons for choosing it are strengthened. Planners can count themselves exceptionally lucky if a choice presents itself to them so easily. But if they fail to do their homework they may miss out, because they have not made the necessary calculations.

5. *There is no sign of any significant section of public opinion, with a direct interest in the matter, which systematically opposes the third airport.*

We may divide opinion on the matter into three groups:

(*a*) *Many people in the London area welcome the airport scheme because they think it will reduce the aircraft noise to which they are now subjected, or at least halt its increase.*

This rests on a number of fallacies, based on the inadequacy of the information now available to the public:

(i) Heathrow and Gatwick are much more acceptable than Maplin for air operations. Under pressure Ministers have admitted that these existing airports will be used to capacity even when Maplin is in operation.

(ii) The number of people subjected to disturbance by aircraft noise would be increased by the extension of that noise to a new area.

(iii) A rail-based solution to European transport needs would mean that in 1980–90 the total amount of disturbance by aircraft noise, in southern England and in Europe as a whole, would be less than it would be under the current plan.

The diversions envisaged in this book would actually reduce the traffic at Heathrow by a greater amount than the reduction foreseen by Roskill through the operations of the third airport. Roskill puts the load for the third airport at around 20 million passengers a year by 1985 and 30 million by 1990.[1] This is less than the number which could reasonably be diverted to railways by that date, in addition to the projection of the number allowed for in Roskill's calculations.

(*b*) *There is no really substantial local opposition to Foulness. Considering the trouble, and the perfectly valid objections, raised by nearly every motorway and other public works scheme, it is marvellous to find a project causing as little trouble as this one.*

It is true that the local opposition in Essex has not been substantial. But the present peacefulness is misleading. It will be a different story when the first plans for the lines of the access motorway and rapid-transport system are published – particularly within London. We have not yet begun to take into account the effects of these complaints on public opinion. Whatever corridor is chosen, the people affected by it will have allies among those not affected : 'Why should these thousands suffer in order that the millions may go by air, when they could have gone harmlessly by train instead, more cheaply and conveniently for themselves and with less damage to the community?'

(*c*) *There is no significant section of public opinion, on a national scale, which systematically opposes the principle of a third airport. Where a piece of government policy is, for once, generally popular, why bother to look at it again?*

Broadly speaking, this argument is correct and a reply to it is not easy. Sir Alec Cairncross, reflecting in 1968 on his experience as the Government's Chief Economic Adviser in the early 1960s, wrote : 'Policy takes shape in a climate of opinion; and without the support of public opinion cannot be persevered in.'[2] As a corollary, when you have a policy which seems to agree with the climate of opinion, don't mess about with it. Ministers are too busy with their difficulties to go back to topics on which they have, albeit only in the short run, a smooth passage.

There has been opposition in plenty, in the pages of *The Economist*, in the press, and in a small minority of parliamentary speeches, but nothing systematic, no full argument presenting the possibilities of an alternative. Public opinion has largely gone by default, because nobody has had time to take a thorough look at the problem on a rational basis.

6. *The present plans for the European Airbus and Lockheed Tristar depend on sales. Public money is already committed to these projects. If the European air market is to be multiplied by only three in the next fifteen years, instead of six, it will not be so good*

for the aircraft industry, on which our prosperity depends, prosperity depends . . . etc. If 10 to 15 billion passenger miles were switched from air the new trains might replace 100 new aircraft of these types for the London–Europe market alone. A similar switch to rail throughout Europe would mean at least 200 fewer aircraft sold.

The reply begins with a question. Does transport exist to subserve one particular transport-equipment industry, or does the whole equipment industry exist to serve transport?

In any case, the European demand for these new aircraft would still be substantial and the world demand would still rise fast enough, in all probability, for it not to need to be fostered by industry-oriented policies. Furthermore, even if we do look to the British and European aircraft industry as an absolute, its prosperity could perhaps be best promoted through a hard, strong push with VTOL or STOL, and that would not be encouraged by a policy of providing long-runway airports for all the expected air-travel demand of the next 20 years. Tristars and airbuses are only a small part of the story. World air traffic outside the Communist bloc amounted to 251 billion passenger miles in 1970. A slowly declining annual 10 per cent growth would put the load in 1980 at 650 billion.[3] If we carry that projection forward we have a figure of about 900 to 1,000 billion for 1985. It can be assumed that by 1985 most aircraft now in service will have been scrapped. Those which will still survive will provide no more than 100 billion of the total passenger miles. On our extrapolation of the IATA estimate, therefore, enough new aircraft would be needed between now and 1985 to provide 800 to 900 billion passenger miles by that year. We have envisaged a switch to rail within Western Europe of about 80 per cent of projected trunk-route air traffic up to 400 miles and 60 per cent between 400 and 1,000 miles, probably amounting to 20 million to 40 billion passenger miles.

The switch to rail would not affect the demand for new aircraft significantly until about 1980; during the 1980s the annual demand for new aircraft would still rise, but slowly. This would hardly be a disaster for the aircraft industry. Also, new types of aircraft could be expected to accelerate the replacement rate, and if VTOL/STOL are successfully developed as major transport-carriers they could have some positive effect on demand after about 1985, unless by that time people had lost enthusiasm for air travel.

What we really need to do is to balance the relatively small ad-

201

vantage of selling Tristars or airbuses against the much greater economic and other advantages which might arise from a change of direction.

If we are concerned with the health of British and European industry, it should be noted that the resources required for construction of the railway vehicles will be an alternative outlet for industrial activity comparable in scope to that which would otherwise be devoted to the manufacture of additional aeroplanes. It should involve British railway-equipment manufacturing workshops. They are now being run down and there is a considerable problem of redundancy which nobody seems to be worrying about. An energetic rail investment policy would bring increased employment in this sector. Particularly at the sub-contracting level many of the same skills are required by both sectors.

What about the economic advantages as between the two industrial activities? Western Europe is relatively advanced in preparing the way for the construction of railway equipment capable of travelling at high speeds. The eventual market for such equipment is not restricted to Western Europe. The scope for exporting material of this kind to other parts of the world may well be superior to the scope for exporting aircraft. Eastern Europe and the Soviet Union, in particular, rely very heavily on railway transport and have been inclined until now to lag far behind Western Europe in the speed and efficiency of their passenger railway-transport systems. There is virtually no prospect of sales of aircraft to Eastern Europe; the prospects of export arrangements with new high-speed railway equipment to this market would appear to be good. A very large Western European domestic railway-equipment industry would be a sound basis for a development of exports not only to Eastern Europe but to many other parts of the world. Western Europe's position in this field seems to be prospectively much better than its position in the aircraft industry.

7. *London airports are great earners of foreign currency. These earnings should not be jeopardized.*

The BAA's Annual Report for 1970–1 (p. 15) includes the statement that the eight million foreign visitors who arrived and departed on international air services through the Authority's airports spent more than £300 million in foreign currency in the United Kingdom. This looks a harmless enough statement, not very significant for our discussion; but when we find the Chairman, Sir Peter

Masefield, telling the Roskill Commission in 1968 that Heathrow alone was responsible for £200 million a year in foreign currency, we have to pay some attention.

Foreign visitors' spending in the UK is made possible by their journeys, but the mode of transport is immaterial. The improved railways envisaged in this book would generate new traffic and increase the amount of foreign currency spent. In any case we have then to deduct spending abroad by British travellers; the last two years have seen a small surplus for the first time since such records began.

If we are to deal with relevant facts we should rather concern ourselves with the statement that in 1970–1 the BAA contributed directly towards the national balance of payments some £10·6 million earned from operations based abroad. By 1985 this could be expected to rise to £50 million at 1970 prices; a transfer to rail of 20 per cent of the total traffic might reduce that figure to £40 million.

That loss is meaningless when considered alone. We should subtract British airlines' spending at foreign airports and add the net foreign earnings of British airlines which would be sacrificed through the transfer to rail. But then we should have to take into account the effects of the railway operations on the balance of payments. As 80 per cent of, say, 15 billion passenger-miles would be on European continental tracks, there could be some disadvantage, though this could be minimized if the rolling-stock were British-owned.

Some of the airports' existing earnings presumably come directly or indirectly from passengers' spending at airport duty-free shops. They may enjoy the joke of receiving what amounts to a bonus of £3 each from purchases of goods which escape tax. But the amounts which they spend, and the profits earned both by the airport authorities and by the concessionaires, are hardly worth considering in a serious calculation.[4]

The airlines also benefit from tax-free sales in flight. An aeroplane seems to be a singularly inefficient and high-rental cigarette and liquor shop by any normal standards, though perhaps not so bad for selling watches and cameras which have little bulk or weight in relation to their value. Both they and their passengers are now enjoying a veritable bonanza at the public's expense.

By 1985 it is quite possible that this gift to human cupidity (and concealed subsidies to air operators) will no longer be dispensed.

It would be distinctly comic if the loss of tax revenue to government and the loss to the balance of payments were regarded as an issue to be taken into account in calculating the economic costs and benefits of alternative transport systems.

It would be absurd and wrong if international air passengers enjoyed this bonus while rail travellers did not.

8. *London's role as a major interchange point for international passengers must not be jeopardized.*

A third London airport would jeopardize this role seriously unless all international traffic were moved there. It is quite clear that any interchange involving a journey between airports is unsatisfactory for the passengers. In London's case it is bad for the local transport system too. With three major airports all in operation, the occasions for inter-airport transfer would be more numerous than with two.

Meanwhile, the increase in total world air-traffic will increase the variety of direct links in all directions. The proportion of journeys necessitating interchange will decline; the absolute number of such journeys may increase, but at a much-reduced rate. However, the choice of interchange points will also grow; there will be a relatively reduced role for London in particular. Some British regional airports might well enter the field, particularly for travellers terminating at other British regional airports, and possibly for some travellers between two foreign airports. If London loses some international interchange traffic to Amsterdam, there will be some immediate loss of foreign-currency earnings at the airport, and indirectly some loss of business for British operators. But a spreading of London's air traffic over more airports will tend to drive people to use other routes anyway. Our final estimates suggest that it ought to be possible to keep the number of terminating passengers at London airports so well within the capacity of the existing airports up to 1990 that there will be plenty of room for accommodating the interchanging passengers who would want to use London in addition. Some net gain of interchangers at Amsterdam is quite likely in any case; the addition of Maplin to London's pattern would be likely to increase Amsterdam's gain rather than to diminish it.

The importance of London's role as an interchange point for international journeys would seem likely to be best served by keeping all the major scheduled traffic at Heathrow; but this object could probably best be achieved if the growth of total London air traffic were restrained through the transfers envisaged in this book.

9. *Paris is just completing its new major airport at Roissy-en-France, to replace le Bourget. London must not fall behind. Its main airport must be bigger and better than any serving Paris.*

In so far as this argument expresses mere childish competitiveness, it cannot and need not be answered. In so far as it is based on fear of loss of foreign-currency earnings, it has been answered above.

10. *The Maplin scheme is important for the plan to reduce the population within the Greater London Council area. A movement of people to South Essex is important to that plan, and the whole development off Foulness Island would help the project.*

First, the airport city would be in South-East Essex, not South Essex – and there is a real difference. Secondly, the existence of the airport will tend to discourage diversion of traffic away from London's airport system. Many travellers would be brought to London, including central London, who would not otherwise go there at all. There would probably be a net addition to jobs in central London and a very large addition to jobs in the South-East.

The building of Maplin in the 1970s would be likely to prejudice those very objectives – highly praiseworthy in themselves – which some London planners wish the airport to subserve.[5]

11. *There have all along been many interests lined up in favour of a third airport and the greatest possible expansion of air travel. Almost all the industrial, commercial and administrative interests involved would have been likely to oppose any serious search for a new transport pattern involving a switch of growth to rail.*

These interests would include :

(*a*) The whole aerospace interest, industrial and commercial, with the possible exception of the VTOL/STOL section of it.

(*b*) The established defence interests, which are identified with aerospace.

(*c*) Road interests and construction interests.

(*d*) Tourist interests, package-tour operators (though a rationalization of routes and modes would do them more good than harm).

(*e*) Several big trade unions.

(*f*) Several Government Departments.

The arguments of most of these bodies might well be sectional and biased, but they seem a formidable array.

No particular producer-interest in Britain would expect to benefit from the abandonment of Maplin airport in part exchange for a perfected Channel-tunnel system. Even for British Rail the rapid-transit line to Maplin holds out the prospect of more passenger miles by 1985 than the perfected line to the tunnel. If Maplin's load attains the predicted maximum of 125 million passengers a year, the mass-transit link will surely need to carry 100 million of them.

From the narrowest point of view the Maplin mass-transit line must look attractive to the railway man. On this short journey there will be no need to use space for catering facilities. Trains with 1,000 seats can be envisaged, and in the conditions of this journey 80 per cent seat occupation should be easily achieved. One would not expect British Rail to rush to give up this huge captive market which, on the present plans, would rise from a billion to 5 billion passenger miles a year during the 1990s, free of any uncertainties and awkwardnesses which might arise from the negotiations needed for the European railway routes.

All this is true. Even the other advantages which British Rail might derive from the absence of an airport, added to the immediate Channel-tunnel traffic, could not be guaranteed to surpass the benefit to their accounts which the mass-transit line could bring. But a cumulation of sectional interests is not always the same as a public interest shared by millions of disparate individuals.

THE ARGUMENTS IN 1973: POSTPONEMENT COSTS

1. *It is already too late to go back on the decision to build the airport. The reopening of the question would do great harm.*

(*a*) *Indecision and vacillation are bad in themselves.*

True, but this is not conclusive with respect to every imaginable case. Ever since the Concorde project began it has been too late to abandon it, and that is the main reason why it survived until 1973. In this case of the airport we would do well to look more closely at the balance of advantage and disadvantage involved in the timing of irrevocable decisions.

(*b*) *Much work has already been done in preparing for the building of Maplin airport. We are already nearing the end of the two years of work on the planning and detailed design of the airport, which Roskill (Report, 5.4) said would be needed before construction could begin.*

The damage and waste caused through going ahead unnnecessarily would infinitely exceed the costs of a decision to suspend activities, even when the pride of those who have committed themselves to the scheme is taken into account.

(c) *A considerable apparatus has been in existence for two years, involving many civil servants, local authority officers and others. It has already made much progress in preparing the plans for runways and buildings, and for the access routes. Is all this work to be thrown away?*

Supposing we do reopen the whole issue. An assessment of the alternative would take time. We do not know what the findings would be. They might find that the first Foulness runway would still be needed by 1980, or that it could be deferred until 1985 or 1988 or some indefinite date after that. The processes now working on it would have to continue in the meantime. What about the morale of the people involved in them? What about the expenditure on their operations?

The reply to this is that we must be, and are, prepared to plan for different contingencies. The process must involve a certain amount of work which seems to be wasted. Some fringe waste is inevitable with most plans. In relation to the total at stake, with economic and environmental factors taken into account, the fringe waste in nullifying the work done so far might well be trivial, even now.

(d) *Various interests have already committed resources to the new airport.*

If we have reached a point at which the abandonment of Maplin would entail heavy compensation payments, the cost of such compensation would have to be weighed against the long-term financial and other consequences. A net saving of many hundreds of millions of pounds might make any compensation seem trivial by comparison.

At this point a compromise solution might envisage only a small single-runway airport on Maplin Sands, dealing with German, Scandinavian and East European traffic, giving some minor relief to Heathrow and Gatwick. It would have some intrinsic merit as a safeguard in case transfer to rail and regional airports ran into trouble; but its main justification would be as a rescue from the embarrassment created by the over-hasty decision of 1971.

2. *Supposing a new inquiry should disclose insuperable objections to a new combination of options? The inquiry would take some*

time. We are not even quite sure that the Channel tunnel can be built; there is no joint agreement on railway development; the arguments about spontaneous transfer to regional airports may be mistaken. If the London airports' traffic overtakes their capacity in 1980, and the new airport is not ready, we shall be in trouble.

We ought to be able to settle these problems by 1975. If the programme of building Maplin had to be put back for up to two years, so that it would be ready by 1982, interim measures, with very little speculative element to them, could hold the London airports' traffic down during the interval. The new fast trains will be running to the North of England and Scotland by that time. A faster rate of switch to rail than Roskill envisaged could give relief up to the equivalent of one year's London air-traffic growth. It would not be unthinkable to distribute up to 3 million London–transatlantic charter passengers among several regional airports with spare runway capacity, e.g. Liverpool, Manchester, Birmingham and Castle Donington, as an interim measure. If they then lost this American traffic on the opening of Maplin any additional capacity created to deal with the temporary transatlantic load would be useful for their own growth afterwards, and would encourage it. All this could produce a little of the relief at Heathrow, etc., which would not come otherwise. Either way, even a losing gamble would be likely to bring overall advantages in the long run.

By 1973 new trends can be seen in the development of demand for runway space at the existing airports. The growth of traffic has slowed down; average aircraft-size has increased and seems likely to continue to rise faster than Roskill expected and allowed for. The previously-expected date of a saturation, even without any changes, already looks likely to be deferred until 1982 or later. There is now time for the reappraisal that was always needed.

3. *Technological developments since 1971 give ground for increased confidence that the menace of aircraft noise will soon be so much alleviated that this ground for objection to the aeroplane should be largely removed by the late 1980s. Why then seek to check the growth of air transport, just as the main environmental damage caused by it is on the point of being cured?*

If anything, this point helps the argument of this book, by reducing the main objection to traffic growth at regional airports. The diversions to rail and regional airports would keep the air traffic at existing London airports within the same limits as the diversions to

Maplin, so new optimism about noise does not affect the London area one way or the other, though the diversions envisaged in this book might well exceed those which Maplin would produce. They would certainly help the Luton area. But this book does envisage a greater increase of air traffic at some regional airports. If the new technology reduces noise the main objection to *those* diversions is removed.

4. *By 1973 the additional schemes for development in the Maplin area were seen to have great merit on their own account. There will be a major port for oil-tankers and container-ships, bigger than any that could go into the existing Thames Estuary docks. The Maplin scheme is meritorious precisely because it is comprehensive, covering transport by sea as well as air, and at the same time developing southern Essex.*

The reply to this argument, as it presented itself in 1971, has been discussed above, on page 34, but some further points may now be added. Taking into account the port facilities, existing, under development or planned, at Southampton, in the Severn Estuary and elsewhere, the need for a Maplin port can be judged only in the light of a full survey of national dock facilities, which must include an analysis of the actual and potential capacity of pipelines and of road and rail links between the ports and the final areas of origin and destination of the oil, containers and other freight concerned. Maplin is well placed geographically for access to the eastern half of the South-East region – an area containing perhaps 10 to 15 per cent of the national population. For all other parts of Britain other port-areas are better. All access to Maplin, except by water, involves new pipelines, rail or road construction. As a comprehensive plan it needs more justification than has yet been presented.

PART THREE

The Airport Question and the Political System

15

The Governmental view

It is one thing to argue the merits of one policy, as against alternatives, on public welfare grounds. It is another thing to expect a Government to follow the same line of reasoning. The sources of its decisions are in general fourfold: values, interests, constraints and information. The sources overlap one another. Where a sectional interest coincides with the Government's own values the two cannot easily be unravelled, and an interest may contribute to the formation of a Government's values. The two together may determine the direction of inquiry in pursuit of information. An instrumental policy, developed to promote a value, may in its turn attain the status of a value in the scheme of motivations.

We may see the following forces at work in leading to the airport decision:

1. *Values*:

   National greatness $\rightarrow$ military power $\rightarrow$ technological achievement $\Big\}$ $\rightarrow$ aircraft industry.

2. *Constraints*:

   Balance of payments $\rightarrow$ support exporting industries $\rightarrow$ aircraft industry.

3. *Information*:

   Aircraft industry $\rightarrow$ airports on existing pattern $\rightarrow$ London airports.

A secondary value entered the picture in the 1960s:
Environment $\rightarrow$ no airport at damaging inland site $\rightarrow$ airport at Foulness.

Neither values nor interests nor constraints promoted any desire to ask whether it might be possible to do without an airport.

The doctrine that a new London airport was needed was an expression of the principle of 'more of the same thing'. The decision was incremental because it was not based on a study of needs as a whole and ignored new technologies and trends. Adapting the Dimocks' words, there was no thought of initiating more urgent and progressive lines of activity to supplement or partially to replace an older one.[1] But this incrementalism had to have a starting-point. The airport dogma was a by-product of a love for aviation and all its works, a love which has three roots – defence, national prestige, and the promotion of exports, visible and invisible. The aviation industry subserves all these ends, and a patriotic value-system might be expected to support it. Aircraft manufacture has been consistently fostered, with the promotion of Concorde as the most spectacular recent expression of this fostering. For many years before 1968 a whole array of beliefs and slogans identifying aviation with the national interest were common currency, scarcely requiring any promotional activity by the manufacturers themselves, and they had a status within the very consciousness of government, a status that had the quality of a mystique.

For some decades around 1900 British policy towards the shipping industry was similarly positive. We may quote from the 1918 Report of a Departmental Committee appointed to consider the position of the ship-building and shipping industries after the war: 'Since the middle of the last century the navigation policy of this country has been based on the great ascendancy of the British mercantile marine. . . The maritime supremacy of the Empire must be maintained at all costs.'[2] The means proposed in that Report involved absence of subsidy or restraint, and the Empire's maritime supremacy was not maintained. Shipping was once part of Britain's greatness. When the special quality of maritime power, with the inter-linking of the navy with the shipyards and civil shipping services, no longer had the same quality as expressions of national sentiment, no longer the same imperial significance, aerospace could arguably be said to have moved imperceptibly into the position which shipping had once held.

Politicians' identification with aerospace, particularly since 1940, has been amply illustrated from ministerial speeches in Parliament. In another context it has been suggested that the Ministry of Aviation's record is 'an awful warning of how, when broader responsibilities are taken away, government agencies can become lobbies financed by the tax-payer'.[3] It looks like an example of the working of C. Wright Mills' military-industrial complex,[4] a danger recognized by President Eisenhower in his speech at the end of his term of office.

The phenomenon was not peculiar to Britain; its character is thoroughly Gaullist. In France, for example, bureaucracy and politicians have consistently been enthusiastic supporters of the Concorde project, with less popular opposition than in Britain. The Labour Party's leadership at least thought seriously of dropping that project on coming into office in 1964, only to be confronted with the advice that their predecessors had left them with no escape clause[5] – and neither Gaullist France nor the Soviet Union admitted rational doubt to ruffle confidence in the supreme piece of promotional activity which the supersonic transport aircraft represents.

Patriotic beliefs can easily produce a mythology of their own, and the Roskill Commission itself declared a positive sympathy with the prevailing view. The final chapter of its Report refers, with more rhetoric than elegance, to an earlier White Paper on London's Airports (Cmnd. 8902, 1953):

The phrase 'London is the Clapham Junction of the air' was no mere chauvinistic cry. It represented the deeply and sincerely held views of the economic and political importance of maintaining the position of this country as one of the two foremost aviation nations of the western world and as the leading aviation nation of Western Europe.

The gratuitous denial of chauvinism leads to just a faint suspicion that there might be something else in all this than sober assessment of economic and social utility.

We have argued that the Government's rigidity on the need for a new airport had a starting-point in a value system within the administration itself; a value system so closely identified with aerospace that it could not readily be modified. That value system may be seen as a response to a number of inputs.

First was the prestige or glamour, call it what you will, of everything to do with aerospace. Many utterances of Ministers,[6] of both major parties, show that they were affected by considerations of this kind, spurred on by international competition in a world in which many other countries foster their airlines with mad abandon. Total losses of all world airlines in 1971 are estimated at £160 million, mainly paid for by taxpayers. (No wonder, when you see a dozen airline offices in and just off Regent Street, occupying 600 feet of the most expensive street-frontage in the world, with 50 visible staff and a dozen customers in all of them put together.)

Secondly, closely connected with this, was the close link between aerospace and military effectiveness.

Third was a public opinion broadly favourable to aerospace technology and to air travel.

Fourth was the ability of aircraft manufacturers and airline operators to earn foreign currency and to make a contribution to the balance of payments which has tended to grow with the increase in air travel, though the overall effect of the whole apparatus on the balance may not be as favourable, when everything is taken into account, as is commonly supposed.

Fifth was the demand of the suppliers of air travel to grow and keep on growing : airlines, the Airports Authority, the aircraft-manufacturers, the companies as institutions (if not as capitalist profit-makers), supported by their trade unions.

All of these demands add up quite clearly to a need for a new airport, maintaining the health of the aircraft industry and London's proud place as the world's greatest centre for international air travel. Together they seem to have evoked in the government machine, political and administrative, a self-standing identification with a given set of assumptions so close that change would have been structurally difficult as well as agonizing.

These assumptions included a special role for London as the Clapham Junction of the air. The provincial airports fell outside the framework and objectives which London's international air market represented. The wave of regional policy, which began about 1962 and was pushed forward, for a time, by the Labour Government, passed them by. Any national policy for airports would have been an excrescence on the London-oriented policy : hence the 'dilatoriness' in developing any plan in the absence of a firm ministerial lead.[7]

Where a value system has become solidly established, the machinery of government which subserves it tends to become an end in itself. A Departmental line may be in theory the administrators' response to the requirements of their political masters, but once a line has been established the defence of the line may attain immense importance to them. They must not suffer the humiliation of being forced to abandon a position, and if they have been objectively wrong their error must be covered up. In the extreme example, the Dreyfus case, the military bureaucracy really believed that an admission of error would destroy the very fabric of authority.

It may be fair to go back to John Stuart Mill, and see in the story of the third airport policy, from Stansted in the 1960s onwards, an example which illustrates some of his fears. Mill suggested that if government was not adequately representative, it could have adequate competence only if it was bureaucratic; yet at the same time he noted the danger that bureaucracies 'perish by the immutability of their maxims'.[8] Committee structures, accommodations between sections of the administration, attain an independent validity of their own.

Modern bureaucracy in its English form is probably distinguished at least as much by something akin to Weber's 'collegiality' as by hierarchy, and the attitudes on the third airport may be regarded as an instance of the group solidarity which may develop among officials, and which R. K. Merton has observed to be a quality that may of itself generate opposition to change.[9] We may also note Philip Selznick's argument that sub-units set up goals of their own which may conflict with the purposes of the organization as a whole;[10] but in this case the major organization could not see the conflict and remained passive.

In terms of the administration's internal value system, structures had been set up in order to serve the general purpose of the growth of aviation, and these in their turn acquired a validity of their own. It was not only that 'Britain needs an expanding aviation: an expanding aviation needs a new London airport' acquired the force of a slogan which must not be questioned. At the same time, a whole system of committees and relationships within the machine had been built up under the umbrella of that slogan. There was no structure within the machine capable of nurturing any criticism of the values or sub-values.

There is ample evidence, from the behaviour of the bureaucracy in the Stansted period, that the need for a third airport had already by then attained the status of an independent value, to be defended against any attack. Service for the cause excused blatant error, even when it was exposed as such.[11]

Aviation policy was formed within one compartment, and where other compartments impinged upon it the relations had to be defined and set into a pattern which reduced the scope for flexibility. Defence had the advantage of being first in the field; physical planning came second and made its impact; synoptic transport-planning had no constituency.

One battle was lost with the setting up of the Roskill Commission, a second with the rejection of Cublington, though this was not resisted. But the fundamental value, that the need for a third airport should not be questioned, was maintained. The limited terms of reference given to the Roskill Commission went most of the way towards ensuring that the inquiry would not make a synoptic analysis of the fundamental question, and when partial questions were raised the partial answers were successful in forestalling any deeper probing. Even in August 1972 the Department of Trade and Industry still reports that about 80 per cent of the national aviation effort is concentrated in the South-East,[12] as though a change in balance through regional spread of air services were both impossible and undesirable. (But, far from being impossible, it is visibly taking place, and other government policy for encouraging the regions ought to welcome such a change.)

The bureaucracy's 'dilatoriness' in starting to prepare a national plan for airports cannot be explained by mere incompetence; it is plausible to suggest that the very process of preparing such a plan would have wrought damage to the third London airport dogma. The entrenched bureaucratic positions were breached in 1968, but only in so far as they insisted on the Stansted site. On the main issue they would have succumbed only to a determined political direction supported from the highest level. It is clear that there was no such direction in 1968, still less in 1971. We have some evidence about the proceedings of 1967–8, but for 1971 we can only note the apparently complete ministerial identification with the airport dogma; only Mr Noble said that he would like to question it, but was convinced that it could not be questioned.

In his 800-page account of Labour's six years in office Mr Wilson makes at least twenty separate references to the aircraft industry, but he mentions the question of the third London airport only once, as one of the seven troubles that beset him in the Whitsun recess of 1967. It is worth quoting this mention in its context. After referring to some overseas problem, Mr Wilson continues:

At home, the conference season saw one union after another pressing resolutions condemning Government policy on prices and incomes. Defeat became certain at the TUC Congress and the Labour party conference. A grumbling row over the siting of London's third airport erupted into a full-scale campaign by the 'not at Stansted' lobby; the issue had not been well-handled by the departments.

On a somewhat lighter side, a campaign developed against the Government's decision to clamp down on the maritime pirate radios, adding a new and mainly youthful element to the demonstrators I had to face whenever I went about the country.

Some of these matters provided a formidable agenda for a fortnight's recess.

This was a few weeks before the Opposition motion of censure, which is not mentioned, and nine months before the Government's decision to abandon its rigid commitment to Stansted after all; there is no reference to the appointment of the Roskill Commission, although Mr Gordon Walker tells us that the Stansted plan, a subject of prolonged discussion in Standing or *ad hoc* Cabinet Committees, was clearly of such importance that it was all along taken for granted that it would in due course be put on the Cabinet agenda.[13] He also tells us that the matter came before the Cabinet in 1967, 'because there was no other machinery for preparatory investigation of such a question'.[14]

The Cabinet found it very hard to reach a decision and considered the matter at length at three or four meetings. The conclusion [ie. to stick with Stansted] was a reluctant one forced upon Ministers by what appeared to be unanswerable arguments.

The eventual decision to set up an *ad hoc* commission of inquiry was made by the Cabinet, though Mr Gordon Walker emphasizes that the Cabinet would have to take the final decision on 'a matter of such high importance'. Mr Wilson's silence about all this suggests that the highest-level direction of national affairs was not very interested.

Harold Wilson reports that one day in 1966 he had a talk with Attlee and asked this Founding Father whether there was any field of policy which Attlee thought had not received enough attention. 'Transport', Attlee replied. Complacently, Wilson comments that at that very time his Government was preparing 'the biggest and most far-reaching Transport Bill in our history' (which has achieved very little of the main objective, to increase the freight-carryings of the railways).[15] He must have written this at the very time that his party's leadership, except for Mr Crosland, was standing on the sidelines over the Roskill Report and the Conservative Government's non-synoptic decision that the airport must go ahead; and his interview with Attlee was at the very time when his own Government might have been taking a more imaginative line, instead of sticking through thick and thin to Stansted. That interview was also a year after Wilson had given up his plan to ask Lord Beeching to undertake a full review of transport needs; 'sectional pressure' in the Cabinet had been too strong then for the Prime Minister.[16]

One serious disadvantage of the Roskill Commission, given its terms of reference, is that it can be taken to have precluded any parallel official examination of its field. While it was devoting nearly all of its energies to the narrow question of choice between airport sites, the Government itself could not appropriately have set up a wider inquiry into the primary issues which might affect the need for any airport.

But at the end of 1970, when the sad message of Roskill was known, ministers seemed merely to be mouthpieces of the modified bureaucratic doctrine that had by then been produced. We have evidence of this from their public statements, but no evidence at all about any questionings that there may have been among them. The irony is that, in settling for Foulness, they did not satisfy the aviation interests' desire for an airport in an operationally good location, but told them, 'This is the best airport that we can give you.' They may have missed an opportunity to seek out a yet wider public good, but in the short-run political sense their decision was a popular one.

For the Government to decide to review transport needs on a broad scale would have been difficult, administratively and politically. Such a review could have been instituted in the middle 1960s, when Labour ministers were preaching integration of transport policy but did not have the time or the will to take effective steps to promote it in this field.

Given the inputs to the political system, and the way these were perceived by the Government's own machinery, an initiative for a wider review needed to come from somewhere, and the source was lacking. Also, the compartments of the administrative machine, with aviation separated from transport, were devised unfavourably to an approach which would see air transport fully in its wider environmental and economic context. As a result, some quite simple and obvious questions were not asked, and the need to ask them was not perceived.

The least troublesome solution is often one that does not innovate too much, one that develops naturally out of past policies. It may compound old errors, but at least the old errors may be less dangerous than the errors of enthusiasts who think they are all-wise when they are not. The first quality that a civil servant needs is a sure feeling for what will 'go', said a mandarin, explaining the inner mysteries. None of Khrushchev's scatterbrained plans. Disjointed incrementalism may be safer in the long run than more positive enterprise, but when it leads you to fight the next war with the weapons of the last it has its limitations.

It may be useful to glance at the model set up by Professor Lindblom:[17]

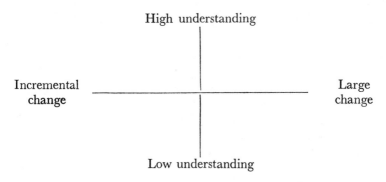

On this model the decision to build a third airport can, paradoxically, be placed in the bottom-left quadrant of low understanding–incremental change. There was low understanding because, although the Roskill Commission undertook its huge exercise in gathering information on the options between airport sites, it did not look thoroughly for all possible options involving substantial deferment of the airport. The terms of reference prevented any such wider inquiry, and the Report drew attention to the vast area of possibilities which it had not been able to cover. But the gap was left unfilled and Government policy so far has been formed without any full assessment of airport capacity or wider transport needs and potential. Unlike Chico Marx in the tipster scene in *A Day at the Races*, Roskill produced the Code Book but then told the Government that it must find the Master Code Book itself, and then the Breeders' Book. This quite often happens with Government-appointed commissions.

The building of the airport would be another increment in un-changing policies of fostering London's air travel; to review trans-port needs as a whole, with a view to finding optimal satisfaction of them, would be a large change in terms of policy. But in terms of real change, resources used, land gobbled up for the access roads, previously untroubled areas subjected to noise, consumption of material resources, the airport, and continued growth of air traffic as projected, involve a much greater innovation than that which could be produced by a heavy new commitment to existing railways and regional airports.

The conflict between disjointed incrementalism and positive search for optimal solutions can be seen in every Government's approach. Much of the literature about decision-making is con-cerned with the extent to which it is practicable for decision-makers to have full knowledge of the consequences of their decisions. As H. A. Simon put it in 1945, the naïve utilitarian view is nowhere more strikingly set forth than by Jeremy Bentham.[18] As far as Simon is concerned, 'rationality is concerned with the selection of pre-ferred behaviour alternatives in terms of some system of values whereby the behaviour can be evaluated.' In this case the Maplin decision is a good one if it upholds and expresses the established and little-criticized values connected with the aerospace industry, at the same time as it strikes the best available balance between the particular interests currently involved. It does not give maximum satisfaction to any, but it probably minimizes dissatisfaction; the decision does after all give the air interests their airport (though not in the place they desired); and although there are some people who currently oppose Maplin on environmental grounds, the weight of that opposition is currently about the minimum that can be expected in relation to any large new construction-project. The trouble over the corridors through London has been put off to the future, and when that breaks out a new generation of politicians and administrators will have to deal with it; they will find it as hard to draw back as the Labour Government found it to abandon Con-corde in 1964, though for different reasons.

As Simon says again, actual behaviour falls short of rationality, because rationality depends on complete knowledge and anticipation of the consequences of each choice, whereas knowledge of consequences is always fragmentary.[19]

It is for these reasons that Lindblom defends disjointed incrementalism as the strategy most likely to work in most circumstances. According to this approach, the desire for a 'synoptic' approach to problems is often unrealistic, because the decision-makers are never fully appraised of all the relevant facts, let alone aware of all the consequences that might follow from their decisions.

The third airport decision deals with the provision of transport in the future. In the terms of Lindblom's discussion its environment is relatively specific; but it is dominated by our ignorance about how the future demand for transport will evolve. It is most unlikely that the currently accepted projections of future demand will be precisely fulfilled, and the likelihood of error increases the further we go into the future. The current figure for 1985 is more likely to be wrong than that for 1980.

Another difficulty about fully rational decision-making is derived from the problem of setting the values by which the decision-makers are to proceed. In most cases there has been no opportunity for a direct expression of public opinion on an issue, and even if such an expression were possible it would be suspect, because much would depend on the manner in which the issue was presented.

An incremental strategy, based on well-tried accommodation of interests, minimizes the danger that decision-makers will insert their own subjective values into the system; it can even be acclaimed as a safeguard for democracy against obvious dangers. On the other hand, the element of mutual accommodation in the strategy depends on the degree of articulation of the interests involved. The values which enter into the argument are derived from the interests of groups of people. In this particular case we suggested above that producer values tended, just for this reason, to take precedence over consumer values and over generalized social welfare.

We may now approach the question by testing the main options which were open in 1971, and by attempting a crude assessment of the diverse consequences which might have been expected to flow from the choice of one or another option. We shall put down a series of consequences all of which would seem to be universally regarded as desirable, and assess the relative prospects of 'good' results flowing from the choice of each option. Next we shall assign weights to the consequences on the basis of different value systems.

We may list the options as follows:

(1) Build the Channel tunnel now and develop the railways quickly. Foster the regional airports to relieve London; defer Maplin for at least ten years; have no immediate cross-Channel facilities for cars through the tunnel.

(2) The plan of 1971: Build Maplin now, but no Channel tunnel; no fostered development of British regional airports in the 1980s.

(3) Build Maplin and the tunnel, develop the railways fully with large new allocations of capital; probably no cross-Channel cars.

(4) Build Maplin and the tunnel, but no special development of railways. The tunnel used very extensively for cross-Channel cars, with huge terminals near Folkestone and Calais.

Options 3 and 4 are not clear-cut. There will presumably be some development of railways in any case; the extremes we may envisage are the full development envisaged above and an absence of special development beyond what has already been approved or implied in present policies.

Options 2, 3 and 4 by definition exclude any fostering of British regional airports as reliefs to London, though increasing traffic generated in the regions will lead to a spontaneous demand for their development.

We shall probably not be far wrong if we identify fifteen main classes of consequences, each of which would be affected by the choice of one or another of the options. There is unlikely to be much dissent from the view that each of these consequences is in some sense a good or bad – not necessarily a universal good, but a good either for the public at large or for some particular groups. It may further be reasonable to rate each of the options in relation to each consequence. Although this process is essentially subjective, there is no great scope for error in assessing the 'goodness' or 'badness' of each option as a likely producer of each consequence. For example, the abandonment of Maplin as proposed in this book would have bad consequences in relation to the satisfaction of currently articulate industrial interests, whereas the Government's present policy would have good consequences. The consequences of building both Maplin airport and the tunnel would be a little better still, but in terms of resource consumption they would be bad.

In some cases there is room for dispute as to the likely consequences of the various options. 'Consumer satisfaction' is measurable in terms of breadth of choice of means of transport, price, frequency, reliability and convenience, which in its turn includes usable daytime hours spent in the total door-to-door journey, frequency, accessibility, amount of hanging around listening for instructions on the loudspeaker, and a variety of other such factors. Much of the material in this book has indicated that a tunnel-and-good-railway-but-no-Maplin solution would give better consumer satisfaction on almost every significant point.

The fifteen main consequences of the choice are listed in Table 20, with a column for each of the four options, indicating in a short sentence the likely consequence of each option with respect to each consequence. In addition to the words a figure is given, which is an assessment of the particular option's likely consequence, with '0' representing neutral or nil consequence, $+10$ very good and -10 very bad.

We do not mention either the financial or the broader economic assessment. This is because we are assuming the situation in 1971, when no attempt was made to compare costs between the options; at that time nobody recognized that there might be an Option 1 at all.

The consequences are not all of equal importance. The trouble is that, even if the validity of the marks, as measurements of the likely consequences, were accepted, there would be disagreement about the relative importance of the different consequences. How is the effect on employment, the local economy and social conditions at Dover to be weighed against the convenience of 40 million travellers or the need for consistency in decision-making?

The difficulty of assigning relative importance to the consequences reflects the difference in values held by different persons or agencies considering the problem. To illustrate the difficulty we shall add a further list, assigning weights to each set of consequences according to two perfectly credible sets of value systems. One of these reflects the preferences of someone who considers the maximization of social welfare as an important objective; he would be anxious to conserve resources and to avoid environmental damage, but he would also be much concerned with the interests of the consumers of transport services. His approach would be greatly opposed to that of the person concerned with means and processes rather than with a true

TABLE 20

Four London Airport Options and their Consequences

Consequence	OPTION 1 *Tunnel, no Maplin. Rail and regional airports fully developed*	OPTION 2 *Maplin, no tunnel*	OPTION 3 *Maplin and tunnel. Rail fully developed*	OPTION 4 *Maplin and tunnel. Tunnel mainly car-transporter. Rail not developed*
A. Consumer satisfaction	V. good. Rail cheap, accessible, frequent for London and regions. Good air service from regions. Adequate air services from convenient London airports	Poor. Good air services from London, but many from Maplin. Rail declining. Poor regional air services	Less good than Option 1. Rail less frequent and higher cost. Some London air travellers use Maplin. Poor regional air service	Similar to Option 2, but with somewhat better rail availability
	+10	+1	+7	+4
B. Environmental damage, general	Not bad. Some disturbance along rail routes. Little effect in Britain; bad in Benelux	Very bad. Maplin environment destroyed. Bad at continental airports. Noise much extended	Evils of 1 and 2 combined	Similar to Option 2, but more damage in Kent on road approach to terminal
	−1	−7	−8	−10
C. Local environment, housing, disturbance in London	Some round new rail route	Airport access route and terminal cause severe damage	Evils of 1 and 2 combined	Similar to Option 1

	Calais			
	0	0	−2	−10
E. Additional use of resources for transport	Moderate demands (−2)	Heavy demands (0)	Evils of 1 and 2 combined (−2)	Evils of 1 and 2 combined, plus more road construction (−10)
F. Effects on British regional employment and development	Great advantage of good direct rail link with continent. Improved regional airports. Employment at Liverpool, etc. (+10)	Wholly negative (−10)	As with Option 1, except for regional airports (+5)	Wholly negative (−10)
G. Effect on road use	Some decrease in growth problem (+10)	Considerable increase in road use through need to go to Maplin (−10)	As with Option 1 (−10)	As with Option 2 (−10)
H. Effect on tourism to Britain	Good. Spreads it around (+10)	Poor. High cost, concentrate on London (−10)	As with Option 1, but higher cost (+6)	As with Option 2 (−10)
I. Employment in aircraft industry	Considerable increase (+5)	Maximum increase (+10)	Slightly more increase than under Option 1 (+6)	As with Option 2 (+10)

TABLE 20—*continued*

Consequence	OPTION 1 *Tunnel, no Maplin. Rail and regional airports fully developed*	OPTION 2 *Maplin, no tunnel*	OPTION 3 *Maplin and tunnel. Rail fully developed*	OPTION 4 *Maplin and tunnel. Tunnel mainly car-transporter. Rail not developed*
J. Employment in rail industry	Maximum increases	Some benefit through the Maplin rapid-transit link	Probably better than under Option 1	Slightly better than under Option 2
	+10	+2	+8	+5
K. Satisfaction to currently articulate industrial interests	Bad	Good	Good	Good
	−10	+10	+10	+10
L. Satisfaction to currently articulate environmental interests	Mixed. Some will complain because they mistakenly think that aircraft noise will be increased at Heathrow, etc. Some pleased in Essex	Some dissatisfaction in Essex	Uncertain; but as Option 2	As Option 2, with additional complaint at tunnel road-terminal
	0	−2	−2	−10

				As with Option 3
M. Satisfaction of chauvinism	Uncertain. Looks now like little satisfaction, but European lead could be made very grandiose −10 to +5	Looks very satisfactory now +8	Even better +10	+10
N. Satisfaction to entrenched bureaucracy	Bad −10	Good +10	Potentially good, but some uncertainties +8	Good +10
O. Political consistency: difficulty of change	Bad −10	Good +10	Good +10	Good +10

welfare function; this last person cares a great deal about preserving entrenched positions and the balance of established interests, the whole apparatus of neutral accommodation involved in decision strategy. It is simplest to call this last imaginary person a 'bureaucrat', though it must be stressed that the use of this term does not imply that it is attached to civil servants as distinct from ministers; it describes an attitude rather than a role, an attitude likely to be engendered in any person involved in the operation of a system with whose processes he is identified. All ministers must be bureaucrats to a certain degree, some more, some less.

The results of the weighting exercise are strikingly different. The maximizer of social welfare prefers the option of tunnel and railway but no new London airport. It comes out about 450 points above the (unrealistic) option of airport and tunnel with full railway development, 700 points above the airport but no tunnel, and 800 above the option of both facilities, with the tunnel mainly as a device of getting cars across the Channel. (See Table 21.)

The model 'bureaucrat' on the other hand is happiest with the unrealistic option involving maximum expenditure. But to placate the Treasury[20] he will surely have to plump for the second-best, airport but no tunnel, which he finds preferable to the airport plus tunnel-for-cars. Of the two main options, he prefers the airport but no tunnel by some 500 points over the tunnel but no airport. But the whole foundation for that preference is built on the interests of the administrative machine in which he is working, considered as an end in itself. The preference may arise from a sound application of Lindblom's strategy; but the results are expensive both for the community as a whole and for the transport consumer.

The process followed here needs a little explanation. It involves setting up two imagined value systems, to which names are given, rational and bureaucratic. As rationality is in Weber's definition a leading characteristic and purpose of bureaucracy, it would seem that 'bureaucrat' is being used in the popular pejorative sense, as distinct from Weber's. This is because the notion of 'bureaucrat' as used here implies the setting of a peculiarly high value on the means used to pursue rational ends. It may be that the notion of 'bureaucrat' is being somewhat confused with that of 'politician', in so far as the object of satisfying currently articulate interests is present. A politician may wish to promote policies which have an ideological basis, but, where he is confronted by options lacking

TABLE 21

Consequences of options weighted for Social Welfare and Bureaucratic Values

Consequence	Unweighted marks Option				wt	Marks weighted for social welfare values Weighted marks Option				wt	Marks weighted for bureaucratic values Weighted marks Option			
	1	2	3	4		1	2	3	4		1	2	3	4
A. Consensus	+10	+1	+7	+4	20	+200	+20	+140	+80	5	+50	+5	+35	+20
B. Environment	-1	-7	-8	-10	10	-10	-70	-80	-100	5	-5	-35	-40	-50
C. London	-2	-8	-10	-8	10	-20	-80	-100	-80	10	-20	-80	-100	-80
D. Ports	0	0	-2	-10	5	0	0	-10	-50	5	0	0	-10	-50
E. Resources	-2	-7	-9	-10	20	-40	-140	-180	-200	1	-2	-7	-9	-10
F. Regions	+10	-10	+5	-10	5	+50	-50	+25	-50	1	+10	-10	+5	-10
G. Roads	+10	-10	+10	-10	5	+50	-50	+50	-50	2	+20	-20	+20	-20
H. Tourism	+10	-10	+6	-10	1	+10	-10	+1	-10	2	+20	-20	+12	-20
I. Aircraft employment	+5	+10	+6	+10	0	0	0	0	0	5	+25	+50	+30	+50
J. Rail employment	+10	+2	+8	+5	2	+20	+4	+16	+10	1	+10	-2	+8	+5
K. Industrial interests	-10	+10	+10	+10	1	-10	+10	+10	+10	10	-100	+100	+100	+100
L. Environmental interests	0	-2	-2	-10	2	0	-4	-4	-20	5	0	-20	-20	-100
M. Chauvinism	-10	+8	+10	+10	-5	+50	-40	-50	-50	10	-100	+80	+100	+100
N. Bureaucracy	-10	+10	+8	+10	1	-10	+10	+8	+10	10	-100	+100	+80	+100
O. Consistency	-10	+10	+10	+10	1	-10	+10	+10	+10	10	-100	+100	+100	+100
						+280	-390	-170	-490		-292	+215	+311	+135

ideological content, he may wish to produce solutions which will give the most satisfaction to existing articulate interests and thus not be likely to thwart his pursuit of ideological goals.

In the case under consideration, there is indeed one obvious ideological factor present, that of the chauvinistic pursuit of national greatness. Through somewhat shallow thought processes, politicians have accepted the view that more London airport traffic subserves national greatness. They may be mistaken in this judgement of cause and effect, but if they do not see the error in it they may prefer a London airport policy in the belief that it will promote an ideological end.

When we suggest that our 'bureaucrat' would set a high value on the satisfaction of articulate producers' interests, and on the maximum promotion of the aircraft industry, while the seeker after a rationally optimal solution sets a high value on 'economizing' and on consumer satisfaction, we have to admit that the actual weights suggested are not weights which every bureaucrat, or every pursuer of rationality, would assign to each of the purposes. It is unlikely that any two politicians would agree in assigning relative weights to the consequences listed here.

On the environmental side both Labour and Conservative ministers have claimed to regard preservation as a very high value indeed, and the choice of the Foulness site in spite of Roskill's recommendations was a most striking proof of this concern. It was a compromise, but a compromise made in the dark.

Incremental and synoptic approaches to decision-making have more concrete expressions in two distinct principles which have been explicitly stated by the Conservative Government which made the decision for Maplin.

One is the Tory principle: the Government should not try to do too much. It may not be obviously relevant to the present case. A consequence is the elimination of functions of the central Government which can be shown to be unnecessary in that they can be carried out by other means. This has found obvious expression already in the denationalization of Thomas Cook and of the Carlisle pubs, and in a hankering after the hiving-off of some nationalized industry functions such as the operation of hotels by the British Rail Board. There is no plan to have a third London airport run by private enterprise, or to sell off BEA. But the philosophy underlying this doctrine might be expected to lead to the view that governmental activity, in the form of building airports or operating airlines or railways, should be content to satisfy observed demands according to 'sound financial princples', without attempting to situate those demands in relation to the overall interests of the community, or even to calculations about the optimal satisfaction of the demands. But 'sound financial principles' demand a weighing of alternatives.

The decision to build a third London airport would be consistent with that philosophy. Confronted with the projections of future demand for air travel to and from London, a Government not wishing to 'do too much' might well think it right to go ahead and build the airport, without asking seriously whether the ultimate transport objective could be achieved by other means at less real cost. If 'not doing too much' implies abdicating responsibility for seeking the most effective means of fulfilling the public interest, well and good; we are back with disjointed incrementalism.

The second theme which may be relevant is a contrary one, proclaimed in slightly different keys by ministers of both parties, as well as civil servants, throughout the past ten years. It is a determination to get the priorities in public expenditure right,[21] expressed concretely through the creation of new pieces of machinery designed to secure that aim. The Public Expenditure Survey Committee was brought into prominence in 1965 in relation to the Labour Government's National Plan. The PESC is still with us, 'concerned with the extent and broad priorities of government use of resources'. The present Government added a complementary device, Programme Analysis and Review, which 'exists for the basic purpose of enabling the Government, in the shape of the Cabinet collectively and individually, to translate their political values as effectively and accurately as possible into specific policies and viable programmes in the major areas'.[22] As Mr Peter Jay shows, this was not a complete innovation, but a development of machinery which had begun to work under the Labour Government.

Mr Heath's reorganization of government departments on a functional basis was an attempt to produce a structure which could handle policies more effectively. He added a further refinement when he created the Central Policy Review Staff, which participates when necessary along with the department responsible for a programme, the Treasury and other Whitehall departments, in preparing Programme Analysis Review reports for consideration in the appropriate Cabinet Committees.

The New Style of Government,[23] which was one of the Conservative Party's themes for the 1970 General Election, was by no means satisfied with incrementalism as a means of settling policies, particularly with regard to the public sector. It was hardly satisfactory, wrote Mr Michael Spicer, for political decisions to be 'one-off, disconnected and crisis-oriented'.[24] The Conservative Systems Research Centre, created while the Party was in opposition, in 1968, sought ideally to identify alternative sets of programmes for achieving objectives, to assess them 'in terms of performance (or output) against cost and other constraints' and to assess 'the effectiveness with which these programmes matched the changing needs/demands of society'.[25] Having described the thoroughly synoptic goals of this exercise within the Tory Party, Mr Spicer notes that in practice 'political action is largely the function of alliances of muddled objectives', but this is only because parties depend upon the support of conflicting interest groups to achieve majorities. But the argument of the need to win votes had nothing to do with the decision, a few months after Mr Spicer had written these fine words, to build a third London airport without having even identified the alternative programmes through which transport might be provided.

16

Parliament and the airport decision

Neither House of Parliament ever defeats a Government in office, but both Houses are among the influences which shape government policy. In the 1950s Christopher Hollis's judgement of 1949, that two flocks of sheep were just driven through lobbies on appropriate occasions, seemed to be validated by events. In the 1960s, and particularly after the 1964 General Election, there was a considerable movement for improving the ability of the House of Commons to control the executive, within the limits of the party system, through the improvement and extension of the ability of small committees to probe. Members of Parliament were to be better informed and thus better able to understand what was being done or proposed, particularly in matters not producing great inter-party battles. Instead of being formed at intervals of ten to fifteen years, Select Committees on Procedure have been set up in every session, and their activities have produced a whole range of improvements to the conditions of parliamentary work. The Library's resources have been greatly strengthened, in breadth and in depth; Members have been given the wherewithal to provide themselves with research assistance; select committees can hire experts to advise them. Parliament's resources are still small compared with those of the United States Congress, but far greater than ten years ago.

In a recent survey of the developments Ann Robinson suggests that there has been a division between those who want Members of Parliament to have a positive role, actually contributing to decision-making, and those who see their role as having a more negative slant, merely checking that nothing absurd is done.[1] Until 1964, ministers recoiled in horror from any suggestion of a positive role for Parliament and were reluctant even to extend the more negative controlling functions, for fear that this would lead to a positive parliamentary involvement which would be incompatible with ministerial responsibility. But after 1964 there was a new open-mindedness; if 'participation' was now valued, Parliament must share in it.

One function must surely be appropriate : to identify any administration's tendency to exalt means rather than ends, to oblige it to examine its own conclusions in the light of this tendency. Closely connected with this, and very important in today's world, is its function of ensuring, on the one hand that decisions are made with adequate consideration, and on the other hand that, when experts have been involved in decisions, they are wisely used in the pursuit of the public interest, not to support positions already taken up.

For its inquiry into parliamentary scrutiny of public expenditure and administration in 1968, the Select Committee on Procedure appointed as its Specialist Adviser Mr James H. Robertson, himself a former civil servant who had spent three years as Private Secretary to Lord Normanbrook. With this previous experience and the experience of advising the Select Committee, he made an interesting comment to an interviewer about the problems confronting Parliament.

What has happened is that a communication gap has come about between say the backbenchers in the House of Commons, the Economists, the Sociologists and the Political Scientists and the data processors. The 'experts' just want to deal with their own technicalities.

The amateur approach is out of fashion, yet there may be a need for a new skill, amateurish enough to see beyond the limits set by the horizons of differing specialisms yet professional enough to be able effectively to argue with the experts in their several fields. Ministers and civil servants should ideally fill this gap, but their own objectives may stand in the way of a will to do so. This is where Parliament can usefully come into the picture, provided that it is equipped both with procedures and with the information needed for the purpose. But the task is very difficult. A complex issue, lacking party content, will interest only few MPs, and they are not well placed for forcing their party leaders to take note of their arguments.

Experts' calculations may be of little use if they are told to exercise their talents on the wrong questions. But, when they produce their answers, non-experts may be daunted from any effective critique of their conclusions. Members of Parliament who seek to raise serious questions can have an impact only if they collect supporters numerous enough to give ministers ground for concern; and even in the context of the newly vitalized committee system, the scope for effective parliamentary action may be limited, particularly when complex calculations are involved.

The London airport question became a first-class political issue in 1967, and the debates on the Conservative Opposition's motion of censure on Stansted, on 29 June, and in the Lords on 11 December, may be regarded as a major contribution to a reversal of Government policy. In the Commons debate the Government gained its majority, but its supporters' lack of enthusiasm for Stansted was clearly shown against a background of local protest. The damage that would have been caused by the Stansted major airport was simple and dramatic, and quite properly dramatized by the press.

The House of Lords made a major contribution at this time and there was a real danger that the upper House might choose Stansted as an issue on which to use its remaining powers. An Order would have been needed, and the Lords looked likely to dare to throw it out. Ministers were not anxious for a constitutional struggle in which they would be defending an unpopular policy.

While the Roskill Commission was at work in 1968–70, local groups were formed to oppose each of the inland sites then under consideration. In July 1970 some Conservative MPs representing constituencies in the area formed a committee to oppose the choice of any of these sites. *The Times* quoted them as stating their conviction that, in default of any overwhelming argument to the contrary, present conditions and future trends dictated that the proper place for a large international airport must be Foulness.[3] When a summary of the Roskill findings was published, together with an indication that Professor Buchanan favoured Foulness, there was a general chorus of support for him.[4] But the argument was still nearly all directed to the choice of site; only a few voices, including those of some aviation experts, suggested that the need for any new airport had become uncertain. They were heard with indifference, and ministers had no need to heed them.

The debates on the Roskill Report, in the Lords on 22–23 February 1971 and in the Commons on 4 March 1971, were important in relation to the Government's decision to reject the Roskill Commission's recommendation of Cublington. In both the Lords and the Commons Roskill was almost friendless, and an exceptional number of Government supporters spoke in both Houses. At this time the Government was not committed and was able to say that the debates in Parliament would help it to make up its mind.

The importance of these debates, even in relation to the siting of the airport, should not be over-emphasized. The Government would probably have decided against an inland site anyway, but the debates did strengthen the case for doing so. No vote was taken in either House, but most of the speakers in both Houses concentrated on the horrors of an inland site; there was near-unanimity in opposing Roskill's recommendation. Five-sixths of the backbench speeches in the Commons were by Conservatives, so the Government had a clear message from its own supporters. The topic did not stir the Opposition very much; only six Labour Members spoke, two of whom mentioned the Trade Union and Labour Co-ordinating Committee in the Thurleigh area which actively wanted the airport there.

Attitudes to Foulness varied. A few thought it a splendid scheme, Roskill notwithstanding. More accepted it reluctantly, as the best solution to a nasty problem, one which would make the best of a bad job. Mr Noble himself, introducing the Report for the Department of Trade and Industry, had talked, as we have seen, of serious thought about the possibility of doing without the airport. But only a few speakers, in both Houses, took up this line.

Several peers made constructive suggestions, to which we shall return. In the Commons debate, ten days after that in the Lords, Mr Crosland led from the Opposition front bench and came near to putting the complete case for deferring a decision on a major airport. But he did not present a complete argument based on a combination of transfers to original airports and rail. During the debates the prospects of VTOL/STOL were mentioned by many speakers; so was the scope for redistributing the future traffic among regional airports. The new railways were given some slight mention, the European aspect very little indeed.

In the Lords debate, which came first and was spread over two days, Lord Beswick (who had been the Labour Government's spokesman in 1967) attacked the principle of a large third airport. He relied on rapid development of short take-off aircraft, claiming that 100-seaters could be operating on routes up to 600 miles by 1978–82, at a seat-mile cost only 5 or 10 per cent above that currently achieved. If he were right, this mode could begin to relieve the long-runway system earlier than the Government expected; but he recognized that his solution would need to be combined with some other new development.[5]

Lord Dilhorne gave the most extended statement of the regional case, but he did not direct his attack specifically to the arguments of Roskill's advisers, and he did not go back to demonstrate how the 1967 White Paper had already been shown to have underestimated the growth of the regional airports' traffic.[6]

In the House of Commons Mr Crosland, opening from the Opposition front bench, referred to the possible contribution of improved railways and of regional traffic pending the large-scale growth of VTOL, but he did not venture any figures;[7] and without any figures such arguments are unlikely to impress.

Two Conservatives with personal knowledge of the aerospace industry followed Mr Crosland's line. Mr Norman Tebbit, a former airline pilot, spoke of both the Channel tunnel and regional airports as reliefs to London until STOL should develop.[8] So did Mr. Wilkinson, Member for Bradford West, who had experience in the aircraft industry and as aviation specialist in the Conservative research department:

It has been an amazing feature of this debate that the more expert people are in aviation the more convinced they are that the third London airport is not necessary. The same was true of the debate in the other place. The noble Lords Lord Beswick, Lord Kinnoul and Lord Kings Norton all argued the same case. The Beswick case, if I may so call it, that 'Foulness, which some see as a solution without tears, would in fact be a gross misuse of public funds' (Official Report, House of Lords, 23 February 1971, vol. 315, col. 939.), is an admirable summary of the matter.[9]

Mr (now Sir Bernard) Braine (Conservative), the Member for South-East Essex, which includes the Foulness area, was glad that Foulness had not been proposed; he did not support an inland site, but referred to the possible role of the Channel tunnel[10] (which Mr Crosland had left out); but Mr Braine did not attempt any estimates. One or two others suggested that VTOL/STOL might make it possible to dispense with a third major London airport, for a time at least. Mr Crouch, Conservative Member for Canterbury, and privately Chairman of the Action Committee against Foulness Airport and of the Sheppey group, spoke inevitably against an estuarial site, mainly on the ground of the disturbance that it would cause to the local population; but his only offering in place of it was to pin faith in the new aeronautical technology.[11] The Liberal speaker, David Steel, also spoke of VTOL, coupled with tracked hovercraft, but without any solid argument or even questions on the timing of these developments in relation to the transport needs of the early 1980s.

Among all these constructive speeches the most notable feature was the lack of statistical estimates. Mr Noble had already given quite convincing arguments against any assumption that the new VTOL/STOL technology could be expected to give effective relief by the early 1980s. No advocate of a VTOL solution could claim or even suggest any substantial evidence for its ability to take up the excess load immediately after 1980; and nobody worked out a comprehensive plan to deal with that timing in relation to other developments. Altogether 41 speeches were made in the eight-hour debate, including the four from the front benches.

Of the 37 backbench speakers in the debate, 15 represented constituencies close to Foulness or one of the South Midland sites, and all but one opposed an airport in his area. Five other speakers represented areas affected by Heathrow aircraft noises; all of these concentrated on complaint against it, and in begging for some release favoured Foulness because it would disturb fewer people than any inland site.

Apart from those who favoured wider redistribution of traffic on the ground of national interest, three regional speakers advocated airport development in their own areas. One Liverpool member, Mr Tilney, followed Lord Royle (a former Manchester Labour MP) who had spoken in the upper House. Both supported the claims of Liverpool airport to take up some of the London load – a sound argument indeed, but not much use without other support, in spite of Mr Tilney's well-argued exposition of the case in a wider context and Lord Royle's sound plan to relieve the main railway to Liverpool.

At the end there was not much to answer; Mr Rodgers, former Minister of State at the old Board of Trade, winding up for the Opposition, offered no conclusion except nationalization of the main regional airports, and Mr Walker's final Government front bench speech was merely cautious, with a brief reference to the difficulty of providing 40 trains an hour to the airport, wherever it might be.

The nearest approach to a telling attack on ministers was in the House of Lords. First Lord Jellicoe, speaking for the Government, presented the case in such a way that many hearers would be likely to take it that the building of a third airport would actually reduce aircraft noise in the London area. He asked peers to remember what deferment of the new airport would mean in lack of relief for the sufferers (from noise) near Heathrow, and referred also to Gatwick and Luton.[12] Lord Dilhorne took him up on this,[13] but the main discussion on this point was left until the next day of the two-day debate.

It is worth quoting the relevant extracts from the Lords *Hansard* of 23 February 1971 :

Lord Sandford:
The Department of the Environment, in which I serve, has wide and complex responsibilities, but two very simple aims : first, the conservation and enhancement of the best in our environment; and secondly, the clearance or the improvement of the worst . . .

I have no hesitation in supposing that your Lordships will agree that one consideration, among many others, in building a third London airport, and in deciding when to bring the first runway of a third London airport into service, should be that of relieving the plight of those 700,000 households which are already daily drenched in the whine of jets at Heathrow . . .

In the light of the forecast of the traffic demands in the London area – only the London area – even in the relatively short term, is not deferment of action on a third London airport bound to lead to increasing pressure to make far greater use of the existing London Airports? (col. 962)

Viscount Dilhorne:
Is the tenor of his argument this : that Heathrow will not be allowed to use its full capacity because of the noise consequences, and that a new airport is necessary to relieve those consequences? If that is so, that is an entirely different case from that put up at the time that this Commission was appointed, and an entirely different case from that considered by the Commission. (col. 968)

Lord Sandford:
The noble and learned Viscount is reading too much into my remarks if he reads that. Everything that I am saying now – everything that all three spokesmen from this bench are saying – must be understood in the light of the fact that the Government have to take their own decisions after very careful consideration of all that has been put before them both by the Commission and by Members of this House and the other place. What I am saying is that, from the point of view of the Department in which I serve, this consideration – that is to say, the noise now affecting $2\frac{1}{4}$ million people around Heathrow – is of con-

siderable importance. I am not of course saying that it is decisive or that it will be decisive in the last analysis. (col. 968)

Lord Dilhorne:
Is the noble Lord saying that possibly Heathrow will not be allowed to be used to its full capacity?

Lord Sandford:
I am not even saying that. What I am saying is that this proposal that the decision should be deferred is bound to lead to increasing pressure to make for greater use of the existing London airports. (col. 969)

This interchange in the Lords must surely create the impression that the Government spokesmen were implying that the new airport would actually bring relief from noise to the Heathrow area, but that they were not prepared, when pressed, to uphold the implication that it was intended deliberately to reduce the Heathrow traffic to any significant degree after the opening of the new airport.

Nevertheless, in the Commons ten days later Mr Noble ran the risk of incurring the same charge of inconsistency. Referring to the mass of complaint about noise around Heathrow, etc., he said: 'The choice and timing of a new airport is closely linked in my mind with a sincere wish to provide some alleviation in these areas at the earliest practicable time.'[14]

It would be easier to be convinced of the sincerity of this wish if it had found concrete expression in a vigorous plan to transfer as much transatlantic traffic as practicable, as soon as practicable, to Liverpool.

What is noteworthy here is the ineffectiveness of Parliament as an instrument even for exposing ambiguity in ministerial use of words on a simple point. Lord Dilhorne's efforts in the Lords debates ought to have penetrated the sensibility of ministers, and of those who give them their briefs, but Mr Noble's repetition of the same line in the Commons ten days later shows that it may be safe to create a convenient but misleading impression without incurring even an effective debating penalty.

The speech of Mr Rippon on the second reading of the Maplin Development Bill in 1973 showed that ministers were still prepared to use language likely to appear to represent the third airport project as a device for taking noise away from those who now suffer from it, and thus to gain popular support for the third airport.

On 8 February Mr Rippon began his second reading speech with

242

the usual incantation about the need 'to maintain Britain's position as one of the world's greatest centres of international aviation'. He went on by saying that it was also, and above all, necessary to ensure 'that people who live in and around our existing airports get relief from noise'. (*Hansard*, col. 664.) He ended his speech with the same theme, but at this point he said that 'only by building a major new airport for London could we . . . [incantation] . . . and at the same time give a firm prospect of relief from *increasing* airport noise to the millions of people who now suffer from it'. (*Hansard*, col. 680 : author's italics.)

There is a very great difference between the two statements. The first provides a basis for enthusiastic support for Maplin from a huge public; the second means very little. The first (by association of ideas, if not by direct statement) implies, and must have been framed so as to imply, an intention to *reduce* traffic at the existing airports after Maplin is opened, the second implies that Maplin will take only the overflow.

In the debate, later the same evening, on the committal of the Bill, Dr Glyn, Member for Windsor, asked for elucidation : with Maplin open, would there or would there not be 'some alleviation of the present level of air traffic in and out of Heathrow?' (col. 802). The ministerial reply, this time from the Under-Secretary of State, Mr Eldon Griffiths, was more frank : 'No one can promise that there will be an alleviation of the noise. It can be said, however, that if the airport is to be built at Maplin the increase of noise, which is becoming intolerable in those areas, will not happen at anything like the same speed. In that sense there can be a material alleviation of the possible distress of the people in that area.' (col. 817).

There may be some gobbledygook in this, but it clearly admits that the opening of Maplin is not intended to produce an actual *reduction* of traffic at Heathrow. Mr Griffiths' statement was made to an almost empty House, at 10.40 pm. Mr Rippon began to speak at 4.15. Meanwhile the public is conveniently left to associate Maplin with relief from noise for those who now suffer it. The evidence suggests that Mr Rippon's opening statement was highly ambiguous. It agrees with evidence of a similar occasion two years earlier, with different ministers. The House did not pursue the point. Only Oppositions want to engage in severe pursuit, and the Opposition was asleep.

If the process of parliamentary debate failed to puncture the Executive's confidence even on this straightforward and easily comprehensible point, it is perhaps not surprising that it failed to convince the Executive of the worthwhileness of a new synoptic approach to the whole question of the need for a new airport. The claims of Mr Ernest Davies' comprehensive planning, set forth four years before,[15] were allowed to go by default, mainly because of the Labour Party's collective abdication. As far as Parliament was concerned, the matter was left dormant throughout 1971 and 1972. The Government was left to go ahead with its plans for building the airport, and at the same time to develop its studies of the Channel tunnel and regional airports as separate issues, without parliamentary complaint at the separation.

Parliament shook the Government's confidence just a little when the Maplin Development Bill was brought forward early in 1973. The Bill was needed to provide the Corporation with powers to acquire land, borrow money, etc. It was a hybrid bill, so a small committee of MPs heard the objections of persons or bodies directly affected by the project, but not the objections of those whose property would be affected by the indispensable access route.

The Second Reading was at first scheduled for 30 January 1973. During the previous week, at a meeting of the Conservative backbench members' aviation group, there was severe criticism of the whole project. According to press and BBC reports, most of the Conservative Members with concern for, and knowledge about, aviation showed grave disquiet.

The Second Reading was postponed to 8 February and duly approved on a two-line whip. The Opposition amendment, asking for a reappraisal, was defeated by 201 votes to 169, the Second Reading approved by 195 to 173. Four Conservative Members voted against it and an estimated 15 abstained. Two-fifths of the House's membership did not vote at all. The two ministerial speakers reiterated the old reasons why the Government was 'convinced' of the need for the new airport, though they did not deal with any of the specific arguments for reappraisal.

One of the main Conservative opponents of the Bill, Mr Robert Adley (Bristol North-East), advocated a synoptic reappraisal, but the content of his speech was not reported in *The Times*, *Guardian*, or BBC's *Today in Parliament* programme. (Mr Adley's speech was, however, reported extensively in the *Bristol Evening Post*. *The*

Times, Guardian and BBC selected less complex arguments for inclusion in their reports.) Several such arguments had been put forward during the previous ten days in a voluminous correspondence in *The Times* and there had been much hostile comment in the press generally. Much of the criticism, inside and outside Parliament, came from aviation experts, including Sir Peter Masefield, formerly chairman of the British Airports Authority.

All this serious comment was simply ignored by the ministerial speakers.

As an expression of preference between sites, the debates of 1971 served a clear purpose, to show that parliamentary opinion, particularly in the Conservative Party, was wholly set against the site which the Roskill Commission had recommended. If Parliament counts for anything at all, it would have been almost inconceivable for the Government to follow the Roskill proposal. Parliament is usually most influential when it does not vote. But on the fundamental issue, the question whether the third airport might be deferred, ministers showed no sign of being prepared to give fresh thought as a result of contributions to the debate. The process of parliamentary discussion was not an effective influence on the Government's major decision.

One reason for this may be that, where a Government's case relies ultimately on intricate statistical calculations, rival calculations can only be produced with much trouble and their validity cannot easily be established. It is unusual for a peer or MP to have the time to do the necessary work, and if he does, or gets some assistance with his calculations, his reward will probably be poor: people will not listen with attention unless they are already sympathetic to the argument.

A special feature of the debates was the lack of interest shown by Opposition Members. The Labour Party's response to the strong lead from its own front benches was less than slight, so that all Mr Crosland's efforts struck no spark among his own supporters. We may well say that this was their fault, not his. The Labour Party may have made fine statements about its planned transport policies,[16] but did not perceive the relevance of the airport question for the goal which it has so consistently set before itself. Even on the Bill of 1973, Mr Crosland obtained only rather half-hearted and fragmentary support from his own backbenchers.

MPs have to dissipate their interests and energies over so many topics that they have little opportunity for concentrating their thoughts. Recent reforms and developments with Select Committees have been aimed in part at improving their opportunities for the concentration which is necessary if they are to have an impact on the administrative machine. Improvement of the means for obliging the Government to justify public spending is one device; a committee on nationalized industries is another. Both of these devices are relevant for an issue such as transport planning, and it may be useful to look at their working. A comparison with a parallel process in France suggests that the very different French processes were no more effective.

Long ago the House of Commons gave up the attempt to control details of government expenditure through the traditional supply procedure, and the abandonment was properly recognized in the reforms of the supply system in 1967. In 1912 a Select Committee on Estimates was set up to fill this gap. It was not very effective before 1939. 'The original formula suggested that the Committee should search for economies simply by scrutinizing the figures themselves.'[17] In 1960 a new Standing Order (No. 80) empowered the Committee to report 'how, if at all, the policy implied in these Estimates may be carried out more economically' (these estimates being the ones which the Committee might choose for examination). Nevil Johnson comments:

The 1960 amendment gives some emphasis to what has been since 1945 characteristic of the Committee's approach to its work, and that its main function is to find out whether administration is effective and economical. This means that it must in many instances first establish what policies are in fact being implemented. Though debarred from then challenging these policies, the Committee must subject them to some degree of critical examination in the course of finding out whether the administrative organization which puts them into effect is efficient, and whether the financial demands which they impose are reasonable. Thus the Committee is now by no means so distant from policy questions as is believed by those who still make a rigid separation between administration and policy. This rather mechanistic view of the process of government makes too little allowance for the fact that administration and policy are often inextricably tied up together, and that a critical examination of the administration of policies can serve as a basis for a re-assessment of the policies themselves, even though they have been exposed to no formal challenge.

246

The reform of 1970, by which the Estimates Committee was replaced by a Public Expenditure Committee with even wider terms of reference, was a further move in the same direction.

But there are still some gaps. The Nationalized Industries Committee is there to take care of expenditure and implied policy in areas falling within the responsibilities of particular corporations, but not to look at the role of nationalized industries in relation to one another in cases of overlap.

The Estimates Committee's study of Transport Aircraft (2nd Report of Session 1963–4) was concerned with expenditure on aircraft research and development, including Concorde, and with the question whether civil expenditure had a useful military by-product.[18] The Public Expenditure Committee could take a wider view, but is likely to follow its predecessor in being reluctant to invade the area of the Nationalized Industries Committee.[19] It might perhaps look at the expenditure on roads to Maplin airport, and in order to do this thoroughly it would need to ask whether the need for the airport had been adequately established. But it could hardly repeat the examination of the BAA's chairman and officers and departmental spokesmen already undertaken by another committee, and if it did, it would probably let itself be convinced by superficial argument even more easily than its opposite number.

It may be that reluctance to talk about figures has been carried too far. Some kinds of governmental activity can only be discussed adequately in terms of comparison of the costs of available options, and this does mean figures.

If the airport question were to be adequately examined from this point of view, it would soon emerge that no attempts had been made to compare the cost of available options, because some options had been neglected. It would seem that a demand that the Government should inform itself about these relative costs would fall within the definition given by the Standing Order of 1960, and even more of the new Standing Order. A Government might reply that the task of obtaining fuller estimates of costs would itself be too time-consuming and too costly, but that reply would itself be subject to questioning. Such questioning might well have the effect of pressing for an approproate series of stages in the estimating process, of which the first might be pilot studies going little further than the gropings of Chapter 13 above.

Nevil Johnson observes that,

One of the main causes of wasted expenditure which the Committee discerned has been failure to review commitments rigorously enough and soon enough. There is an inertia in the spending process, and once something has been started it becomes difficult to stop it, even though the need for it may have changed or the costs have risen to an unacceptably high level.[20]

In fact the notion that there must be a new London airport was formed long before the new railway technology introduced a potential new series of options for the 1980s, and before STOL/VTOL had begun to offer further options for the 1990s. Lindblom's doubts about the possibility of ever having adequate knowledge might justify a decision to go ahead, because *something* must be done, without further inquiry (which leads to further inquiry still) in some cases, but in this particular case we seem to have grounds for suggesting that there is evidence of that 'need to review commitments regularly and to be prepared to sacrifice commitments if the cost has become embarrassingly high' which the Estimates Committee often emphasized.[21]

Parliament's weakness as a check on compartmentalism would not necessarily be cured by an extension of the committee system. Unless there were a committee dealing with transport as a whole, it is difficult to see what committee structure would help. The Select Committee on Nationalized Industries has been in existence since 1956, and its ambit covers railways, the nationalized airlines and airports. It is thus quite well placed for having an overall view of transport problems involving all these corporations – better placed, one might think, than any single department. However, a synoptic picture of airport requirements in the context of broader transport policy does not depend on the fact that the main services concerned are nationalized. It just happens that they are nationalized, and the fact that they are nationalized could well create conditions favourable to a synoptic view, though it has not yet done so.

In 1969, when the Select Committee took up the British Airports Authority, it was ten years since its last inquiry into British Railways. Its membership had wholly changed and the new railway technology had just appeared on the scene. During the hearings of Session 1969–70 and again in the resumed hearings of 1970–1, some members did take up the possibility of transfer of future passengers from air to rail, and also that of the regional airports' future contribution to a lightening of London's load (see Chapters 5 and 6). But

248

when spokesmen of the BAA and the DTI replied that first this and then another individual item of transfer could not, by itself, hold up the saturation of the London airports by more than one or two years, no Committee member pressed the respondent to add all the potential transfers together. The Committee's members were not searching enough, and collectively they agreed[22] to paragraph 38 of the Report, which wholly deferred to the wisdom of Roskill and the Government:

The Roskill Commission decided unanimously . . . that the first runway of the Third London Airport must be operational during 1980. This conclusion is supported by no less than twelve quarto, double columned pages of closely reasoned argument, and your Committee is clearly in no position to challenge it.[23]

It can be assumed that members of parliamentary Select Committees give most of their time and thought and energy to other aspects of their parliamentary activities. In his analysis of the Nationalized Industries Committee's work up to 1963, David Coombes found that 'even the Committee's normal programme called for diligence. So while making periodic full-scale enquiries, the Committee has not had much chance to follow up earlier inquiries, or to take up special investigations into controversial issues, even if it had wished to do so.'[24] Coombes noted the weakness of the Committee's own research support,[25] though he quotes a former Chairman's statement that he had briefed himself by discussion with economists and, where appropriate, 'an expert consultant.'[26] By 1970 the Committee as a whole had the benefit of expert advice. Professor Maurice Peston was appointed to assist it on 25 November and was present during the meetings mentioned in this account, and at the meeting of 10 February 1971, when the draft report was considered and approved. A Committee member wishing to be well informed can read the relevant corporation's annual reports, various memoranda, and, during the actual inquiry, the transcripts of former meetings. 'Not all the members', says Coombes, 'may be able to grapple with the whole of this material.'[27] Research assistance may be useful, but only to a member who has the time and the dedication to put it to use. It may be that a weakness of Parliament is too much verbalizing, crowding out reading, thought and hard work on figures. Barker and Rush have noted the same weakness in their more recent study of MPs' sources of information.[28]

249

The fundamental argument against the ability of the railways to give significant relief, which seems to have been accepted without question, was put by Mr (later Sir Peter) Masefield, Chairman of the BAA, during the hearings of the Select Committee on Nationalized Industries:[29]

Mr Kerr:
When you have gazed into the future has any account been taken of the development apparently taking place in the field of high speed surface transport? This might affect some of your thinking about the future?

Mr Masefield:
We try to keep in touch with this and the two areas where it might affect us. One is the domestic trunk routes London/Scotland and the second is if a Channel tunnel were ever to be built, London/Paris. We have made assumptions and assessments with and without these developments during the hearings of the Roskill Committee. The result is surprisingly marginal because the really big growth is coming in two other directions, long haul over the North Atlantic and tourism in Europe which would not be affected by these developments. So ten years from now they will not make a substantial difference.

The answer does not prove that improved railways cannot produce a significant reduction in London's air traffic, and the question was related to that possibility. Even if the really big growth is to be on American and longer (non-railable) European routes, the potentially railable proportion will hardly fall below 40 per cent by the early 1980s; the DTI Working Party's projections assume that the European and domestic total will still be two-thirds of the whole.

If the traffic with the remoter parts of Europe does have much bigger growth than that with near-Europe, the biggest growth will be in the form of British holiday-makers' journeys to Spain, Greece, etc. In that case the main growth will be accounted for by people residing outside the South-East, and they will be numerous enough to justify a far greater switch to regional airports than Roskill allowed for, and thus slower growth of London traffic.

No member of the Select Committee pressed Mr Masefield on this. True, another member, Mr Price, asked about the loss of traffic to air on the London–Manchester route after electrification had cut the rail journey-time from $3\frac{1}{2}$–4 hours to $2\frac{1}{2}$–3 hours. Mr Masefield replied that the air traffic had gone down by only 20 per cent and that even before this reduction the London–Manchester route was only 2 per cent of BEA's total traffic. In view of the prospective improvements on other domestic routes, and of the Channel tunnel's potential effect on future air traffic with Europe, Mr Masefield's reply invited further questioning. However, the Committee dropped the matter and the case against the conventional wisdom was allowed to go by default – as it was, very nearly, in the big parliamentary debates on the Roskill Report during the next three months.

MPs were indeed not informed about any relevant facts about action taken or omitted by the Government with a view to determining the potential sources of relief to the London airports, but they did not succeed, either in the House or in the more favourable conditions of a Select Committee, in insisting on a full analysis of the figures on which the Roskill Commission had estimated the timing of the need for the airport.

Barker and Rush describe the devices for improving the information to Select Committee members. Under the Labour Government in 1964–70 some improvement was made in the services available to them. Persons with technical and scientific knowledge could be called upon. Their role is to supply 'for the purpose of particular inquiries, either . . . information which is not readily available or to elucidate matters of complexity within the committee's terms of reference'.[30] The House of Commons Library had already set up 'an embryonic abstracting service based on the staff's judgment of what is worth covering.'[31]

But neither Coombes, nor Barker and Rush, nor indeed Nevil Johnson in his study of the Estimates Committee, succeed in giving a real impression of the depth of commitment of members of Select Committees to these special activities. The task would be very difficult. We may note though that neither Mr Price nor Mr Kerr, who had put their questions about possible reliefs to London airports, during the hearings in January 1971, and had received inadequate replies, caught the Speaker's eye in the debate in the House on 4 March to return to the attack.

A gap still remains. When a huge and complex issue has been passed to experts, and they produce their answers, there is a tendency for lay people, including Ministers and Members of Parliament, to think that the experts might be right. When experts have used all the vast array of skill and techniques available to them, a critic using mere common sense, and without either expertise or time to go over the whole report from beginning to end, must feel daunted at the prospect that any conflicting judgement he may offer will be pushed aside. This happened during the discussion of the timing of the need for the airport.

It is not clear that a mere thoroughgoing committee system like that of the United States Congress would fill this gap. In his 1966 study of the Appropriations Committee of the House of Representatives, Richard Fenno has a section on 'role and role behaviour' of sub-committee members. 'The overarching norm' which all sub-committee members are expected to follow, he says, is *'hard work'* (Fenno's italics).[32] Individual members specialize and members 'are expected to acknowledge each other's specialization and defer to it.'[33] The system probably does give more scope for an inquiring and enterprising individual Congressman to develop ideas and to ensure that no wool is pulled over his eyes, but the strong pressure for compromise within a sub-committee, as the price of its unity in the face of the full committee, may well tilt the scales in the direction of incrementalism.

The French system of parliamentary committees, even under the 1958 Constitution which restricted their powers, still provides a form of parliamentary work which is potentially far better adapted to provide for an effective parliamentary contribution to public investment-planning than the British system.

Each departmental estimate of expenditure, or vote, is submitted *pour avis* to one of the six *Commissions* (committees). Plans of nationalized industries may be dealt with. For each vote a member of the committee is appointed as *rapporteur*; the *rapporteur* prepares a document, typically of about fifty pages, which examines the actual figures in detail. A deputy appointed as a *rapporteur* thus has an individual task to perform quite without parallel among the functions of British MPs. In due course the committee devotes one or two sessions to the *rapporteur*'s draft *avis* on a particular vote, and in some cases the appropriate minister, or a junior minister, attends a committee session to answer questions or give explanations. A defect of the system is that the committee discussion is not reported in full; only a brief summary is reported, and it appears that the discussion tends to be fragmentary and of little effect. The *rapporteur*'s draft tends to propose acceptance of the departmental estimate, subject to some generalized recommendations of principle.

In the autumn Session of 1971 the Commission de la Production et des Echanges alone dealt with nineteen votes (e.g. Agriculture, Housing, Tourism, Protection of Nature and of the Environment). Each of the committee reports forms a volume (*Tome*) of Document No. 2015 of the National Assembly's document series for 1971–2. Apart from volume 19 (on the mercantile marine), three of these volumes deal with aspects of transport which concern us here: volume 9 with equipment (roads, inland waterways and ports), volume 17 with land transport, volume 18 with civil aviation.

Each of the report volumes provides a mass of valuable information, including relevant statistics of expenditures, passenger-kilometres, ton-kilometres, etc., and some international comparisons. M. Fortuit's report on land transport mentioned that, in March 1971, an interministerial committee had set up 'les organes d'une politique coordonnée des transports',[34] but did not pursue the question of co-ordination or overall planning. On the contrary, a long section of the report dealing with the plan for a new rail route bebetween Paris and Lyon deals with this important project only in its immediate local context; the main argument is that the existing two-track route over the first 200 miles (Paris–Dijon) is likely to be saturated by 1978. But there is no discussion of the potential role of the new Paris–Lyon route as a part of a European railway system.[35]

There is also a discussion of the *aérotrain* project, currently being planned by French technologists, for building some completely new *aérotrain* routes using vehicles capable of 150 mph (perhaps more at a later stage of development), but carrying no more than 80 passengers. There is a mention of schemes for developing this device on a number of sections, each of less than 100 miles, including Paris–Orleans and Lyon–Grenoble, but no discussion of its significance for the development and extension of the existing railway system, to which the aérotrain system might or might not be inimical; and there is no discussion of the potential output of the new system in comparison with that of conventional railways as they might be developed.[36]

The report mentions the Channel tunnel as a desirable project, but only in the context of the existing railway system on land, through which the London–Paris journey could be cut to four hours; there is no mention of the option of combining the tunnel with new connecting railway development, which could cut the journey to $2\frac{1}{2}$ hours and thus wholly alter its role.[37]

The full committee of 150 members devoted a session to the discussion of M. Fortuit's draft report on the budget, but no minister took part. The discussion is recorded in a two-page summary which mentions the names of those who intervened and the topics with which they dealt. The Chairman (M. Lemaire) welcomed the increase in rail traffic which had followed from the increase in speed, and claimed that the railway system was by no means saturated. The record shows that a number of minor worthy hobby-horses were disjointedly trotted out : let the trains be better cleaned, let foreign cars using French roads be taxed, let speeding car-drivers be sought out and suppressed. But of any pursuit of a conscious transport policy there is no evidence.

The same committee's report on the civil aviation budget for 1971–2, drafted by M. Labbé, is also full of useful statistics, but reads like a piece of sales talk for the civil aviation industry. There is much about Concorde, balancing some doubts about its economic viability with emotional phrases about its technological splendour. (If you condemn the Concorde project on economic grounds you are not only ignorant of the political, psychological and technical outcomes, but *incapable de saisir les problèmes dans leur véritable dimension*.) The *Airbus* and *Mercure* projects are also mentioned with enthusiasm; the report then goes on to the need to prepare for a third Paris airport, on the assumption that soon after 1980 Orly with 15 million passengers and the new Paris-Nord at Roissy with 30 million will be reaching the limit of their combined capacity. By 1985, the argument goes, the third airport should be dealing with 5 million passengers a year, and £100 million to £200 million should have been invested in it by then, the exact amount depending on the site chosen. It was necessary to begin soon to prepare for 140 million passengers at the Paris airports by 1990, say 25 million at Orly, 50 million at Roissy, and 65 million at the third airport ultimately to be developed.

The increase envisaged for the 1980s here is sharper than that currently foreseen for London, but the difference would correspond with the faster projected growth of Paris's population and purchasing power. There was even less indication than in the official British material of even a sideways glance at the overall shape of transport in the future. There is a breakdown of Paris airport traffic by origin and destination, showing that 56 per cent in 1970 was with other EEC countries, London or domestic, but there is no mention of the fact that the whole of this traffic will be potentially railable in the 1980s. Only 26 per cent of the total in 1970 was long-haul. Yet there is an assumption of a twelve-fold increase in the total air traffic by 1990, with no reference to possible diversion of part of the traffic to rail during the 1980s. This report dealt with civil aviation and stuck very narrowly to its brief, in sharp contrast with the contribution made by the Director-General of Air France to the book on transport co-ordination mentioned earlier.[38]

The report did however include a discussion of a national policy for airports, which had been submitted to regional consultation in the summer. A long-term plan should envisage the concentration of long-haul traffic at the Paris airports and four or perhaps six others (which were named). Internal scheduled air services were currently served by 28 provincial airports, which were listed. By 1985, 32 or perhaps 43 others would be needed in addition; these too were named in a list.[39] But the possible effect on Paris airports of development of regional airports as long-haul terminals was neglected (and the French distribution in 1970 resembled the British).

The draft reports on both rail and air transport were discussed and approved by the same committee, but there is no record of any comment by any committee member on the compartmentalism of the two reports. One parliamentary question had been put down two years earlier, referring to the constant talk about co-ordination of transport in the public interest, combined with the absence of any action; but the question was never answered.

The asker of this question in 1969, M. Catalifaud, was himself the *rapporteur* for 1971–2 on the estimates under the heading 'Equipment: roads, inland waterways and ports'. His draft report[40] did not use the opportunity for demanding a broader view of transport as a whole; on the contrary, he concentrated on the need to develop the road programme, to aim at the completion of 150 to 300 miles of new motorways per year, and to improve the maintenance work on existing main roads. The same committee discussed this report, and also the reports on scientific development and environmental protection. The report by M. Herzog on the first of these complained bitterly about the lack of information given to Parliament,[41] but no report or committee discussion records any serious pressure for integration of transport facilities.

The French parliamentary committee-proceedings recorded here took place before the publication of *Pour une Politique Economique des Transports*,[42] in which the heads of the French nationalized transport undertakings show, in varying degrees, a consciousness of the overlap between modes. The recognition by the head of Air France that Europe needs to bring some order to competition in transport is particularly significant, and provides the basis for a substantial contribution by a parliamentary assembly which may think it worth taking the trouble.[43]

The story illustrates the gaps between experts and both politicians and administrators. The latter ask the experts to undertake a limited task, and this they do. Their answers suggest a solution to a problem, but that solution may not be the only one. To propound an alternative solution it is necessary to have solid information, but if the administrators or politicians lack it they have no answers of their own. They may be loath to try their hand at providing themselves with adequate alternative information, because they are ill-armoured against the experts' private language. Also, they have no time.

Those British MPs, like Mr Tebbit and Mr Wilkinson, who followed Mr Crosland's arguments for a wider view of the whole transport problem, were not able to offer any figures in support. Mr Walker did not answer them in the debate of March 1971, and they have never been answered. Nor have the similar arguments put forward in many newspapers and journals from time to time.

The figures offered here are based on straightforward, simple calculations, both as regards transfer to regional airports and rail and as regards the cost, and on all these counts they are only tentative. Anyone can follow them; there is a danger that experts would discard them just because of their form and pedigree. They dissent from Roskill's findings only on the potential future distribution of traffic among airports, and there is a temptation to think that Roskill must be right, because of the quality and scale of the research that went into the Report. But Roskill's questions were incomplete. It would have been safer here to do no more than point to the questions Roskill and the Government have left unanswered, but in order to question the validity of their claims we need to produce some evidence, whatever risks that process may involve. If nobody tries to fill this gap, the gap must remain unfilled.

17

Conclusion

This book set out with the prime purpose of looking for a solution to a particular problem which would conserve resources and reduce environmental damage and yet not exact too great a cost in terms of desired satisfactions foregone. Most such exercises involve difficult balances and choices. Such a choice faced the Roskill Commission itself when it found (albeit on inadequate evidence) that it must weigh the social, environmental and economic merits and demerits of the available airport sites. It found a formula on which to base its choice, but articulate public opinion rejected the outcome and the Government, in doing likewise, showed that it gave more weight in the balance to the environmental side of the equations than Roskill's formula had done.

But the solutions propounded here raise no such difficult questions. On *prima facie* evidence at least, the environmental benefits seem to be there for the taking, bringing a wider and more satisfying range of options to consumers, a greater prospect of operation at lower cost and even of financial viability. As a contribution to economic theory the discussion has been of little value. Crude calculations have been used, with no respect for the techniques established by professional economists. But are they so much more likely to be wrong than more respectable procedures, if in their turn they are based on speculative foundations which may throw their findings all askew?

As a case-study in political science it has been possible to use a little published material to suggest reasons for the set of decisions that have been made. It may seem that the argument has claimed to discern a public good distinct from the sum of private goods, but the real message is more simple: that the sum of private goods is not always correctly expressed by interests which are currently articulate. Some are not articulate yet, because the future options are not yet well perceived; some are not articulate because their nature precludes effective organization.

On another plane it has been suggested that decision-makers become identified with their own solutions and may tend to dig into positions which have become familiar. Some evidence is offered in support of this not very original suggestion. Signs of incrementalism and compartmentalism in the decision-making process have been identified, and judgments have been offered indicating that these syndromes may at times militate against sound decision-making. But it cannot be claimed that any new theory has been propounded.

This study has claimed to show that there seems to be a strong probability that, within one area of decision, the public good and the sum of private goods would be better served by a solution different from that which the Government has decided to adopt. That situation is familiar. If only more people would use public transport in towns instead of cars, the public transport could be improved until even today's car-users were better off. If only people would see the inflationary effect of wage claims and restrain their claims accordingly, inflation would be reduced. At many points where a public good is easily discernible the action needed to achieve it may not be practicable within the limits of accepted beliefs about the proper limitations on the use of power.

It is unwise to try to lay down general principles to cover the whole field. In the case which we have been considering there is no problem about the use of power. The problem is rather how far a Government can go in seeking to identify options which may not obviously present themselves at all. The only power to be used would be through decisions about the direction of public investment, made by several Governments in concert, perhaps supported by a structure of airport charges designed to influence individual choices – a principle which has already been accepted. The real problem here is much less profound, one concerned with the bridging of the gap between groups of experts, each identified with its own solutions, who have found an overall solution which represents a compromise which they all are prepared to accept. In this case politicians, responding to several sets of articulate opinion, have influenced the compromise. Many amateurs, including backbench Members of both Houses of Parliament, have perceived that there may well be a solution more productive both of private and of public goods, but the Government's situation has failed to produce a will to see the nature of the gap in its own calculations. The parliamentary contributions of Lords Dilhorne and Beswick, and Messrs Crosland, Wilkinson and Tebbit were disregarded, partly because a parliamentary speech gives no scope for a full exposition of a complex case, partly because mere rational advocacy of a public good may be unimpressive. Such advocacy if too short cannot make its case; if too long the administration has no patience for it; and too long and too short overlap.

If the experts and the interests have left a gap which only amateurs can fill, the amateurs have little hope. The expected need to do battle for the environment, and for conservation of resources, turns out to be no battle at all if economic and environmental arguments both produce the same conclusion. The battle then is against the political system's tendency to work within the assumptions which have become familiar, to listen to and balance only those arguments which have solid interests behind them and, when it thinks it has reached a solution, to set up its own spiral of ever-deepening commitment.

The Government's own failure to see the scope for a wider analysis could be attributed in part to its prejudices, but also to its mode of operation. In 1968 Mr Denys Munby set out clearly the reasons for the inadequacy of the machinery of government for setting out alternatives as rationally as possible, to aid politicians in their final choices of priorities:[1]

Within the British system of government, basic responsibility rests within departments and is borne by the Minister. The department exists to serve the Minister, not the public, nor the Cabinet, nor the House of Commons. If the Minister wants to hide things from his colleagues, his department abets him; it covers up for him; it promotes his policies; it tries not to let him down, and hopes in return that he will support their established shibboleths. It is not surprising that a department keeps its own files, which are not open to other civil servants, and only releases such information to other departments as it thinks they ought to know. Co-ordination is in theory achieved by inter-departmental committees, but these are in practice meetings of sovereign powers. If the sovereign powers want a sensible overall solution of a problem, then of course all the relevant information will be provided and the problem will be objectively assessed. Not surprisingly this is rare, as most problems requiring inter-departmental committees involve the established interest of departments and the political prestige of Ministers. Information is then suppressed (or not provided because of 'pressure of time'), and attitudes formed *a priori* are put forward as bargaining points for inter-departmental diplomacy. The top-level civil servants on these committees with their keen nose for the realities of political and personal power (which is their real professionalism, misunderstood by many of those who think they know or should know about 'administration' or problem-solving) are able to assess, as any diplomat, to what extent such phrases as 'Our Minister will never stand for that' mean what they say and to what extent they should be translated as 'Under no circumstances will we let our Minister know that there are any serious arguments for any other case than the one we are committed to as a department'. In the last resort, the compromise achieved in the report which is sent to Ministers depends on the relative political power of Ministers. A weak department with a weak Minister will find its point of view minimized, if not ignored completely, however sensible it may be.

The airport decision is a concrete illustration of this process at work.

In project-planning three parties are involved: producers, consumers and the passive general public, whose interests may be affected by the production and consumption. Their relationship with government may be described as a sub-system, never wholly self-contained; and that sub-system generates interests, not necessarily compatible with one another. Within our culture there is a tendency to rate the interests in an accepted order: producers first, consumers a poor second, society virtually forgotten (except when it appears sometimes in a special form as *national* interest understood competitively). Those who are offended by the values of The System within which we live may be concerned by this ordering of priorities. The producers are well placed to have influence on the centre of power; they are an organized group already, or rather two well-organized sub-groups (managers and the working mass) and a third (the unorganized owners) whose interests the managers interpret and express.

The consumers have no voice, but the producers could not exist as such without them; in the case of this matter of transport, the consumers of the future are mathematical projections of the consumers of today, and the producers embrace them.

Society at large has a mainly passive role in this relationship. A narrow circle of it is intensely affected by the activities of a particular set of production and consumption processes. People in a series of wider circles are affected with declining intensity until we reach the great outer circle on which the effect is so remote that perception requires insight which is not widely distributed. In our political system inner-circle complaints have the best chance of producing a response. Articulation of misgivings by the outer circle tend to be seen as merely academic. Its attack on environmental pollution is made more effective by the fact that most people, including ministers and civil servants, find themselves from time to time in the innermost circle – as when, twenty years ago, they choked in smogs or now in a lorry's fumes.

If The System's critics are asking that it should always put society's interest before the producers', they may, in some degree, be asking the impossible. If a Government really claimed a capacity to perceive the common good and to pursue what it perceived, the errors of its prejudice or misunderstanding might well cause more harm even than today's pluralist attempts to satisfy the scattered demands of man-as-producer. But this does not mean that there are no areas of activity in which the effects of choices on the common good can be identified and promoted; the choice of transport options for the next few years presents some real challenges and opportunities.

That which involves the London airport plan is a case whose nature is particularly favourable to a firm and positive public-interest orientation, though the opportunity was not used.

The government machine has responded twice to articulation of passive public interest in this matter, against the specific wishes of the producers. First at Stansted, then at the other inland sites, inner circles of resistance sprang to life, with a wider circle of enthusiastic supporters; the Conservative Government quickly decided on the Foulness site instead. Here there was no significant inner circle of complaint, and no outer circle to demand a review of the whole reasoning behind the decision that the airport would be needed by 1980.

There will soon be an inner circle, consisting of householders and farmers who will be displaced or disturbed by the access route from London. Until the line or lines have been published they will not know their fate. When they do they will become articulate, and outer circles will bring support to their complaint.

But just as there is as yet no inner circle of persons whose immediate interests are damaged, so there is no outer circle, at any level, prepared to argue that the consumers' interest may have been misjudged and an easily discoverable general interest overlooked.

The ecologists' demand for conservation receives little support for practical measures within the political system as it works today. Nobody wants to do without any of the goods and services that he can buy, and everybody wants more, not less. Aspirations to consume are approved and consumption is admired. The economy too is geared to increasing production and is not ashamed of waste. Any sermon about cutting down now for the sake of future generations can be expected to have the same effect as any other hortatory sermon. A Conservation Party's candidates would lose their deposits, even at by-elections.

Is there then nothing to be done? Must we just continue as we are and hope the gamble will succeed? Not quite. A practicable conservation policy could make a realistic start with a careful search for places where it will not hurt, with some concrete applications of a kind already made familiar by some of the land-use plans which we have already achieved. An approach to demands for transport which would satisfy the demands, more cheaply and at lower real social cost, without requiring any real sacrifice from the consumers, seems a good beginning, and we must be prepared to look at the question in a severely practical way. Maplin airport is a big project when looked at parochially, small in global terms. As an example of the kinds of real choices which face us now it has a wide significance.

When environmental arguments are attacked for being 'hysterical' the criticism can usually be reduced to a judgement that the arguments are over-general and unrealistic; we cannot reverse overnight the universal desire of individuals to increase their consumption of goods and services. 'It is not necessary to stop economic growth altogether', writes David Marquand.[2] 'What is needed is a way of stimulating "good" growth and curbing "bad" growth, and of making sure that the environmental costs of "bad" growth are taken into account before the damage is done.' Marquand argues that the taxation system is a powerful weapon in the hands of government and that it should be used, in addition to direct regulation and control, to discourage harmful activities. He is concerned with whole classes of activities, which may quite easily be identified, and he cites examples.

This book looks for a realistic way of rationalizing part of the transport system in the direction of Marquand's 'good growth'. Such rationalization could probably be achieved without help from the tax system, but the tax system could help it to work if necessary. Curiously, it looks as if the rationalization advocated here would have involved no conflict between any of the real objectives that the public want. It is necessary, somewhere and soon, to begin a dialogue between the banalities of today's immediate demands on the one hand, and the long-term problems of survival on the other. The London airport question is a severely practical one, affecting only a tiny part of the long-term issue; but it is one of the biggest enterprises ever planned in Britain, big enough to have quite serious environmental consequences, yet immediate enough to be eligible for examination in severely practical terms. The decision to build it may have been made without adequate thought, but the urgency of the question does not make it any the less useful as an illustration of the long-term problems of policy-making.

Notes

Preface

1. David Braybrooke and Charles E. Lindblom, *A Strategy of Decision*, New York, Free Press, 1963, and London, Collier-Macmillan, 1970.

1. The Background: from Stansted to Maplin

1. Cf. R. E. Wraith, 'The Public Inquiry into Stansted Airport', *The Political Quarterly*, July–September 1966, vol. 37, pp. 265–80; Olive Cook, *The Stansted Affair*, Pan Books, 1967.
2. Civil Aviation Paper 199 of 1964.
3. The inquiry took 31 days. Wraith (op. cit., p. 265) quotes a leading counsel as saying that it cost some £2,000 daily in taxpayers' and privately subscribed money.
4. Cf. R. E. Wraith, op. cit., pp. 266–7. The point is also discussed in R. E. Wraith and G. C. Lamb, *Public Inquiries as an Instrument of Government*, Allen & Unwin, 1971.
5. Appendix 7, para. 54; cf. paras. 55 and 77.
6. *Hansard*, 29 June 1967, col. 815.
7. Ibid., cols. 769–84.
8. *Hansard*, 22 February 1968, col. 671.
9. Ibid., col. 672.
10. *Hansard*, 20 May 1968, col. 38.
11. Cf. R. E. Wraith and G. C. Lamb, op. cit., p. 207.
12. *Hansard*, 20 May 1968, col. 33.
13. Ibid., cols. 33–4.
14. Ibid., cols. 36–8. These two Members, both Labour, represented Northern constituencies. Both were defeated at the 1970 General Election and were thus out of the House when the Roskill Report was debated.

2. The Snags of Maplin

1. Select Committee on Nationalized Industries, HC 275 of 1970–1, Minutes of Evidence, 19 January 1971, Q. 107. Sir Peter put similar arguments, updated, in letters to *The Times* and the *Daily Telegraph* on 2 February 1973.
2. Ibid., Q. 121. These statements by the British Airports Authority's Chairman, rather than statements made to Roskill, are quoted because they were more recent, made after time for further reflection and at a time by which it was generally expected that the Government would choose Foulness rather than any inland site – though they might still have opted for a further, wider inquiry into the possibility of dispensing with any third airport for some years more.

3. Roskill Report, Table 12.1.
4. J. Parry Lewis, 'The Forecasts of Roskill', Occasional Paper No. 11, Centre for Urban and Regional Research, University of Manchester, 1971. See also John G. U. Adams, 'London's Third Airport', *The Geographical Journal*, vol. 137, December 1971, p. 473.
5. BAA Evidence to the Roskill Commission. Roskill Papers and Proceedings, vol. 2, pp. 17–22.
6. Roskill Report, 5.23.
7. Ibid., 5.23.
8. Ibid., 5.23.
9. Ibid., 5.28. Cf. Document 6022, p. 2.
10. Ibid., 10.71.
11. Ibid., 1.23.
12. James Fenton, *New Statesman*, 26 May 1972, quoting the *New Scientist*.
13. See P. R. Odell, 'Europe's Oil', *National Westminster Bank Review*, August 1972, pp. 6–21.
14. See T. E. M. McKitterick and T. C. Shaw, letters to *The Times*, 12 and 19 May 1972. Both show that a West coast site would be better for an oil port. Mr McKitterick reports that a thorough survey of possible sites had been made, occupying two years, and that 'Foulness came out badly in comparison'.
15. W. A. Robson, 'The Missing Dimension of Government', *The Political Quarterly*, vol. 42, July 1971, pp. 233–46.
16. *Hansard*, 4 March 1971, cols. 1919–20.

3. A Preliminary Discussion of the Alternatives

1. *Hansard*, 4 March 1971, col. 1914.
2. Roskill Report, Appendix 6, para. 21.
3. Ibid., para. 22. For more detailed discussion, see Chapter 5, p. 62.
4. E. Davies, 'Labour's Transport Policy', *The Political Quarterly*, vol. 38, 1967, p. 421. In the Commons Mr Davies had been Chairman of the PLP Transport Group from 1945 to 1959, except for an interval when he held a government post.
5. N. Tien Phuc (ed.), *Pour une Politique Economique des Transports*, Paris, Eyrolles, 1972. See pp. 15, 69 (Robert Guibert, of SNCF, and P. D. Cot, of Air France), and 187.
6. 'I hope that here Members will not make the mistake of believing that the speed of trains is the whole answer, as the frequency of the service is equally critical to door-to-door times.' (*Hansard*, 4 March 1971, cols. 1916–17.) Nobody took this up in the debate. True enough, speed of trains is no more use than the power of a 150-mph car, if track occupation prevents its use. But that obstacle could be surmounted, and the cost of surmounting it deserves examination.

4. The Original Projections Reconsidered

1. Roskill Papers and Proceedings, vol. 8, part 2, Table 4.5, p. 86.
2. Georg Leber (Minister of Transport for the German Federal Republic), 'Europe's Need for High-Speed Surface Transport', *Railway Gazette International*, May 1972, p. 169.
3. See David Fairhall's discussion of Graham's paper in the *Guardian*, 29 November 1972.

5. *Relief from other British Airports*

1. *Hansard*, 24 January 1946.
2. 'British Air Services', Cmd. 6712, December 1945.
3. Select Committees on Estimates, 1946–7, Sixth Report, 'Civil Aviation'; cf. R. S. Doganis, 'Airport Planning and Administration: A Critique', *The Political Quarterly*, vol. 37, 1966, p. 418.
4. R. S. Doganis, ibid. The history of government policy towards airports, together with that of the establishment of the BAA is set out in the Report of the Select Committee on Nationalized Industries, HC 275 of Session 1970–1, paras. 7–29.
5. 'Civil Aerodromes and Air Navigational Services', Cmnd. 1457, 1961.
6. R. S. Doganis, op. cit., p. 433.
7. His memorandum submitted to the Edwards Committee on Civil Air Transport, was also printed in the BAA Report and Accounts for 1968–9, pp. 158–63.
8. HC 275 of Session 1970–1, *British Airports Authority*, Q. 140–53. Cf. Evidence taken in Session 1969–70.
9. *The Political Quarterly*, vol. 42, 1971, p. 425. Cf. the Select Committee Report itself, para. 37 (reprinted below, Appendix 1, pp. 284–5).
10. DTI, Observations by the Secretary of State for Trade and Industry and by the BAA on the First Report from the Select Committee on Nationalized Industries (HC 275 of Session 1970–1), Cmnd. 5082.
11. BAA Report. Cf. Select Committee on Nationalized Industries, Report (HC 275 of Session 1970–1), para. 25.
12. HC 275, op. cit., Evidence, 19 January 1971, Q. 90.

6. *Regional Airports in a National Role*

1. Roskill Report, 5.44, quoted in Chapter 5, p. 63.
2. HC 275, op. cit., Evidence, 19 July 1971, Q. 99 and 106.
3. City of Liverpool, Department of Transportation and Basic Services, *Report: The Development of Liverpool Airport* (1970), 9.3; cf. Appendix D.
4. HC 275, Evidence, 26 January 1971, Q. 148.
5. *Hansard*, 26 April 1971, col. 36. This was in agreement with the principles proposed by the House of Commons Select Committee on Nationalized Industries (HC 275, 1970–1, para 75), which positively recommended that the possibility of discriminatory charges should be studied afresh.
6. HC 175, Evidence, Q. 169.
7. As defined by the International Urban Research Group in *The World's Metropolitan Areas*, University of California Press, 1959.

7. *The New Capabilities of Railways*

1. G. Leber, 'Europe's Need for High-Speed Surface Transport', *Railway Gazette International*, May 1972, pp. 169–71.
2. See the GLC consultative document *Channel Tunnel London Passenger Terminal*, November 1972.
3. National Assembly, 1971–2, 1st Session, Document No. 2015, vol. 18 (Report of the Committee of Production and Exchange on the Budget: rapporteur M. Labbé), p. 36.
4. The Ministry of Transport's *Study of a Rail Link to Heathrow* (1970), p. 17, estimates that passengers intending to depart from Heathrow should, by

1981, allow 83 minutes from Westminster if travelling by Piccadilly Line
train, 95 minutes by coach, and 71 minutes by car.
5. DTI Working Party on *Traffic and Capacity at Heathrow*, 1971, 4.3.5.1.1.

8. The Rail-Air Comparison

1. This information is derived from a paper read by Dr Sydney Jones, a
member of the British Rail Board, to the Bristol Institution of Engineers
on 11 April 1972. Cf. *Railway Gazette International*, March 1972 and
December 1971 (reporting an interview with Mr Marsh and Dr Jones).
2. Ministry of Transport, Survey of Road Goods Transport 1962. Final Results,
HMSO, 1964. Quoted in M. Chisholm and G. Manners, *Spatial Problems
of the British Economy*, Cambridge University Press, 1971, p. 227.
3. EEC Statistics. Cf. French National Assembly, 1971–2, Document No.
2015, vol. 9, p. 14. This committee report cites comparisons for the whole
of Europe.

Percentage distribution in ton-miles of freight traffic,
excluding pipelines, 1969

	Rail	Road	Water
Britain	25	74·9	0·1
Italy	23·6	76·4	—
W. Germany	43·1	37·4	19·7
France	46·3	43·6	10·1
Belgium	29·2	43·5	27·3
Netherlands	7·7	54·3	38

4. Dutch Ministry of Finance document *Re-orientation of Policy 1972–5.*

9. The Scope for Future Diversions from London Airports

1. BAA Report 1970–1, p. 198. Excess provision of aircraft space on this route
has been notorious for the past few years. Load factors below 50 per cent
on scheduled flights cannot continue for long.
2. By 1985 there will probably be large numbers of British holiday-makers
travelling to Tunisia, Morocco, etc. The majority can be expected to live
outside the South-East, and to be numerous enough to find direct flights
at regional airports.
3. French National Assembly, Session 1971–2, Document No. 2015, vol. 18
(Report of the Committee of Production and Exchange on the Budget).
4. BOT *Passengers at London Airports*, 1970, p. 33.
5. At all four BAA airports the total was 20,164,000. From this we must
deduct the Prestwick figure (327,000). (BAA Report, 1970–1, pp. 118–19).
The Luton figure is taken from p. 125.
6. British Railways Annual Report, 1970, p. 19.
7. DTI Working Party, p. 31. (Appendix I, para. 4.3.4.)
8. Ibid., p. 37. The range suggested is from 9.9 million to 16.4 million.
9. Ibid., p. 106.
10. Air might be quicker, even on journeys between London and northern England, for people whose provincial terminal points were easily accessible to
the local airports. Here it should be observed that large expenditure on

roads leading to the provincial airports may have involved large concealed subsidies to air travel. In contrast, little has been done to improve road access to city railway stations or all-day parking at them. A station specially for road users was opened at Bristol Parkway in 1971. Nearby motorways had no signposts to it for a year, though they had numerous signposts to Bristol Airport, even 15 miles away from it.

11. Michael Baily, 'Inter-city–British Rail's Blue Chip', *The Times*, 14 September 1970.
12. According to the DoE's *Highway Statistics 1971* (pp. 50–2) the average daily traffic flows on the M1/M6 in 1971 exceeded 33,000 vehicles on 95 per cent of the London–Manchester distance. Assuming the traffic to increase in 1971–85 at the same rate as on all classified rural roads, and allowing for relief from planned new roads, the average daily flow by 1985 will spread between 60,000 and 100,000 vehicles over the road's length. Experience with M4 London–Heathrow suggests that such an average load produces congestion-delays in a significant number of hours a year.
13. *Roads for the Future*. Cmnd. 4369, 1970.

10. *The Switch to Rail and the Quality of Transport*

1. Roskill Report, Appendix 6, para. 24.
2. The Channel Tunnel Green Paper gave no estimates of numbers of passengers after 1980, though its estimates of revenue (para. 8.13) would seem to imply $5\frac{1}{2}$ to 7 million rail passengers through the Tunnel by 1985, half of them diverted from air, and thus around 3 to $3\frac{1}{2}$ million continuing and generated surface travellers, of whom not more than 2 million would be on the Paris route. But it did not raise the question of a really good railway service.
3. DTI, op. cit,, p. 37.
4. Ibid., p. 107. Cf. Appendix 2.
5. Harold Wilson, *The Labour Government*, Weidenfeld and Michael Joseph, 1971.
6. Cf. Chapter 9, p. 134.

11. *The Channel Tunnel*

1. *Proposals for a Fixed Channel Link*, Cmnd. 2137, 1963.
2. Cmnd. 5256.
3. H.C. Debs, 8 February 1973, col. 667.

12. *New Rail Investment in London and the South-East*

1. GLC, op. cit., 5.1.
2. Ibid., Fig. 4.
3. C. D. Foster and M. E. Beesley, 'Estimating the Social Benefit of Constructing an Underground Railway in London', *Journal of the Royal Statistical Society*, vol. 126, 1963, pp. 46–58.

13. *What about the Costs?*

1. The British Government's anger at the *Sunday Times* disclosure of the contents of a departmental paper on possible future closures of railway passenger services was itself scandalous. *The Times* of 9 October 1972 published a map, showing the routes which were under consideration. It showed that the lines from Middlesbrough to both Northallerton and Darlington were under consideration for closure; but these short branches

are part of the route between Teesside–Wearside and the whole of the rest of England outside the North-East. But in 1985, if the 20 miles between Teesside and Northallerton were still in use, an urban population of 800,000, or 10 per cent of the whole population served by the main King's Cross route, could have access to London by train in around 2 to 3 hours. This market would be relevant to the investment policy towards the route as a whole. If that branch were closed, travellers from this area to London would have to go by road either to Darlington or to the Teesside airport, thus increasing their door-to-door journey time and adding both to road movement and to the demand for London airport-space. This is no doubt recognized, but secrecy at the early stages of calculations reduces public confidence in the plans themselves.

2. Seat occupation is now normally much lower by rail than by air, partly because a train's load factor changes as it stops along its route. With non-stop trains this would not apply. A revision of the aircraft seat occupation to 60 per cent would affect our calculation only slightly.

3. BEA Report, 1970–1, p. 55.

4. In the 20 years 1950–69, air operators' real costs on domestic trunk lines in the United States fell by an average of 1.8 per cent per passenger mile per year. Cf. A. S. de Vany and Eleanor Garges, 'A Forecast of Air Travel and Airways Use in 1980', *Transportation Research*, vol. 6, March 1972, p. 14.

5. The maximum load might well be much more than this, if the traffic was highly homogeneous, at least within long periods per day.

6. Schriftenreihe des Bundesministeriums für Verkehr, Hegt 40. Battelle-Institut e.V., Frankfurt, *Die Beurteilung von Investitionen im Fernreiseverkehr der Deutschen Bundesbahn und im Luftverkehr der Bundesrepublik Deutschland bis 1980* (2 volumes).

7. West German Railways in 1970 carried twice the freight traffic carried by British Rail, measured in ton-miles. Rail freight was 43 per cent of all freight traffic, as compared with 25 per cent in Britain. As inland waterways accounted for a further 20 per cent of all West German freight ton-miles, the German roads, including 3,000 miles of motorways, carried only 36 per cent of the freight ton-miles, compared with the 75 per cent carried by the British roads. West Germans are intending to spend more on their roads than the British in the next few years; it seems that West Germany has consistently applied different standards of the quality of inland transport-infrastructure.

8. The analysis by sections of routes, given in *Beurteilung von Investitionen*, vol. 1, pp. 165–7, lists 19 sections which were loaded in 1970 at 90 per cent of capacity or more, given the existing mix of use.

9. B. Pilz and D. Wilken, *Beurteilung der Investitionen . . . auf der Grundlage der Kosten-Nutzen Analyse,* research paper, Deutsche Bundesbahn, 1972.

14. *Further Arguments and Answers*

1. Roskill Papers and Proceedings, vol. 1, 3.1, p. 286.

2. A. K. Cairncross, 'The Work of an Economic Adviser', *Public Administration*, vol. 46, 1968, p. 5.

3. Cf. IATA, 17th Technical Conference, 1967, Paper no. 3.

4. Sir Peter Masefield explained some of these processes to the Select Committee on Nationalized Industries in 1970. The BAA, he said, fixed the prices in the duty-free shops:

Notes

Sir Peter Masefield:
We feel it is our responsibility to ensure that the right standards are maintained in these respects, especially as these people are paying us rents and sometimes, of course, a percentage of turnover as well.
Mr Mikardo:
How do you decide on the rents or percentages of turnover or is it just a horse trade?
Sir Peter Masefield:
It is a horse trade, but on a basis of making sure that the people who are in the horse trade are capable of doing the job . : . We fix the prices . . . partly on what is a fair and reasonable price in competition with overseas airports and partly on what we can get because this is commercially a very important part of our business.
HC 275, op cit., Evidence, 5 February 1970, Q. 268–76.
5. See P.J.O. Self, letter to *The Times*, 31 January 1973

15. The Governmental View

1. M. and G. Dimock, *Public Administration*, Holt, Rinehart and Winston, 1964, 3rd ed., p. 131.
2. Cd. 9092 of 1918 (Booth Committee Report), p. 51.
3. *The Times*, leading article on the question of the possible creation of a Prime Minister's Department, 24 August 1972.
4. C. Wright Mills, *The Power Elite*, Oxford University Press, 1959; S. Lens, *The Military Industrial Complex*, New York, 1970.
5. See Harold Wilson, op. cit., p. 61f.
6. The Second Reading of the Maplin Development Bill, on 9 February 1973, opened with the usual ministerial incantation. Using almost the same words that Mr John Davies of the DTI had used in announcing the decision for Foulness airport 22 months before, Mr Rippon, recently translated from Britain's European Entry to the Secretaryship for the Environment, began: 'It is necessary to maintain Britain's position as one of the world's great centres of civil aviation.'
7. R. S. Doganis, 'British Airports Policy', *The Political Quarterly*, vol. 37, 1966, and HC 275 of 1970–1, Report, para. 37.
8. J. S. Mill, *Representative Government*, 1861, Liberal Arts edn., New York, p. 90.
9. R. K. Merton, 'Bureaucratic Structure and Personality' (1940), reprinted in Merton *et al.*, *Reader in Bureaucracy*, The Free Press, Glencoe, Illinois, 1952, pp. 361–71.
10. Cf. P. Selznick, 'An Approach to a Theory of Bureaucracy', *American Sociological Review*, 1943, and the summary by M. Albrow, *Bureaucracy*, Macmillan, 1970, p. 55.
11. The assurance, still being given to the public in 1967, that a new airport would be needed by the early 1970s, was belied by the Roskill findings. When the Civil Aviation Authority's assessment, as reported in the Press in April 1973, showed that the saturation-date would not arrive till 1985, the ministerial reaction was blunt insistence on the Maplin plan. (H.C. Standing Committee on the Maplin Development Bill, 1 May 1973.)
12. Cmnd. 5082, op. cit., p. 4. See Chapter 5, p. 68.
13. Patrick Gordon Walker, *The Cabinet*, Fontana, 1972 edn (first published 1970, p. 118.

14. Ibid., p. 166.
15. Harold Wilson, op. cit., pp. 246f.
16. Ibid., p. 184. Cf. Chapter 10, p. 156.
17. David Braybrooke and Charles E. Lindblom, *A Strategy of Decision*, New York, Free Press, 1963, and London, Collier-Macmillan, 1970, p. 67.
18. H. A. Simon, *Administrative Behaviour*, Macmillan, 1945, p. 61.
19. Ibid., p. 81.
20. We may quote Sir Richard Clarke, then Second Secretary, H.M. Treasury, writing in 1966 about future economic planning for the public sector: 'The advances in the next five years will be in determining what are the most worth-while uses of resources in each part of the public sector, in other words in getting the best value for money, rather than in determining how much resources each part of the public sector should get.' (*Public Administration*, vol. 44, 1966, p. 69).
21. For a discussion of this theme, cf. the articles by Sir Samuel Goldman, Second Secretary, H.M. Treasury, in *Public Administration*, 1970, pp. 247–61; and by Karl M. Hettlage and Philippe Huet, ibid., pp. 263–88, relating to Germany and France.
22. Peter Jay, 'P.E.S.C., P.A.R. and Politics', *The Times*, 31 January 1971. Cf. Michael Spicer, 'Towards a Policy Information and Control System', *Public Administration*, vol. 48, 1970, pp. 443–8.
23. David Howell, *A New Style of Government*, Conservative Political Centre, May 1970.
24. Michael Spicer, 'Towards a Policy Information Control System', *Public Administration*, vol. 48, winter 1970, p. 443.
25. Ibid, p. 444.

16. Parliament and the Airport Decision

1. Ann Robinson, 'Select Committees and the Functions of Parliament', McGill University PhD thesis, unpublished typescript, 1972.
2. Interview with Mr James H. Robertson, quoted by Ann Robinson, op. cit., p. 241.
3. *The Times*, 15 July 1970.
4. *The Times*, 19 December 1970.
5. *Hansard*, 23 February 1971, cols. 936–9 (House of Lords).
6. Ibid., cols. 943–9.
7. *Hansard*, 4 March 1971, cols. 1923–6.
8. Ibid., cols. 2028–30.
9. Ibid., cols. 2064–5.
10. Ibid., col. 1969.
11. Ibid., col. 1986.
12. *Hansard*, 22 February 1971, col. 833.
13. Ibid., col. 835.
14. *Hansard*, 4 March 1971, col. 1913.
15. See above, p. 42.
16. E.g. Ernest Davies, 'Labour's Transport Policy', *The Political Quarterly*, vol. 38, 1967, p. 421.
17. Nevil Johnson, *Parliament and Administration: the Estimates Committee, 1945–65*, Allen & Unwin, 1966, p. 19.
18. Nevil Johnson takes this Report as one of his three case-studies (op. cit., pp. 94–111).
19. Nevil Johnson, op. cit., p. 47n.

20. Ibid., p. 125.
21. Ibid.
22. The Minutes of the Committee's meeting of 10 February 1971 record that the whole of the draft of the first 60 paragraphs was agreed.
23. Report, HC 275 of 1970–1, op. cit., paragraph 38.
24. David Coombes, *The Member of Parliament and the Administration*, Allen & Unwin, 1963, p. 70.
25. Ibid., p. 76–80.
26. Ibid., p. 80, quoting the article by Sir Toby Low (Lord Aldington) in *Public Administration*, vol. 40, 1962, pp. 8–9.
27. Coombes, op. cit., p. 80.
28. A. P. Barker and M. Rush, *The Member of Parliament and his Information*, PEP for the Study of Parliament Group, Allen & Unwin, 1970.
29. HC 275 of 1970–1, Evidence, 12 January 1971, Q. 57.
30. Barker and Rush, op. cit., p. 333.
31. Ibid., p. 304.
32. Richard J. Fenno, *The Power of the Purse: Appropriations Politics in Congress*, Boston, Little Brown, 1966, p. 160.
33. Ibid., p. 162.
34. National Assembly, 1971–2, Document No. 2015, vol. 17, p. 5.
35. Ibid., p. 25.
36. Ibid., pp. 53–4.
37. Ibid., pp. 55–6. London–Paris railway traffic through the tunnel in the early 1980s is put at $4\frac{1}{2}$ million passengers annually, together with $4\frac{1}{2}$ million tons of freight and $4\frac{1}{2}$ million passengers 'sitting in their own motor-cars' on the cross-Channel shuttle service.
38. Ibid., part 4, pp. 32–5. Cf. above, p. 43.
39. National Assembly, 1969–70, Debates, Question 7260, 13 September 1969; see Tables 1969–70, p. 162.
40. National Assembly, 1971–2, Document No. 2015, vol. 9.
41. Ibid., vol. 5, p. 27.
42. N. Tien Phuc (ed.), Paris, Eyrolles, 1972.
43. Ibid., p. 187.

17. Conclusion

1. D. Munby, 'The Assessment of Priorities in Public Expenditure', *The Political Quarterly*, vol. 39, 1968, pp. 375–6.
2. *New Society*, 30 March 1972, p. 656.

APPENDIX 1

EXTRACTS FROM MINUTES OF EVIDENCE TAKEN BY THE
SELECT COMMITTEE ON NATIONALIZED INDUSTRIES ON
26 JANUARY 1971 (HC 275 OF SESSION 1970–1), AND
FROM THE COMMITTEE'S REPORT

During the House of Commons Session of 1970–1 the Select Committee on Nationalized Industries studied the British Airports Authority, and most of its hearings related to matters not concerned with the third London airport. The passages quoted here contain a series of questions put by MPs as members of the Committee, to Mr J. E. Barnes, who was then Under-Secretary, Civil Aviation, in the Department of Trade and Industry.

These passages relate to the absence of government action to plan air-transport needs on a nationwide basis, and are concerned in part with the scheme to set up a Civil Aviation Authority, a piece of machinery which would make such planning possible. They are of interest as an indication of the administration's perception of the problems facing it.

The relevant section of the Select Committee's Report is also included. It shows a perception of the need for a national plan as a basis for a decision on the airport needs of the South-East; its perception would have been heightened if there had been detailed questioning of the figures on which the estimated need for the third airport was based.

The Department's reply to this part of the Report is extensively discussed in Chapter 5 of this book. The Civil Aviation Authority was set up in 1972, but the choice of this particular type of machinery is not directly relevant to the main purpose of this book.

Members present : Sir Henry D'Avigdor-Goldsmid in the Chair. Mr John Biffen, Mr William Clark, Mr David Crouch, Mr Dormand, Mr Peter Emery, Mr John Golding, Mr Green, Mr Alec Jones, Sir Donald Kaberry, Mr J. T. Price.

Appendix 1

Mr J. E. Barnes, Under-Secretary, Civil Aviation, Division 3, Mr H. J. Holdsworth, Director, Accountancy Services (Civil Aviation Branch), called in and examined.

Q. 139. *Chairman (Sir Henry D'Avigdor-Goldsmid)* : Is it still the policy, as laid down in the White Paper I have mentioned, to set up a Civil Aviation Authority?
Mr Barnes : Yes, it is, subject to Parliament, of course.

Q. 140. *Chairman* : You would presumably be putting a plan before Parliament in connection with this? It would be your Department's responsibility?
Mr Barnes : Yes, we would introduce a Bill.[1]

Q. 141. *Chairman* : Therefore you would in fact seek to set up a Civil Aviation Authority?
Mr Barnes : Yes.

Q. 142. *Chairman* : Would it not be correct that such an Authority would have the responsibility for a United Kingdom airport plan?
Mr. Barnes : Yes, that is one of the duties which we should give it, but I think it would be largely an indicative plan, in other words, it would give guidance to the very many individual airports that there are in this country. It would not have a liberal supply of funds to impose its pattern on the nation at large, nor would it be given powers of planning permission which would remain with the Department of the Environment. Planning permission, I may say, is one of the very great obstacles that anyone compiling a national airports plan has to jump. It is very easy to do in-house planning but very difficult to get planning permission in face of the often understandable opposition we meet on any airport development.

Q. 143. *Chairman* : Would a national plan not facilitate this to some extent?
Mr Barnes : I would hope so, but I would very much doubt it. I think everyone hoped two and a half years ago that the Roskill Commission would in effect plan a very great part of our aviation infrastructure, that is the south-east and the areas adjoining the south-east. But we do see today the kind of controversy that that report has engendered, and I fear a wider plan covering the whole of the country would simply multiply that controversy by perhaps two or three times. A plan before it is published and made known is all things to all men, when it is made known it can be an extraordinarily unpopular plan.

Q. 144. *Chairman* : Are you in fact telling us that you do not intend to produce such a plan?

Mr Barnes : No, Sir, what I am saying is that we cannot hope that such a plan would be a trouble-free guide to airport development in the United Kingdom for the next ten or twenty years. Certainly we expect the Civil Aviation Authority to do broad indicative planning, but subject to the powers of the Department of the Environment to say yes or no to individual planning permissions.

Q. 145. *Chairman* : Is there or is there not any plan on the stocks for the creation of this Civil Airports Authority?

Mr Barnes : Yes, indeed, there is a plan, but its main function will lie in the field of the regulation of air services, although this, I agree, in turn blows back on airport planning . . .

Q. 146. *Sir Donald Kaberry* : I like your frankness, but are you saying that you avoid making or helping to make a national airports plan because it may prove unpopular in certain sections?

Mr Barnes : No, Sir, I am not saying that. What I am saying is that to prepare such a plan would first of all, to do it properly, be a very time-consuming effort. The Roskill Commission, admittedly, over a very important area of our civil aviation, laboured for two and a half years at a cost of £1·5 million, I reckon, to the taxpayers, plus the cost of the parties that appeared in front of Roskill. To prepare a plan one must have public participation. Whitehall cannot do it in-house, there must be public participation at each and every stage. I am saying that it will be a very long and expensive process, and at the end of the day I do not think we should delude ourselves that it would give unanimous satisfaction. But certainly I believe that road ought to be trodden.

Q. 147. *Sir Donald Kaberry* : The Roskill Commission was not asked to formulate a national airports plan, am I not right?

Mr Barnes : Absolutely.

Q. 148. *Sir Donald Kaberry* : In the meantime there are many other airports around the country with different authorities, controlling them, each trying to multiply and to develop haphazardly. I cannot resist putting the specific case I have in mind of Yeadon between Bradford and Leeds in Yorkshire, where they have been refused permission to extend a runway, and the campaign against Thorne Waste in Yorkshire by those who wish to preserve that area. All these matters, Leeds, Bradford, Liverpool, Manchester, the East Midlands, or wherever you go around the country, all the local airports could be resolved if there were a national airports plan?

Mr Barnes: I doubt, with respect, whether it would be resolved to everyone's satisfaction. Luton, for example, which is now suffering very badly from noise, sees a national airports plan as entailing the closure of Luton. To them it is self-evident. Those living round Gatwick see a plan as meaning no second runway at Gatwick. Those in Liverpool see the Government in some way, whether by bribery or direction, boosting the traffic very greatly at Liverpool.[2] I am sure the respective owners of Prestwick and Abbotsinch see an answer to their problem. But I would not like you to think that there is no conscious planning at all. Certainly we have deliberately planned a major international airport at Manchester and, until the BAA took over, a major international airport at Prestwick. There, we have, down the spine of the United Kingdom, two major airports ready and anxious to obtain business. Equally, although our powers are very limited, they are limited to planning permission and loan sanction, we have in that negative way restrained some development at various places. You yourself have mentioned Leeds and Bradford, a decision that is unpopular with the pro-aviation lobby but doubtless popular with the environmentalists. In that sense the Government has done a little relative shaping. I think we have dissuaded Liverpool, for example, from spending even more money than the sums they have committed at present. But given the diversity of ownership which stems from the policy in the White Paper of 1961, obviously centralized planning becomes that much more difficult. We cannot have both local ownership, local responsibility and a highly centralized direction on what is to happen to airports. But in various negative ways I think we have tried to shape the pattern a little, and certainly, to come back to Manchester and Prestwick, we have created — at a cost to the taxpayer as to 60 per cent in the case of Manchester — two very fine airports.

. . .

Q. 150. *Mr Green*: You mentioned a negative shaping, but is this in fact not shaping the destination of a huge public investment? How can it be said that the siting of a new airport or the major extension of an existing one, as perhaps in the case of Manchester, is a negative action? Does this not presuppose a positive piece of policy thinking on the part of the Department? After all, there are hundreds of millions of pounds involved here overall?

Mr Barnes: I mentioned negative in particular because our powers to do anything positive are restricted. It might be, for example, and, indeed, I do believe it to be the case, although there are site difficulties,

276

that it would be sensible to replace Prestwick, Abbotsinch and Turn-house by a single central Scottish airport. Certainly as part of our back-room planning we have looked at that. We have found the difficulties on site overwhelming. But assuming that we found this was a sensible idea, then one is bound to ask, where would the money come from in effect to liquidate three airports and construct a major new one? It is no secret to say that money for aerodrome development from the taxpayer has been very limited since 1961.

Q. 151. *Mr Dormand* : Is Mr Barnes saying in effect that they will not produce a positive plan? He said in an earlier answer that it really would not be worth a candle, if I can use that expression. Is Mr Barnes saying that an overall plan can be produced by negative planning? I can see some virtue in this, incidentally. But so far as a positive plan is concerned, he did mention cost and he did lay stress, I think quite properly, on the opposition which such a plan would receive. Is there to be a positive plan? I am not quite clear from the answers given as to whether there is to be a positive plan?

Mr Barnes : I hope that in emphasizing the point that a plan is not a panacea for all the ills of airport development I did not move to the other extreme and suggest that there was no point at all in pre-paring a plan. This is a job that we shall ask the Civil Aviation Authority to embark upon, but it is a very slow, long and costly process especially as there must be, I think everyone would agree this is necessary, public participation both at local and at national levels. It is very easy for in-house planners, perhaps men like myself with assistants, to begin to draw circles on a map and say, 'We will develop here and close there', but the reality is very different. One does run into, and rightly, public opposition, or indeed disappointment that they have not got a bigger circle on the plan. But certainly I think the Civil Aviation Authority will be charged with the job of preparing what I call an indicative plan. It does not mean a plan that the Government is hell-bent on imposing on the map of the United Kingdom no matter what it costs either in money or in terms of planning permission, but what I would call a broad indicative plan.

Q. 152. *Mr Crouch* : That is more helpful than the first answer you gave, because I was a little dismayed to think that your Department had lost some of its nerve in making a recommendation which might or might not be accepted by the Government and by Parliament as, for example, on Stansted by the Board of Trade in the past. After all, the White Paper we are talking about does refer to the Civil Aviation Authority as thinking in broad structural terms. Could I ask you to let your hair down about this and tell us frankly what are the thoughts of the Department on this very big problem of the structural plan of air communications, which is airlines, routes, airports, some run by the BAA and some by municipal authorities, and, of course, surface transport as well? It is an enormous planning problem with enormous economic problems and potentials. Obviously it involves the Department of the Environment, obviously it involves the Department of Transport. Could you say whether you do not think yourself, or whether it is not thought in your Department that your Department should not perhaps fly a kite here? You do not have to expect your recommendations to be accepted by Parliament, but at least you are concerned with economic achievement for the country and you have a duty to look ahead and then perhaps some of those other Departments can come in and criticize you?

Mr Barnes: I think, for the reasons you have given, that the preparation of a sensible plan would be the very long and costly process that I have mentioned. Certainly I would not like to pretend we have got the sort of resources available to us that were available to the Roskill Commission. It is not a case of planning airports in isolation, you have then got to think about, in effect, the planning of air services, to what extent you are going to allow commercial or market factors to determine this pattern, or to what extent you are going to try to distort it by either direction or outright subsidy. Then you move a little to the next stage. You have got to think in terms of surface transport and possible developments there, and, more widely, what one might call general regional planning and possible growth points at various parts of the United Kingdom. So although you may modestly think you are starting with an airport plan, gradually the pebble in the pond begins to spread over a very wide area indeed, and this is why I say it is a long and expensive process calling for a lot of scarce resources to help to get it. It is not something that can be done in six months.

Q. 153. *Mr Crouch*: I do appreciate the size of the task, but you are not suggesting to this Committee that such thinking would not take place, are you?

Mr Barnes: No, I am not suggesting that at all, and indeed we ourselves, within the limits of our resources, are already beginning to get some of the basic elements of such a plan, that is the origin and destination of passengers by particular areas in the United Kingdom, both surface and air. This again we think is the first step to the construction of a rational plan. But it is a long, slow, expensive process, and at the end of the day none of us must delude ourselves that this is a panacea, because even the basic concept of airport planning is bitterly contested as between the economist, on the one hand, who has one objective for airport planning, and what I might call the town and country planners on the other. The Roskill Commission have very neatly drawn attention to this sort of basic gulf between what planning is in aid of, the economists, on the one hand and the countryside on the other.

Q. 154. *Mr Jones* : It seems to me what you are saying is that the disadvantages of a very detailed national plan outweigh the advantage which could accure from it but you would support a less detailed plan. Would you confirm this? Secondly, you did say that you are able to influence negatively the position at certain airports. Could you give us some idea as to whether you are really able to influence those air-ports which are controlled and owned by local authorities as to whether they should be expanded or whether they should be contracted, or provide different services?

Mr Barnes : The answer to your first question is yes, I do think an attempt should be made to produce a broad national plan, but, I am sorry to repeat myself, I do think because it is so complex and spread over so many factors it is not an easy thing that someone can do in six months. It is a long, slow costly process. As regards local authorities, yes, we can and have influenced local authority develop-ment mostly, I am sorry to say once again, in a negative way because that is where our powers lie. For example, loan sanction is something that local authorities have got to come to us about, and indeed before they make formal application we do advise them not to embark on a particular piece of development. At the other end of it the Department of the Environment when deciding on planning permission do allow aviation to express a view. We have seen, happily for some, the results at Bradford. It has happened at Southampton and it has happened at Southend where aviation, for environmental reasons, has not been allowed its head. On the positive side, we do rather grudgingly, rather cheeseparingly, I admit very rarely, make grants to local authority aerodromes. We did make a grant to Newcastle, we did make a grant to help Teesside get established. In regard to some other aerodromes which were formerly in our ownership, we still have contractual liabilities to them on capital expansion, Birmingham is a case in point, I think the one remaining case. Therefore by virtue of the power of the purse we can either aid or not.

Q. 155. *Mr Crouch* : On this question of grants, are the grants which you make as a result of the local authorities first approaching you, or are there any occasions when you have made the first approaches yourself?

Mr Barnes: I certainly cannot bring to mind a case in which we have gone round with our cheque book in our hands, as it were, positively thrusting money on local authorities. But, for example, in the case of the establishment of the Teesside airport, there was the idea of taking over the Middleton St George old R.A.F. aerodrome and more or less simultaneously there was the thought that the Government ought to give something to get it started.

Q. 156. *Mr Price*: Mr Barnes made a passing reference a few moments ago to an overall plan for the future. Is it not a fact that if we were starting *de novo*, from scratch, as it were, and making such a plan, many of the airports, particularly the marginal or peripheral airports, would never be there at all? They have grown up in a most haphazard way without any rhyme or reason, often from grounds of local prestige or other factors which could no longer be justified either on environmental grounds or on economic grounds. Is it not useful in this context to compare the experience of this small islands of ours, less than 1,000 miles long overall, with the experience of metropolitan France? We have in this country a vast network of railways which are being electrified to a large extent, the main lines being made more efficient. We have the densest road traffic in the world, yet we have perhaps more airports proportionate to our area than any of the countries of Europe. Is it not time we had a sorting out of all this morass of haphazard airports which could no longer justify themselves? And is it not in the minds of our officials in the Ministry who have to advise at top level on these matters that the French Government would no longer allow an airport, for example, at a small town that happened to be on a main line railway with a first-class service? These are conflicting elements. There is also the environmental point, the growing resistance of large numbers of our people in every part of the country to whatever you propose so far as flying is concerned because of its destruction of the environment. So you want fewer airports, and not more?

Mr Barnes: Obviously it is fair to say that to some extent the growth of our airport structure was haphazard. This is true of so much of our industrial infrastructure, of our road system, of what remains of our railway system, of some of our industrial conurbations. I think we can see the unhappy legacy of the past in many of the infrastructures of the United Kingdom, certainly many of the aerodromes we are talking about have, in aviation terms, a very long history. If we were starting with a clean sheet today with the knowledge that we have got I doubt, for example, whether we would have an airport at both Prestwick and Abbotsinch, although a good deal of planning went into that at the time. I doubt whether we would have an airport at Birmingham and Coventry; it is arguable whether we would have an airport at Liverpool and Manchester and perhaps arguable whether we would have an airport at both Southampton and Bournemouth. But for the rest, I think we would have those airports. I have picked out what we call the 'terrible twins' where, if we were starting with a clean sheet, we might have one airport rather than the two that exist at the moment. But which of the twins would be the winner, or whether we would close them both and build on a virgin site, is a more open question. But certainly one can point to that kind of perhaps unhappy duplication. However elsewhere, for example, in the Highlands and Islands, Newcastle, Teesside, I would think the spread is not a wasteful one.

Q. 157. *Mr Emery*: I would like to ask two questions on the planning side, one on the background information. In cross-questioning Mr Peter Masefield last week he made it quite clear that the catchment area, in their judgment, for the major section of flying was the south-east, and he went on to say that they were able to show that only about 15 per cent of those people coming into London went on by other means of air transportation. Therefore they wanted to come to London was the assumption that was drawn from this. He did not take up the point which I had hoped he would take up which was whilst people were not going on by air, a very large section of this other 80 per cent coming into London were not just coming to the south-east, they were going on by other means of transportation to Birmingham, to Bristol, to other areas. I was very worried that there did not appear to be any information that could be given to us about that further transportation of incoming passengers. I therefore ask, has any study been made about it? Are the Ministry considering this? Can you add to what Mr Peter Masefield said? Secondly, I was very concerned about the negative influence. In the south-west we are inclined to feel there has been a most positive negative influence about the enlargement of or about the encouragement of Exeter, or any airport in the south-west, including the Plymouth study and everything else. I am worried about this negative influence as it affects the south-west. I wonder if you could say something about the position of the south-west in any airport structure?

Mr Barnes: If I could turn back to the south-east, I believe that what Mr Masefield said or intended to say was that 80 per cent of the people passing through the London airports had their final origin or destination in the south-east. In other words, the great weight of traffic being handled by, in effect, Luton, Gatwick and Heathrow is in respect of people who are starting or ending their journey in the south-east, a very large number of them, of course, are overseas tourists. Fifteen per cent would probably be coming from other parts of the country, or perhaps other parts of the continent, coming to Heathrow to inter-line with other services. Some of those 15 per cent clearly would come from other parts of the country, and so would the balance, the 5 per cent or 10 per cent who may be travelling on to some other part of the United Kingdom. This is really the obstinate fact that we meet, that most of the traffic that we are trying to cater for at London's airports is really south-eastern traffic, a lot of it overseas tourist traffic, the rest is fragmented over the rest of the country, and unhappily it is the case that those sort of droplets are not really big enough, except in the case of Manchester, to be able to command international services both by a reasonable spread of the destinations and by a reasonable frequency of service;[3] to have one service a week between, say, Manchester and Marseilles is a nonsense, people do not want to know that, they come down to London. But Manchester, I am glad to say, is growing, and it is certainly our intention in the airport field to see that those services are not frustrated by lack of capacity. In the north and in Scotland it is simply, I fear, a commercial issue that the airlines do not see the traffic there in sufficient numbers to mount the sort of services that we on the airport side would dearly love to see. We would like to see the load taken off London. With regard to the south-west, we did try a little positive planning there in that through the South-Western Economic Planning Council we did commission a study to which we contributed to see what was the right answer to the aerodrome problem of the south-west. . . .

Q. 164. . . . It is certainly not part of our policy that one should erect an enormous aerodrome, such as the one suggested at Thorne Waste, in the hope that it will be a growth point in the area in question, because again, if I can perhaps quote from the Roskill Commission, they said in order to act as a stimulus for growth the airport must first of all fulfil its primary purpose, and that is be successful and suitable as an airport.

Q. 165. *Mr Biffen* : But in the decision as to whether to take the weight of one set of factors, namely, those related to economic growth, or another set of factors, namely, environment or defence, do you accept that this is really the area in which a political judgment is made?
Mr Barnes : I think in the middle of that, but not at the extreme.

Q. 166. *Mr Biffen* : The question all this leads up to is, to what extent are you equipped to, as it were, cost for the politician who has to make this judgment as to what extent environmental and defence considerations shall be taken into account? To what extent are you equipped to cost the options?

Mr Barnes : We ourselves are not equipped at all in terms of resources of manpower and skills. We have got some, but certainly we would not pretend to the battery of skills and indeed the money cost of running to the kind of work that the Roskill Commission did. This is something that, over time, might perhaps be remedied, but we have not got anything equivalent to their research team or the funds to pay for it.

Q. 167. *Mr Biffen* : If you do not possess these skills, do they exist anywhere else in the machinery of Government in the context of a plan, indicative or otherwise, for a national airport?

Mr Barnes : I think such a team could be assembled were there the will and the money to assemble it, just as Roskill assembled his research team and in turn used consultants, and so on. Certainly I think there is sufficient knowledge to provide a central direction. We do know the sort of things that need to be done. What I am saying is we have not got the numbers, we have not got the money, we have not got the experts available to put on to this task in a high, wide and handsome way. We hope, over time, the CAA will have such people.

Notes
1. This legislation was passed in 1972. The Civil Aviation Authority was then set up and instituted a survey of the airport needs of the Midlands, Lancashire and Yorkshire, with the possibility of taking in the South-West. By then, the decision to build a third London airport already made it impossible for this survey to contribute to the Government's objective, as stated by Mr Barnes in his reply to Question 157, to 'see the load taken off London'.
2. Thus Liverpool's potential as a relief to London was not being considered seriously. The Select Committee's discussion did not pursue that question.
3. This refers to the situation in 1971. It does not take into account either (*a*) the fact that by the mid-1980s these 'droplets' will be immensely bigger, or (*b*) the likelihood that traffic terminating outside the South-East will increase faster.

EXTRACT FROM THE SAME COMMITTEE'S REPORT, PARAGRAPHS 34–39

National Airports Policy
34. The Department of Trade and Industry is responsible for civil aviation policy, of which airport policy forms a minor, but vital, part.

The 1969 White Paper on Civil Aviation Policy accepted that there had been a lack of clarity about the objectives of civil aviation policy.[1] Your Committee found a similar ambiguity in the general strategy of providing airport facilities beyond the proposition that airports should not be provided directly by the State.[2] The Authority stated the long standing need for a national airports plan.[3] Mr Goronwy Roberts, then Minister of State at the Board of Trade told the Sub-Committee that he believed that the whole question of airport provision, its organization and management needed to be looked at. He envisaged two main alternatives; a national airports authority or the continuation of the present mixed ownership, with the advantages of the participation of local patriotism. In the latter case, he saw overall co-ordination being provided by the proposed Civil Aviation Authority.[4] Meanwhile the policy of decentralized aerodrome ownership, adumbrated in the 1961 White Paper still obtains, blessed by the concurrence of the Edwards Committee of Inquiry into Civil Air Transport.[5] The Government cannot compel either the Authority or the municipal authorities to go beyond what each thinks proper in developing airports, but it can exercise a negative control both by its powers over the licensing of services and, in the case of the Authority, by its controls over capital expenditure, and in the case of municipalities by its powers of planning consent and of loan sanction. It can also provide grants for airport facilities.[6] In these ways the Department has influenced airport development, but without the guidelines of an overall plan.

35. More recently Your Committee were told by the Department that they were not equipped to prepare an airports plan, although, if it were required, they could assemble a team capable of performing this task.[7] Their intention was to entrust the Civil Aviation Authority, when it was established, with the task of preparing an indicative national airports plan.[8] Whoever did it, it would be a long and costly task. The decision on the Third London Airport would probably precede the formulation of even an indicative national plan.[9]

36. The Department had hoped that the Roskill Commission would, in effect, produce the south-eastern part of a national plan.[10] The Commission, however, regarded this as being beyond their terms of reference[11] and limited themselves to considering the best site for the Third London Airport.

37. The situation appears to be that, because the formulation of

a national plan would take much time and skill, and because neither the Department nor any other body is yet preparing itself to undertake such a task, the decision on the siting of the Third Airport will be taken before there is a national plan. This, when it is prepared, will have to be built round the existing fact of the Third Airport. Your Committee regret the present dilatoriness in starting to prepare a national plan. To have one would greatly assist airport planning not only in the south-east but also in Scotland and elsewhere and they recommend that this work be started in earnest without waiting for the establishment of the Civil Aviation Authority, whenever that may be.

The Third London Airport

38. The Roskill Commission decided unanimously, for Professor Buchanan in his note of dissent expressly stated that he accepted his colleagues' forecast of the timing of the need, that the first runway of the Third London Airport must be operational during 1980. This conclusion is supported by no less than twelve quarto, double columned pages of closely reasoned argument, and Your Committee is clearly in no position to challenge it. But the implication of its acceptance is that a decision on its location is urgent; to delay it is to aggravate the very problems it is meant to solve. If the decision is delayed, then in the Authority's view saturation at the existing London airports is inevitable, and 'we shall have to start turning traffic away from these islands'.[12] The decision, with its fine balance of argument between environmental and commercial considerations, must be taken at the highest level, and it is not for Your Committee to seek to advise those responsible. Nevertheless, Your Committee thought it right to ask the British Airports Authority to comment on the Roskill conclusions, and they also took evidence from the Department on the financial implications of a decision that a Third Airport was to be built, irrespective of where it was to be sited.

39. The Authority stated that all of the sites were too far from London, and hence not one was to be preferred.[13] Your Committee has no remit to comment on the attractions of one location as against another, and will therefore avoid doing so; except to note that the Authority agreed with the Commission that neither direction of airlines nor subsidy of surface passenger movements is the answer to an inaccessibly sited airport.[14]

Notes
1. Cmnd. 4213, para. 7.
2. See, for example, Evidence, p. 2.
3. Q. 100.
4. Q(A). 1041.
5. Cmnd. 4018, paras. 903–9.
6. See also Q. 148, 154.
7. Q. 166–7.
8. Q. 151.
9. Q. 152–4, 204.
10. Q. 143.
11. Commission on the Third London Airport Report 2.12.
12. Q. 106.
13. Evidence, p. 16; Q. 94.
14. Evidence, p. 17, para. 9.

This Working Party consisted of representatives of the Board of
Trade (which was incorporated in the Department of Trade and
Industry in 1970), of BEA, BOAC, two independent airlines, and the
British Airports Authority. (Para. 1.3.)

The meeting that led to the formation of the Working Party was
held on the day on which Mr Crosland made the first announcement in Parliament of the decision which led to the setting up of
the Roskill Commission. (Para 1.1.2.1.)

Although the Working Party was primarily concerned with the
problem of traffic at Heathrow in the 1970s, it also extended the
scope of its investigation so that 'material could be provided which
would assist the Commission in their consideration of the timing
of the need for the Third London Airport'. (Para 1.1.2.2.)

The Working Party's methods in making projections up to 1980
are described in the extract from the Report which follows: 'The
extension of the forecasts to 1985 was obtained by continuing the
predicted growth of the international travel market and sea traffic
for a further 5 years with further reductions in the rate of increase
in domestic air traffic.' This exercise was 'not given the same amount
of thought [as the projections to 1980] and it should be regarded
as an extrapolation rather than a forecast'. Later the Working Party
produced revised figures (only up to 1980) in the light of developments during its work. The reasons for the revision are given on
page 103, which is reproduced below in full.

The North American figure for 1980, in millions of passengers,
was revised upwards from lower/likely/higher projections of
6.8/8.4/9.6 to 9.3/11.0/13.0. If this had been carried forward to

1985 the most likely figure for that year would have been 18 million, instead of 13·9 million in the original forecast.

The domestic forecast was revised downwards from 7.5/9.0/10.8 to 6.5/7.8/9.3. A further extrapolation to 1985 would have produced a revised 'most likely' figure of 10 million instead of 12·8 million.

Thus the most likely 'revised' global total for 1985 for Heathrow and Gatwick was 88 million; the revised figure would be around 90 million. This agrees with Roskill's Working Party figure of 82·7 million, which was arrived at *after* allowing for small reductions specifically attributable to transfer to rail within Britain and to regional airports.

This book has not criticized, or seriously dissented from, either the Roskill Commission, or their advisers, or the DTI Working Party, in respect of their figures for 1980. What it has done is to insist that the Government ought not to have been satisfied with the extrapolations of these figures for the years after 1980. Improving railways and the spontaneous development of regional airports are likely to bring new elements into the situation after 1980, even if the Government does nothing about it. But it was open to the Government in 1971, and was still open to it in 1973, to take action, by studying the possible effects of investment in railways (co-ordinated with the French and Benelux Governments) and a positive approach to regional airports, particularly to Liverpool for North Atlantic traffic. This option could turn out to be preferable to a third airport for very many reasons, for the sake of the economy and of a broad public interest.

The DTI Working Party's explanation of its methods is reproduced here in order to illustrate the Government's irresponsibility, in 1971 and again on the Maplin Development Bill in 1973, in simply asserting a conviction of the need for the third airport, on the basis of these calculations, without examining the options open to it.

. . . About four-fifths of the passenger traffic at London's airports is international and this traffic is more than three-quarters of the international air traffic at all United Kingdom airports. More than 60 per cent of passengers entering and leaving the United Kingdom travel by air; this proportion has been growing and is likely to continue to grow. London area air passenger traffic is, therefore, closely linked with total international passenger movement.

4.3.3.2. Leaving aside traffic across the land border with the Irish Republic which is mainly local, the UK international travel market is made up of sea and air travel. In many ways these two transport modes cater for different kinds of demand for travel, yet the numbers of passengers carried by each have changed in ways similar to those that would have been expected of a single market composed of two parts — sea transport and air transport — with substitution at the margin.

4.3.3.3. The rate of growth of passenger traffic by sea and air together into and out of the United Kingdom has been remarkably stable at about 9 per cent a year over the last 15–20 years. We reviewed the forces at work, or expected to come into play in the next decade, that might operate to accelerate or retard the expansion of international passenger travel. On the side of buoyancy, the largest international markets – those to and from Europe and to and from North America – have been growing faster than total travel between the UK and the rest of the world. The increasing importance of the faster growing markets could raise the rate of increase of total international travel, although to the extent that these markets are gaining at the expense of slower growing markets the scope for these above average rates of growth will lessen. Continued growth of international travel at rates of similar order to those of the past implies an increasing share of disposable income spent on international travel by those groups of people from which travellers into and out of the United Kingdom are mainly drawn. However, consumers' expenditure on travel and associated items is a sufficiently small proportion of domestic income for this to impose no restraint on traffic growth at past, or somewhat higher than past, rates even though there will be other growing demands on consumers' discretionary income.

4.3.3.4. The Working Party decided that there were no strong reasons for forecasting the most likely growth of international passenger travel at a rate other than the 9 per cent of the past; any reasons that there were for taking a different view were covered by the inevitable uncertainties of forecasting — uncertainties arising from the errors of estimating underlying growth rates in the past and from the imprecision of any calculation of current trend values. In setting limits within which we have a high degree of confidence the traffic will lie, we took account of the consequences for international travel of the recent slower growth stemming partly from policies at home (including devaluation) designed to achieve a permanent shift in the allocation of resources from consumption to exports and investment. Some of these policies, such as devaluation, may have the effect of increasing the number of overseas visitors to the United Kingdom; but these are fewer than the number of United Kingdom residents who travel abroad, and the boost to foreign traffic is not likely to outweigh the adverse effect on overseas travel by UK residents.

4.3.3.5. Methods and reasoning similar to those employed above in the context of total international travel have been used with some modifications to project international travel in each of the main markets and to estimate sea travel within the total. The modifications recognize that for the longer journeys there is less substitution between sea and air travel. This is what we would expect on general grounds and is in accordance with the evidence from the past.

4.3.3.6. International air passenger forecasts can now be made. Over the period 1968–1980 traffic growth is forecast at rates commencing at about 12 per cent a year and declining to about 11 per cent a year by the end of the period. These rates also apply to the large European market. Traffic to and from Ireland is likely to grow less quickly, at rates falling from about $8\frac{1}{2}$ per cent a year to about $6\frac{1}{2}$ per cent a year, whilst in the North American market they might run from 15 per cent a year down to about 11 per cent a year. Other long-haul traffic is forecast to expand at about 13 per cent a year. These forecasts continue the slow decline in the rate of growth of all passenger traffic carried by air that has been observed in the past. Within the total the forecast for the North American routes is, on the information available to us, consistent with the forecast of North Atlantic traffic now being made for ICAO. Most of the international air traffic to and from the United Kingdom will pass through London area airports. The proportion of total international air traffic that uses these airports will continue to rise as a consequence of the changing market pattern of the traffic, since the fast growing long-haul services are more concentrated at the major international airports than are short-haul services.

4.3.4. *Passenger forecast: domestic*

Domestic air traffic is more difficult to forecast. It is, however, a relatively small part of air traffic at London. The United Kingdom is limited in size and there is a network of railways and roads linking the main centres of population and industry. With easy and fairly rapid surface transport the proportion of total domestic traffic carried by air is very small. Considerations of what might happen to the total market are of little value in forecasting air traffic. For this same reason no sudden incursion of air transport into the markets of surface operators can be foreseen. There have been periods of rapid growth in domestic air travel in the past. These seem to have been associated with large fare reductions or special cheap tickets; domestic air fares have risen sharply in recent years and there may be further increases to come. Domestic air transport is little used by holiday-makers so that the buoyancy expected in international travel will be absent.

Though domestic traffic may grow less quickly than international traffic there is evidence of substantial interlining between domestic and international services. Various estimates of the scale of this interlining at London have been made from the results of surveys made for other purposes. The estimates centre on a figure of about one-third of domestic journeys being for the purpose of making an air connection. This suggests that the growth of international traffic may prevent the growth rate of domestic traffic from sinking far. We decided to predict growth of domestic traffic at an average rate of $8\frac{1}{2}$ per cent per year, with outer limits of 7 per cent and 10 per cent per year, until 1980, with a slowing down of the rate of expansion similar to that forecast for international traffic.

Appendix 5 to the Report begins as follows:

Revision of Traffic Forecasts
In the year since the forecast was first made for this Working Party and submitted in evidence to the Roskill Commission, events have led to a change of view on the ways in which the air transport market is developing, calling for some revision of some aspects of the forecast. The main events which have been considered are the large increases in traffic with North America in 1969 and the continuing slow growth of domestic traffic in that year. The demise of British Eagle resulted in a loss of service at Heathrow on the domestic trunk route to Glasgow and on charter services to Europe, North America and other long-haul routes. Gatwick's fast growth in 1969 is attributed largely to the transfer of some of these services from Heathrow to Gatwick, where they were taken up by other operators.

In the future, the start of BEA Air Tours operations at Gatwick is likely to lead to some reshuffling of traffic between operators at Gatwick, some diversion of charter traffic from other airports in the London vicinity such at Luton, Stansted and Southend and a small transfer of inclusive tour passengers from scheduled services at Heathrow to charter services at Gatwick. A one per cent diversion of Heathrow's scheduled traffic to Europe has been incorporated in the forecast but no specific allowance has been made for other changes. If a quarter of a million passengers were to be attracted to Gatwick in 1970 from other airports not included in the forecast, and this block of traffic were to stay at Gatwick in the future, the Gatwick forecasts of European traffic would need to be increased by about ten per cent. Other changes may flow from BUA's change of ownership but these are too uncertain to enable any worthwhile estimates to be made of future traffic developments.

Appendix 2

Traffic demand

North America traffic increased by a quarter in 1969, including a two thirds increase in charter traffic. Further buoyant traffic growth is likely, boosted by route expansion and new promotional fares. The previous forecasts incorporated annual growth rates which declined steadily over the next decade because of the small potential for diversion from sea traffic : this decline has now been postponed five years. Domestic traffic growth has been retarded in the last five years to an average annual growth of less than four per cent. Some recovery is expected, but taking into account fare increases and the planned extension of railway electrification to Glasgow, domestic growth rates have been reduced to a most likely seven and a half per cent per annum with a range of plus or minus one and a half per cent.

The overall effect, shown in table 1, is that total traffic in 1975 is forecast at much the same level as previously, but the 1980 passenger forecasts have been increased by about two and a half per cent.

SOURCES

The sources used for this study have been very varied. The main materials consulted (not necessarily all quoted in the text) are divided into two main groups: first, Government publications, books and articles related to the choice between building a new airport now and deferring it; second, material related to the decision-making process in general.

I. THE CHOICE

A. Official Publications (all HMSO unless otherwise stated).
The first three mentioned provide the main source-material.

Commission on the Third London Airport (The Roskill Report), with Appendices, Papers and Proceedings.
Department of Trade and Industry: *Report of a Working Party on Traffic and Capacity at Heathrow* (1971).
Ibid., *Observations in Reply to the Report of the Select Committee on Nationalized Industries (British Airports Authority,* Cmnd. 5082, 1972).
British Air Services, Cmnd. 6712, 1946.
Select Committee on Estimates, 1946–47, Sixth Report, *Civil Aviation.*
Civil Aerodromes and Air Navigational Services, Cmnd. 1457, 1961.
Ministry of Transport: *Study of a Rail Link to Heathrow* (1970).
Ministry of Transport: *Proposals for a Fixed Channel Link,* Cmnd. 2173, HMSO, 1963 (reprinted in abridged form in D.L. Munby (ed.), *Transport,* Penguin Modern Economics Series, 1968).
Report of the Public Inquiry into a third London Airport at Stansted (1967).
The Third London Airport, Cmnd. 3259, 1967.
Board of Trade: *Civil Aviation Policy,* Cmnd. 4213, November, 1969.
Report of the Committee of Inquiry into Civil Air Transport (Chairman, Sir Ronald Edwards), 2 May 1969 (Cmnd. 4018).
British Airports Authority: Annual Reports and Accounts.
British European Airways: Annual Reports and Accounts.
British Railways Board: Annual Reports and Accounts.
Deutsche Bundesbahn: Geschäftsbericht (Annual).
National Statistical Yearbooks.
French Embassy, London: Information Bulletins.
Cook's Continental Timetable: Airline Timetables.
Greater London Council: *Channel Tunnel London Passenger Terminal*: A Document for Consultation, November 1972.
City of Liverpool, Director of Transportation and Basic Services, Report, *The Development of Liverpool Airport,* 1970.
Ibid., *Liverpool Airport Market Research Study,* 1970.
Battelle-Institut (for West German Transport Ministry), *Die Beurteilung von Investitionen im Fernreiseverkehr der Deutschen Bundesbahn und im Luftver-*

Sources

kehr der BRD bis 1980 auf der Grundlage des Kosten-Nutzen Analyse. Frankfurt, 2 vols, 1972.

The Channel Tunnel Project; Cmnd. 5256, March, 1973.

Civil Aviation Authority: *Airport Planning: an Approach on a National Basis,* December, 1972.

Parliamentary debates and reports

Commons: 29 June 1967, on Stansted.

Lords: 11 December 1967, ibid.

Commons and Lords: 28 February 1968: Announcement of new inquiry.

Ibid., April 1968: Announcement of appointment of Roskill Commission and terms of reference.

Lords: 21 and 22 February 1971, debate on Roskill.

Commons: 4 March 1971, ibid.

Commons and Lords: May 1971, Statement on the Government's decision to choose the Foulness site and to go ahead as soon as possible; cols. 34–44.

Commons: 8 February 1972: Debate on the Second Reading of the Maplin Development Bill.

Select Committee on Nationalized Industries: First Report, HC 275 of 1970–71, *'The British Airports Authority'*, (especially Minutes of Evidence, 19 and 26 January 1971).

France: *Journal Officiel,* 1971–72, Document 2015 (Reports of Committees on the Finance Law); Volumes 17 (rail), 18 (air).

B. Books

M. Chisholm and G. Manners (eds.): *Spatial Problems of the British Economy,* Cambridge University Press, 1971. Notably—Peter Hall: *Spatial structure of metropolitan England and Wales* (pp. 96–125); M. Chisholm: *Freight transport costs, industrial location and regional development,* pp. 213–44).

Olive Cook: *The Stansted Affair,* Pan Books, 1967.

John Davis: *The Concorde Affair,* Leslie Frewin, 1969.

R. E. Dickinson: *The City Region in Western Europe,* Routledge, 1967.

Friends of the Earth: *The Maplin Manifesto: The Case against a Third London Airport,* 1973.

Gunther John: *Ermittlung und Analyse der Investitionen und des Anlagevermögens im Verkehr der BRD,* Berlin: Duncker & Humblot, 1971.

E. J. Mishan: *The Costs of Economic Growth,* Penguin, 1967.

P. R. Odell: *Oil and World Power: A Geographical Interpretation,* Pelican, 1970, 1972.

N. Tien Phuc (ed.): *Pour une politique économique des transports,* Paris: Eyrolles, 1972.

C. Articles

Ronald Wraith: 'The Public Inquiry into Stansted Airport', *The Political Quarterly,* 1966, pp. 2–14.

R. Doganis: 'Airport Planning and Administration: A Critique', *The Political Quarterly,* vol. 37, 1966, p. 418.

Ernest Davies: 'Labour's Transport Policy', *The Political Quarterly,* vol. 38, 1967, pp. 421–34.

Sir William Hildred: 'British Air Transport in the Seventies', *The Political Quarterly,* vol. 40, 1969, pp. 316–8.

294

Sources

W. A. Robson: 'British Airports Authority', *The Political Quarterly*, vol. 42, October-December, 1971, pp. 423–8.

Ian Fulton: 'Civil Aviation's Quantum Jump', (the statement of the case for very rapid commitment to VTOL), *The Political Quarterly*, vol. 42, April-June, 1971, pp. 133–49.

Peter Self: 'Nonsense on Stilts', *The Political Quarterly*, vol. 41, 1970, pp. 249–60.

Ibid.: 'The Roskill Argument', *New Society*, February, 1971.

John G. U. Adams: 'London's Third Airport: from TLA to Airstrip One', *The Geographical Journal*, vol. 137, part 4, 1971, pp. 468–504.

J. Parry Lewis: *The Forecasts of Roskill*, University of Manchester, Centre for Urban and Regional Research, Occasional Paper No. 11, 1971.

Brian Dixon: 'The Case for a New Yorkshire Airport', *Town and Country Planning*, July, 1971, pp. 351–4.

I. Little and K. McLeod: 'The new pricing policy of the BAA', *Journal of Transport Economics and Policy*, 5/72, 101–8.

A. H. Watson: 'Investment Appraisals: The Channel Tunnel', *Public Administration*, 1967, pp. 1–22.

Georg Leber: 'Europe's Need for High-Speed Surface Transport', *Railway Gazette International*, May 1972, pp. 169–71.

Robert Crow and Jean Longeot: 'A Forecasting Model of the Market for New Aircraft; the Case of Concorde', *Transportation Research*, vol. 6, September 1972, pp. 211–20.

T. F. Golob, E. T. Canty, R. L. Gustafson: 'An Analysis of Consumer Preferences for a public transportation system', *Transportation Research*, vol. 6 (3/72), pp. 81–102.

A. S. De Vany and Eleanor Garges: 'A Forecast of Air Travel and Airway Use in 1980', *Transportation Research*, vol. 6 (3/72), pp. 1–18.

R. J. Gronau: 'The effect of travelling time on the demand for Passenger transportation', *Journal of Political Economy* (8) 1970, pp. 377–94.

P. R. Odell: 'Europe's Oil', *National Westminster Bank Review*, August 1972, pp. 6–21.

Derek Ezra: 'Possibilities of a World Energy Crisis', *National Westminster Bank Review*, November 1971, pp. 22–33.

C. D. Foster and M. E. Beesley: 'Estimating the Social Benefit of Constructing an Underground Railway in London', *Journal of the Royal Statistical Society*, vol. 126 (1963), pp. 46–58.

D. Specialist periodicals

International Civil Aviation Organisation Bulletin.
Railway Gazette International.
Modern Railways.
La Vie du Rail.

II. DECISION-MAKING: PARLIAMENT AND ADMINISTRATION

A. Books

Peter M. Blau: *The Dynamics of Bureaucracy: A Study of Interpersonal Relations in Two Government Agencies*, Chicago, 1963 ed.

David Braybrooke and Charles E. Lindblom: *A Strategy of Decision*, New York, 1963, Free Press; London, 1970, Collier-Macmillan.

Sources

Nigel Despicht: *Policies for Transport in the Common Market*, The Garden City Press, 1964.

Robert A. Dahl and Charles E. Lindblom: *Politics, Economics and Welfare*, Harper, 1953, Torchbook edition, 1963.

Marshall Dimock and Gladys Dimock: *Public Administration*, New York, 1953, 1966 (3rd ed.) Holt, Rinehart.

Charles E. Lindblom: *The Intelligence of Democracy*, Collier-Macmillan, 1965.

James G. March and Herbert A. Simon: *Organisations*, Wiley, 1958.

Gunnar Myrdal: *Objectivity in Social Research*, Nelson, 1970.

Charles Schultze: *The Politics and Economics of Public Spending*, Washington, D.C., Brookings Institute, 1969.

A. P. Barker and M. Rush: *The Member of Parliament and his Information*, PEP, 1970.

David Coombes: *The Member of Parliament and the Administration: The Case of the Select Committee on Nationalised Industries*, Allen & Unwin, 1966.

Nevil Johnson: *Parliament and Administration: The Estimates Committee, 1945–65*, Allen & Unwin, 1966.

Anne Robinson: *Committees in Parliament*, Montreal, McGill University PhD Thesis, 1972.

B. Articles

Sir Charles Cunningham: 'Policy and Practice', *Public Administration*, vol. 41, 1963, pp. 229–38.

Sir Richard Clarke: 'The Machinery for Economic Planning: The Public Sector', *Public Administration*, vol. 44, 1966, pp. 61–72.

Sir Samual Goldman: 'The Presentation of Public Expenditure Proposals to Parliament', *Public Administration*, vol. 48, 1970, pp. 247–62.

Michael Spicer: 'Towards a Policy Information and Control System', *Public Administration*, vol. 48, Winter 1970, pp. 443–8.

Rudolf Klein: 'The Politics of PPB', *The Political Quarterly*, vol. 43, 1972, pp. 270–81.

Michael Ryle: 'Parliamentary Control of Expenditure Taxation', *The Political Quarterly*, vol. 38, 1967, pp. 435–46.

E. Leslie Normanton: 'In Search of Value for Public Money', *The Political Quarterly*, vol. 39, 1968, pp. 156–68.

Lewis A. Gunn: 'Politicians and Officials: Who is answerable?' *The Political Quarterly*, vol. 43, July, 1972, pp. 270–81.

Denys Munby: 'The Assessment of Priorities', *The Political Quarterly*, vol. 39, 1968, pp. 375–82.

E. J. Mishan: 'Economic Priority; Growth or Welfare', *The Political Quarterly*, vol. 40, 1969, pp. 79–89.

W. A. Robson: 'The Missing Dimension of Government', *The Political Quarterly*, vol. 42 (1971), pp. 233–46.

ATE DUE